PHAIDON GUIDE TO
ANTIQUE WEAPONS AND ARMOUR

PHAIDON GUIDE TO
ANTIQUE WEAPONS AND ARMOUR
ROBERT WILKINSON-LATHAM

Illustrated by Malcolm McGregor,
Peter Sarson and Tony Bryan

Prentice-Hall, Inc., Englewood Cliffs, New Jersey 07632

Library of Congress Cataloging in Publication Data

Wilkinson-Latham, Robert.
   Phaidon guide to antique weapons and armour.

   Bibliography: p.
   Includes index.
   1. Arms and armor-History. I. Title.
U800.W64 1984   623.4'41   84-8258
ISBN 0-13-661935-5

Frontispiece: Man in Armour, ascribed to the Florentine Piero di Cosimo, c. 1462–1515.

Published by Phaidon Press Ltd, Littlegate House, St Ebbe's Street, Oxford

Planned and produced by Equinox (Oxford) Ltd, Littlegate House, St Ebbe's Street, Oxford

Copyright © Equinox (Oxford) Ltd, 1981

10 9 8 7 6 5 4 3 2 1

ISBN 0-13-661935-5

This book is available at a special discount when ordered in bulk quantities. Contact Prentice-Hall, Inc., General Publishing Division, Special Sales, Englewood Cliffs, N.J. 07632.

Design by Adrian Hodgkins

Composition in Palatino by Filmtype Services Limited, Scarborough, North Yorkshire

Illustrations originated by York House Reproductions Ltd, Hanwell, Middlesex and MBA Ltd, Chalfont St Peter, Bucks

Printed in Spain by Graficromo, S.A., Córdoba

Prentice-Hall International, Inc., *London*
Prentice-Hall of Australia Pty. Limited, *Sydney*
Prentice-Hall Canada Inc., *Toronto*
Prentice-Hall of India Private Limited, *New Delhi*
Prentice-Hall of Japan, Inc., *Tokyo*
Prentice-Hall of Southeast Asia Pte. Ltd., *Singapore*
Whitehall Books Limited, *Wellington, New Zealand*
Editora Prentice-Hall do Brasil Ltda., *Rio de Janeiro*

CONTENTS

PREFACE

There have been many glossy picture books about fine weapons, a few on armour, and numerous technical and specialist works covering particular topics. It is hoped that this book will fulfil the need for a compact treatment of the whole subject of western arms and armour – which will appeal alike to students, collectors and a more general readership.

After the sticks and stones first used for self-defence and for hunting, the cutting edge and the penetrating point prevailed for thousands of years – the knife, the sword and the spear, together with the club, the arrow, and the stone projected from a sling. It was in response to these weapons that the first armour developed – the helmet and the shield, body defences and greaves.

Weapons and armour in the years following the fall of the western Roman Empire, the starting-point chosen for this guide, owed much to their predecessors of classical times. The brief Introduction to this book deals with the earlier history, and indicates the interrelationship between, for example, developments in weapons and body defences, and the impact of these changes on military tactics, on industrial techniques, and on the history of art.

The main part of the book is arranged in the form of a guide to the development of personal armour and the different types of weapon for the individual. There are sections on staff weapons, blades, and bows (perhaps, with the sling, the oldest of projectile weapons). The firearm, which was introduced as the skill of the armourer was approaching its height, has largely replaced other weapons and rendered armour virtually obsolete. But some older weapons retain their validity today: the knife survives as a military weapon, and personal armour endures in the form of flak jackets and riot control shields.

The specially commissioned artwork which accompanies the text will provide an aid to the identification and understanding of the pieces which may be encountered in the museum, saleroom or history book. Each section of the guide is introduced by drawings which explain technical terms to be used in the text.

Robert Wilkinson-Latham

INTRODUCTION

It has always been said that necessity is the mother of invention and this was never more true than in the field of arms and armour. When early man had to compete in the animal world, he found himself at a serious disadvantage. He was slow on the ground, very poor at camouflage, not particularly agile in climbing and above all had no natural weapons as other animals had. He had, however, one power that animals lacked, that of reason, and with this he was able to arm himself for offensive and defensive fighting. He naturally chose the objects around him that suited the purpose, such as sticks and stones, and from these primitive beginnings arms and armour slowly evolved. Weapons and their advantages and failings obviously dictated the way men fought each other or hunted. By the time of the bronze and iron ages, these factors not only dictated weapon and armour design, but played an important part in the tactics of battle formations used.

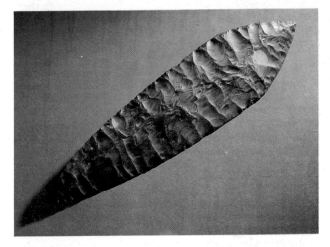

The Stone Age produced a remarkable number of weapons, considering the lack of a really suitable medium. Flint, mainly used for knives and arrowheads, could be easily knapped but it was unsuitable for any long-bladed weapon such as a sword. Various other stones proved highly efficient as clubs when mated to a wood shaft.

The Bronze Age witnessed big advances in weapon technology and also the beginnings of basic armour. Before, "armour" had been provided by wooden shields, but the introduction of the working of bronze in the Near East some time before 3500 BC not only allowed armour to

Right. *A laurel leaf spearhead of the late Stone Age Solutrean culture in Burgundy, eastern France. Finely flaked, and some 12–13 inches in length, these are among the most sophisticated of flint weapons.*

Introduction

flourish but also heralded an artistry in weaponry which was to last for thousands of years up to the present. The amalgam of copper and tin to form bronze enabled weapon-makers to employ different designs. No longer hampered by the frailty of flint and other stones they could, with their casting methods, produce swords, daggers, arrowheads and spearheads. What was perhaps more significant was that they could mould and cast protective armour and helmets. Copper is a soft metal which, while ideal for casting in shaped moulds, does not hold an edge. Because of its properties it had to be cast thick and the edge fashioned by hammering. For this reason central ribs on blades of this period are common as a means of providing added strength. Helmets, shields and armour, on the other hand, could be cast and hammer finished, and craftsmen could work the metal into artistic, often embossed designs.

For weapons the most significant step forward was the discovery of iron smelting and forging with all its infinite capabilities, and the spread of the knowledge west from Anatolia, from about 1200 BC. At last sword blades could be made of a suitable length, arrowheads instead of being flint could now be in iron (copper was too valuable for such an item with such a short life) and helmets and armour could be, if not so decorative, more practical and more effective.

Armour in the ancient Greek world was mainly in bronze (although many-layered linen corselets and greaves were used), consisting of headdress and leg protection. A complete suit of body armour from Dendara dates from the 15th century BC, but the use of bronze

Introduction

cuirasses of "bell" or "muscled" forms dates from much later – the large shields that were carried also gave full protection. The Romans developed armour in a more methodical fashion, and while using a variety of other materials, such as *cuir bouilli* and bronze, produced a first-class standard defensive armour that was both easy to wear and effective. This was the *lorica segmenta*, the banded armour of the Roman legionary. Like the helmet which afforded skull, neck and cheek protection, the *lorica*

Below. *"Achilles slaying Penthisilea", a vase painting from Attica, c.540 B.C. The weapons are spears and swords, and the armour includes large circular shields, a cuirass, greaves, and helmets, one of "Corinthian" type.*

Right. *A bronze helmet from Olympia. An inscription tells that it was dedicated to Zeus after its capture from the Corinthians by the soldiers of Argos.*

Below. *A 2nd century bronze statuette of a Roman legionary wearing lorica segmenta body armour.*

segmenta was of superb design and craftsmanship.

The manufacture of this Roman type of armour was an art that was to disappear during the centuries which followed the fall, in AD 456, of the West Roman Empire. Many of the artistic designs which flourished under the Greeks and Romans were lost during the "Dark Ages", and plate or plate-style armour gave way to mail, which proved for a short period to be more effective, cheaper and lighter. At the same time, however, the capabilities of the weapon-makers had also advanced. The battle between the makers of armour and of weapons continued with the final abandoning of bronze for armour and shields, and the adoption of iron for both defensive and offensive purposes.

The tactics and formations used by different armies evolved over the years, some of the best known being employed by the Greeks and the Romans. The later Greek soldier, the hoplite, was armed with helmet, shield and bronze breast and backplate, and carried a spear and a short sword. The fighting formation of the Greeks was the phalanx, a solid square of men. The success of the phalanx lay not only in the use of long spears but also in the sheer weight and size of the formation. The Romans on the other hand used a line formation, and the legionary was trained to throw his spear when near the enemy and then close with him with his short cutting sword drawn. The Romans made greater use of their shields, often using them to form an armoured box-like formation of men called a *testudo*, or tortoise. This was especially successful in advancing on a fortified enemy position, as it protected the men from stones, arrows and spears raining down from above.

Both Greeks and Romans laid the main emphasis of their fighting techniques on the foot soldier. Later, following the introduction of the saddle in the 4th century and learning from the invaders from the East, much more use was made of the mounted man, and this is clearly shown in the increased activity of the armourer and the swordmaker after the 11th century.

Design and decoration have played a large part in the making of arms and armour. Bronze was an easy metal to mould into shapes, and many bronze weapons incorporated the typical art forms of certain areas and countries. With the almost universal use of iron, engraving became the most popular method of enhancing a blade or a piece of armour. Emphasis was also put on the inlaying of stones and gems, especially in sword hilts, and a combination of precious metals often embellished what seems to be a very basic shape such as the cross-hilted straight-bladed sword. Etching, which makes use of the action of acid on metal, was used by Italian armourers in the late 15th century to ornament their work, before its adoption as a technique for making prints. Acid-resistant wax was applied to the metal in a thin layer and the design then drawn with a sharp stylus through the wax, leaving a thin channel through to the metal. Acid was poured or wiped over the openings between the wax, and ate away the metal beneath. When the required depth of etching had been achieved, the piece was thoroughly washed with water to stop the action, the wax was removed and the metal given a gentle polish. This method became a universal means of decorating armour and sword blades, and in sword-making survives to this day. The "modern" version of the method, dating from the 1830s, is however slightly different. It originally involved painting on acid-resistant paint to preserve the bright portions, leaving the bare metal to be attacked by acid. Later, when blade decoration became uniform and regimented, wax transfers were (and still are) used.

Heraldry was probably introduced in Germany in the late 12th century. It was both decorative and functional, for wearing a closed helm which hid his face meant that the 13th-century armoured knight could only be identified by the coat of arms shown on his surcoat. Although this flowing gown usually covered the mail hauberk, coats of mail

A late Iron Age British ceremonial shield, of bronze. The repoussé work is inlaid with red glass.

Right. *In this early 15th century version of a crusader seige of Jerusalem, the weapons include swords, pikes and halberds, and longbows. Early cannon are in evidence (left).*

Introduction

were sometimes relieved a little by having a wavy lower edge, or borders made of brass rings. The great helm itself might be either gilded or covered with fabric or painted, and was often surmounted by its owner's family crest as a further means of identification.

During the 14th and the 15th centuries, when true plate armour emerged from the coverings of jupon or surcoat, the beauty of polished steel began to be appreciated and the surface of the plates was left unadorned. Sometimes, however, armour was given a lustrous blue-black finish, often shown in contemporary paintings. Decoration was confined to applied strips of brass bearing religious inscriptions and scroll work. However, the real beauty of the armour of this period lies in the form of the plates which make up a superbly balanced and articulated covering for the whole body. Later in the 15th century German armour was decorated by a combination of fluting or ridging of surfaces and piercing and fretting of the overlapping edges of plates, a style known as Gothic, after its general resemblance to late Gothic forms in the other arts.

The wealthy nobility of the 15th century were always prepared to spend a great deal on a good and reliable armour. However, there came a time when reliability and technical perfection was no longer sufficient and by the reigns of Maximilian I and Henry VIII ostentatious decoration began to appear on armour. One of Henry VIII's armours is silvered and engraved all over. At first most armours remained functional as well as decorative but some were embossed with decorative motifs or in imitation of textiles and some were recessed to hold panels of silverwork. In these instances functional propriety was clearly offended, for now the smooth surfaces of the armour, designed to ensure that an opponent's weapon simply glanced off, had become pitted with decoration which thus ruined the utility of the design. This fancy-dress or parade armour became increasingly popular with powerful men who saw it simply as a status symbol. Nevertheless, throughout the 16th century some workshops, such as that at Greenwich, continued to produce armours whose ornament was consistent with use in the field and the tilt yard.

The entry of gunpowder and firearms on the battlefield in the 14th and 15th centuries did not, as one might assume with the rush of the modern age, drastically alter battle tactics or even military thinking. The tactics of armies depended heavily on their weapons and on the importance attached to individual arms. The emphasis on projectile weapons usually meant that an army fought either from

Tournament armour of the 14th century, with bascinet and mail aventail, great helm, mail body armour, and plate armour on the elbows, knees and shins and plate

gauntlets. The helm crest, surcoat, shoulder ailettes, pennant, shield and horse coverings bear the arms of the knight. From the Luttrell Psalter.

defensive cover or in a tight formation.

Projectile weapons had been used successfully by the English at Crécy and Poitiers, when the English longbow decimated the French army, and they were to be used

Introduction

again by the British army in the Peninsular War and at Waterloo when the British infantry discharged its pistols rank by rank and then retired without attempting to exploit gaps in the wall of pikes or to close with the infantry. Thus, because of the adoption of the pistol, the most essential feature of cavalry tactics – the use of the sheer force of a charge to disrupt an enemy formation – was forgotten. It was not until the 17th century that commanders such as Gustavus Adolphus of Sweden, and, in England, Cromwell, Prince Rupert and Marlborough instilled into their mounted troops the paramount importance of the sword and the relative uselessness of firearms in cavalry attacks.

The introduction of new weapons did not therefore always result in an early adaptation or change to appropriate tactics. However, the combination of firearms and bladed

An early 17th-century woodcut showing the combination of pike, musket and cavalry. While the pikeman maintains some body armour, notably a cuirass, and the cavalry has "lobster" armour, the musketeers are not so protected, although all wear a peaked morion and musketeers and pikemen carry sword and dagger. "Pyramid" shaped powder flasks are also in evidence. From John Derricke, The Image of Ireland.

weapons was later considered to be more successful, and even today when nuclear bombs, missiles and jet aircraft dominate the military scene, the footsoldier still has his rifle with that bit of "cold steel" fitted to the barrel. The cutting edge is a fundamental necessity for man whether for offensive use or for survival, and despite modern advances will still be considered as a front-line weapon.

Armour fell increasingly from favour as the firearm established its apparent supremacy as a weapon on the battlefield. But there were other reasons for the decline in the use of armour, including the need for greater mobility on the battlefield and, as wars become more wide-ranging, the need to march further and faster to engage the enemy. The increasing expense of warfare caused by the increasing size of armies also made it financially impossible for most troops to be equipped with armour. By the 17th century even cavalry were not always armoured, although they did tend to retain helmet and cuirass (breast and back) long after armour had been completely discarded by the infantry. In the past the cavalry had been the preserve of the nobility who usually provided their own armour. In such circumstances armour was as much a symbol of prestige, power and social status as a source of protection. But now, as a contemporary observer remarked "the most of the Horsemen as well as of the Foot (are) composed of the scum of the Commons". With changes in the social composition of armies, the need for armour as a sign of rank had also disappeared.

Today, despite the reasons for the decline in its use, armour has thanks to modern science reappeared on the battlefield. The steel helmet has always been in use with the cavalry, but in the infantry it disappeared in the 1600s and did not re-appear until 1916. The cavalry for some reason clung longer to the idea of armour and the French in particular still armoured their cavalry at the beginning of the First World War. Today's armour is universal and makes no distinction between services. History goes in cycles, and in the case of arms and armour there is no getting away from the fundamental weapons of the soldier – the gun, the knife, and armour – even if they re-appear in different styles and in new materials; the basic weapons remain the same.

In the firearms and armour of today's fighting troops there is no decoration, but the skills of the engraver and etcher are still to be seen in swords and sporting guns, and the craft of the bladesmith in hunting knives and in presentation swords. The craft of the armourer survives,

Introduction

having been revived in the 19th century, in the handful of men and women who make the ceremonial helmets for bodyguard troops. The gunmaker and the various branches of his trade still produce works that rival the work of the past.

Invention and innovation have played a large part in firearms development, but less so in edged weapons, because of the simplicity of their form. All these developments have in one way or another altered the course of history. Of course, the development of warfare cannot be regarded simply as an interaction between weapons and tactics. Social and economic factors have always been of great importance. The French Revolutionary and Napoleonic Wars differed from the earlier conflicts of the 18th century not because of any change in weaponry but because of the increased military capacity released in France with its doctrine of a whole nation in arms. The professional armies of the legitimate monarchs were swept away by vast, ill-trained armies for whom casualties were of little consequence. Similarly the development of arms and armour cannot always be seen simply as an interaction between new and old weapons.

In this book the reader will find illustrated a great variety of forms of armour, edged weapons, crossbows and firearms. It is hoped that this selection, and the text which accompanies it, will help an appreciation of the decorative and artistic merit, the capabilities and the usefulness, even sometimes the absurdities of these objects.

ARMOUR

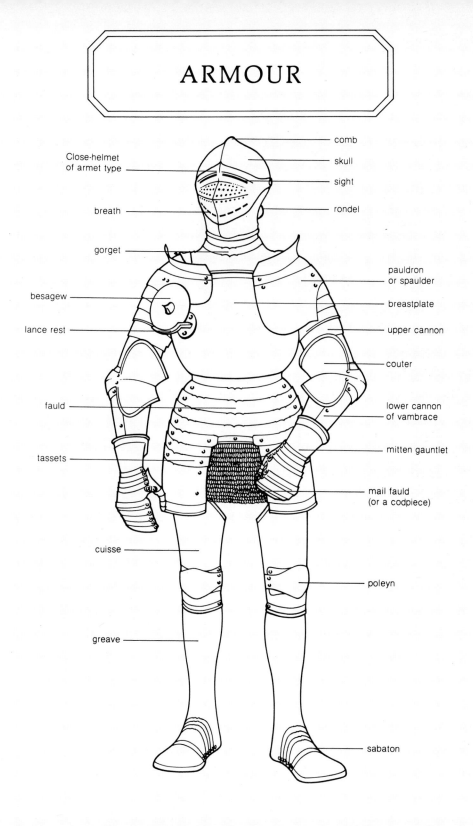

comb

skull

Close-helmet
of armet type

sight

breath

rondel

gorget

pauldron
or spaulder

besagew

breastplate

lance rest

upper cannon

couter

fauld

lower cannon
of vambrace

tassets

mitten gauntlet

mail fauld
(or a codpiece)

cuisse

poleyn

greave

sabaton

Armour

Left. *A helmet modelled on the late Roman style, with nose and eye protection, skilfully constructed with bands of brass over an iron skull. The brass bands are decorative but the comb covers the join between the two halves of the skull.*
Below. *Typical Saxon warrior, with mail shirt, shield and leather headwear.*

In the long period which followed the overturn of the power of Rome, the expertise of the Romans, although often poorly understood, was nevertheless a major influence on the armour styles of the northern invaders. This is perhaps more evident in the helmets of the time than in survivals from the metal body armour of the earlier Roman legions. Mail survived and prospered as a simple (if laboriously assembled) form of body protection, as did "scale" armour. Despite the evidence of those that survive from burials, such as the restored Sutton Hoo headdress, the helmet was usually not ornate, and certainly not the type we are used to seeing depicted with horns each side! Such forms did exist but it is thought that they may have had some religious purpose. The normal helmet was conical in shape and sometimes fitted with a nasal bar. Those of more high-ranking men had a more elaborate face protection, as in the 7th-century helmet from Vendel in Sweden. This had an inner skull of iron over which was riveted brass comb- and lattice-work on each side. The facial protection consists of a half-mask with two eyeholes and a nasal bar, again in iron trimmed in brass. Another helmet of this type excavated in Sweden has a heavy dome and central comb to the skull and an eyehole-type mask with "eyebrow" visor above each eye-slot. The lower part of the face to the neck is protected not by the usual facial bar but by a curtain of mail.

One helmet that has survived from Saxon England is

preserved in Sheffield Museum. It was excavated at Benty Grange in Derbyshire. The inner skull, now missing, was of plates of horn which were fitted inside a skeleton frame of iron decorated with brass. Each of the six horn segments was riveted to the inside of the iron framework. The iron nasal bar was also decorated in the same style. The helmet was topped with a bronze figure of a boar embellished with a piece of silver and eyes of garnet. Being the emblem of the ancient Norse goddess of the Saxons, Frigg, it was one which would give protection to the wearer.

The armour of the Normans who conquered France, Britain, Italy and other Mediterranean lands differed very little from that worn by Saxon warriors. It consisted of body and head protection, body armour in the form of a mail shirt or hauberk. The Bayeux tapestry shows this garment in use. It was worn over an undergarment of the same length. The hauberk had short sleeves open to the elbow, and it reached down to knee level at both front and back. At the centre of the front and back it was divided by vents for ease of movement on foot and horseback.

In some instances, as illustrated in the Bayeux tapestry, mail appears to have been worn on the legs in an extension of the hauberk or as separate leg protection, but most armed Normans seem to have worn fabric hose. The Norman hauberk was sometimes distinguished by a form of

Armour

rectangle on the upper chest. Starting beneath the neck, it comes down to chest level. There is evidence of ties and laces, usually coloured, but the exact purpose of the panel is still uncertain. One theory is that it unlaced for the head to pass through when putting on the armour, but another has it that at this vulnerable point reinforcing was needed, and so the rectangle was an extra panel of mail.

The head was protected by a metal helmet, worn in many cases over a mail hood that was similar in shape to a knitted Balaclava helmet, protecting the neck. In some instances the mail hood or coif was omitted. The helmet had a conical skull which was usually hammered out of a single piece of metal with no seam or joints. To this skull was fitted a rim around the lower edge in the front of which was a nasal protection bar. However, some types of this style of helmet are depicted with bands running not only round the base but also up the centre and at each side, giving the appearance that the helmet was made up of segments with the bands to cover the joins – a survival of Dark Ages practice.

Some helmets, beside having the front nasal protection bar, had a similar one at the back to protect the neck.

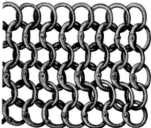

Left. *A helmet, forged in one piece, with a nasal protecting bar, in this case with decoration. It is said traditionally to have belonged to St. Wenceslaus, who died in 935 AD.*

ETCECI DE

Above. *Norman versus English knights, a scene from the Bayeux tapestry (c. 1100). Both sides are portrayed in the same style of helm and mail protection.*

Left. *The interlocking links of chain mail. Note the flattened ends of the rings and the rivets by which each link is attached to four others.*

Mail was made up of a series of interwoven links. Each link was made by twisting a length of drawn wire around a mandrel in a spiral fashion. The spiral was then cut with a chisel to form individual open rings, whose ends were made to overlap and at the same time were flattened. The ends were then pierced with a punch and the rings interlocked with each other in a row, linking with the row above and below to form a series of panels of mail. Usually, if one ring is examined, it will be seen that four other rings pass through it. Once the rings were in place, the two ends of each ring were pulled together and a rivet passed through the holes and hammered down. By this method a shirt, hood and leggings could be fashioned. Beneath the mail, an undergarment was worn to prevent chaffing of the skin from the unlined suit.

Armour

Left. *A relief from Rheims Cathedral showing a knight in full mail with a surcoat. Both hands and feet are fully covered, the ultimate in mail covering before plate was introduced.*

Above. *The Seal of John de Montfort, 1248. This shows an armoured knight of the period with surcoat over mail, a heavy helm, triangular shield, and typical sword.*

The equipment of the Norman knight remained unchanged until well into the 12th century. The chief aspect of the evolution consisted of armouring the man more completely than the early Normans had done. The sleeves of the hauberk were extended and mittens added. These were made like two small bags, one for the thumb and the other, larger, for the fingers. The inner palm was made from cloth or leather, and the mitten was so devised that while it was attached to the arm of the garment by one part, it could be slipped off when not required and left hanging. Leg protection was now also more important. This took the form of complete stockings or "hose" with waist-belt, or shin-pad type mail fastened at the back of the leg by thongs. A cloth surcoat, later emblazoned with an heraldic device, was worn over the mail defence, which now incorporated the hood, shirt and arm protection in one piece.

There was also an evolution in the helmet. While the Norman style continued, other helmets had added neck and ear protection. The forging of these helmets out of one piece often took in additional neck protection, and visors were fixed to the front in place of the nasal bar. While it gave adequate protection against sword cuts etc., the visor had also to provide the wearer with a good field of vision and allow him to breathe. This was done by the addition of slits for view above perforated holes for breathing; both of these features continued when the closed helm became popular.

Right. *This illuminated letter shows a number of knights in round helmets over their coifs, surcoat over the mail, and mail mittens without finger protection. From the Winchester Bible, 1160–70.*

25

Armour

Other forms of helmet came into use during this period. They included the round-topped kettle hat with a brim. There was also the round helmet or skull cap, and the "saucepan-shaped" flat-topped helm, both made with or without a nasal bar.

The 13th century saw the first move towards plate armour supplemented by mail. Mail up until this time had been the prime protective covering but, as the plate workers' skills developed, so gradually plate came to be the principal armour and mail the secondary protection. The mail hauberk still continued very much in use, with long sleeves and hood or coif. Under the coif, a padded quilted cap was worn tied beneath the chin. This gave extra protection and acted like a shock absorber when the helmet was struck by the sword of an adversary.

The helm had evolved and had become deeper back and front, giving protection to both head and neck. There were slits and vents at the front of the flat-topped, all-enveloping helm, the slits often being reinforced with strips of metal which also ran from top to bottom at the front of the helm – in the place where the old nasal bar would have been fitted. However, the helm was not universally popular and many still wore the mailed coif or hood on its own or with a round-topped kettle hat, sometimes with a nasal protection bar.

The most vulnerable part of the mounted man was his legs. Quilted thigh defences (*gamboised cuisses*) were worn; mail hose worn by some gave the legs some protection, but they were still vulnerable. Solid metal plate knee-caps came to be fitted over the quilted thigh protectors, and by the end of the century these two components were combined as leg defences.

Another form of armour was the *cuirie*, a waist-length garment sometimes reinforced with metal plates, being, as the name suggests, made of hardened leather. Other continental forms of armour included the coat lined with plates, best known from excavations on the site of the battle of Wisby, Gottland (1361). It was topped with a mail coif.

The foot soldier wore the hauberk with a kettle hat, skull cap or just the coif. He rarely wore protection on the legs. Most foot soldiers could not afford new mail but were probably given older mail hauberks by their masters, or got them as spoils of war.

A full flat-topped helm with the additional protection of frontal bars to protect the nose and eye area.

A soldier in a kettle hat, from a contemporary French manuscript, also showing the mail worn under the surcoat, and early plate greaves.

Armour

From Mail to Plate

Increasingly from the middle of the 13th century, improvements and additions were made to armour in the form of either extra padding of undergarments or the use of plate on the knees, and concealed in garments. The helm too had altered in shape and the amount of protection it offered greatly increased.

In body armour, leather garments with plate appeared and contemporary accounts refer to added protection for the neck, made of mail with underlying plates. In place of the mail hauberk, a *brigandine* with iron scales, sewn on in an overlapping arrangement, was often worn. Square plates (*ailettes*) were now worn on each shoulder by mounted knights; these bore the knight's arms as borne on the shield and were doubtless chiefly ornamental.

By the end of the 13th century some gauntlets were not just two joined bags made of mail, one small for the thumb and the other shaped like a mitten, but had separate fingers; in some European countries gloves protected by plate came into use, as did elbow-protectors in the form of metal plates similar in form to the small shields called bucklers.

Another addition at this period was plate protection for the lower part of the legs and for the forearms. This was worn over the mail and consisted of curved metal plates which were strapped into place. First worn on the front or outside only, they soon developed into a complete hinged tube affording protection all round, and the elbow and knee protectors already worn were fashioned so that when the joint was bent, protection was complete.

But plate was not the only material with which the armourers were experimenting. Leather or *cuir bouilli* (leather boiled to soften it for moulding, after which it set hard) had been a favourite armour for many years; it was now used as added protection over mail.

Others continued to use and experiment with quilted and lamellar armour. Heavily padded and quilted garments were worn because they had some, though not all, the advantages of mail while having little of the weight. Worn on their own, they afforded little protection from a direct hit with arrow, but because of their bulk they were useful in deflecting glancing sword-blows. Quilted thigh protection and horse protection were used with mail.

Lamellar armour was made up of a number of small plates joined by a system of lacing and worn under a leather jerkin or other garment. A similar type, again made up of small plates, was not laced but riveted inside a leather jerkin. Originating in the East, this form of protection only became popular in Scandinavia and Eastern Europe.

Armour

The development of head protection was taken to great lengths before once again it simplified, with the more open helmets of the 16th century. In one sense – that of massive protection – the great helm was perhaps the furthest that helmet design went. The weight alone dictated that as a helmet for combat it was not entirely suitable, but it lasted in the tournament and the joust because of the extra protection it gave.

In the 14th century, however, a different type of helmet was designed in place of the cumbersome great helm. These were open-fronted helmets, forged from one piece, with rounded or pointed skulls. The bucket-like shape of the great helm had a great disadvantage in that there were no glancing surfaces. The increase in armourers' skill, facilitating the forging of a helmet in one piece, assisted the development of this innovation. The skull on the new helmet was not only rounded but came to a point at the top. This afforded maximum protection from a glancing blow and in theory ought to have deflected a straight-on cut. The bascinet, as the new type of helmet was called, became a most popular form of head defence, incorporating as it did good head protection with the improvement of glancing surfaces.

At the beginning the bascinet was worn over the mail coif, but this soon gave way to mail protection fitted to the rim of the helmet; many surviving examples show the rivet holes where the aventail was fixed. The helmet was ideal protection, as it came down the back of the head and over the neck and curved around over the cheek. The only vital area not protected was the central facial part.

Developments in weapons and armour have always been closely linked. Where one advanced to protect, the other, the sword or some other edged weapon, advanced to defeat the new form of protection.

The first visors were simple affairs, slightly rounded face protectors with small slits for vision, but they soon evolved into more rounded shapes with ventilation holes, and into pointed versions. Some tomb effigies of knights show the visorless bascinet being worn and the knight's head resting on his great helm – in battle both were worn together. With the great helm being abandoned visors were added to the bascinet, early visors being hinged at the top (as in the *Klappvisier*), later stronger visors being hinged on both sides, with a pivot and removeable hinge pin so that the bascinet could be worn "open", without danger of the visor falling down. Good quality helmets retained this feature until the 16th century.

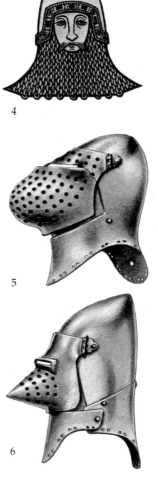

4

5

6

It was during the 14th-century that the great helm began to give way to the bascinet, except for use in the tournament. The increasing popularity of the bascinet with its movable visor is shown in the number of variations in design.

1. Great helm, round-topped and fully enclosing the head. English, 1375.

2. Late 14th-century bascinet, with visor missing.

3. Italian bascinet with pointed visor and mail aventail, 1390.

4. Bascinet without visor, from the effigy of Sir Peter Courtnay, 1409.

5. Late 14th-century bascinet with bulbous visor.

6. Late 14th-century bascinet with pointed visor.

1

3

2

Armour

As the weapons improved to combat mail, so armour had to be improved or reinforced to answer the new menace.. Armour for the trunk would have to give increased protection as this area was the most obvious killing target for arrows, staff weapons and of course swords. Little armour of this period survives, and our knowledge chiefly derives from representations in manuscripts and churches – tomb effigies, brasses etc.

While the mail hauberk still formed the basic garment, other forms of added protection were soon worn over it, among them leather armour, the reinforced surcoat and quilting. Parallel to mail there was another development – the scaled hauberk, in which small overlapping metal plates took the place of interlocking rings.

Shoulders and elbows were a vulnerable area; a severe blow to the former could incapacitate a man, and a wound to the latter was guaranteed to disarm him. Added protection for these areas was provided by some with small round plates, which were strapped on. Metal plates were also used to reinforce the gauntlets or mittens, both these of course made of mail. At the time of these developments, scale armour seems to have all but disappeared.

For the mounted knight, the legs, always easy prey for the soldier on foot, were among the first parts to be given extra protection. Initially this took the form of adding pads that stretched from the knee to the thigh, but presumably these were found not to be the answer and by about 1220 small metal plates were fitted to these pads to cover the knee.

At this time body plate armour was beginning to be introduced in Europe. It consisted of a number of large plates, as in the armour found on the site of the battle of Wisby in Gottland (1361), and was worn between the hauberk and the surcoat.

Changes in fighting styles had also affected the helmet and the vital throat and neck areas. The mail coif had been reinforced with a stiffening, but the answer lay in a helmet development in which the metal of the helmet reached over the neck at the back, while the throat was protected with a stiffened collar, the forerunner of the gorget and bevor. The 14th century was the age of the most rapid development in armour, and plate was progressively to encompass the knight.

The preoccupation with armourers at this period was to supplement mail protection.
Right. *An early 14th-century monumental brass, showing the increasing use of plate on limbs and over joints. The surcoat conceals the development in body armour.*
Far right. *A set of plates for back and front excavated from the mass grave at Wisby in Gottland. Note the front portion made in three parts.*

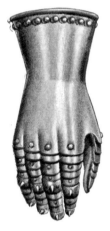

Left. *A monumental brass (of Sir John Aubernoun in Stoke d'Abernon church, England) of 1327. Mail still predominates on the inside of the arms and the back of the legs, and plate is only to the fore.*

Above. *A solid "hourglass" gauntlet of the period with articulated fingers, the plate now replacing mail protection for the hands.*

From Mail to Plate

The most rapid change in the outward appearance of the armoured fighting man was the appearance at various strategic points of solid plate protection. We have seen the introduction of rudimentary plate armour to protect knee, elbow and shoulder and also the use of the coat of plates, but by the early 14th century gutter-type limb defences had appeared. For the arm these consisted of a gutter-shaped plate to protect the outer upper arm – often with an exten sion to protect the shoulder, when it was called a *spaudler*, an elbow piece (*couter*) with a round plate (the shoulder was similarly protected), and a "gutter" worn on the inside of the lower arm. These plates were held in position over the mail by leather straps, and are known as a *vambrace*.

This form of protection was extended to the legs, cover- ing the shins. The plate for the kneecap (*poleyn*) was worn over this greave, the elbow piece over the arm portions.

The armoured man of this period wore three layers of body protection. First he put on the aketon, a quilted dress to prevent the mail from rubbing and also affording protec- tion. Then came the mail hauberk, and over that a shirt of body armour. This was a leather or cloth shirt inside which was sewn a number of plates all overlapping – hence its name of "coat of plates". To these were added the arm protection, shoulder and elbow guards, and the knee guards over the greaves and the padded thigh protection. Over all went the surcoat (not always over a coat of plates).

At about this period the padded thigh defences were improved by the addition of metal plates with the knee protectors on occasion riveted to them but more usually strapped on. Extra protection to the foot was provided by a number of overlapping plates fitted to the mail sock.

At this juncture the garment with plates sewn inside developed further and a single plate to protect the breast started to appear. At first this was purely for the front, but by the late 14th century a plate for the back was provided as well. While the breastplate was a single piece, the skirt (*fauld*) was, for ease of movement, made from a series of horizontal plates fitted together with leather and rivets.

Arm and leg defences had also improved by the last years of the 14th century and arm defences were now made so that upper, lower and elbow defences were linked together with strips of metal termed "lames". With loose riveting and leather straps, a degree of flexibility was provided. Gauntlets had developed from having an additional strap on the cuff to having the whole made in one piece of an hourglass shape. Both knee and elbow defences might have side wings to protect the joint.

Breastplates, backplates, laminated skirts, arm and leg defences were soon made from plate, with hinged joints for movement.
Left. *A monumental brass of 1412, showing plate armour, two styles of bascinet (one with a plate gorget), swords (note the pommels) and daggers. The articulated spaudler at the shoulder, the winged couter replacing the metal disc, and metal cuisses for the thighs are clear.*
Below. *The typical leg harness of the period.*

As has been seen, the armourer of the late 14th century was providing additional protection for the mounted man with the introduction of plate in various shapes and at various places to protect the wearer. In addition to the breastplate, held with straps, a complementary backplate had been introduced.

Other parts of the body that had already been given some defence, the arms and legs, were better covered. In place of the single plate, the whole upper and lower arm were encased in plate. The inner and outer gutter plates were hinged along one edge and strapped on the other. These surfaces, and that of the elbow couter, were designed not only to withstand but, with their curved nature, to deflect a blow. The armourers' preoccupation with deflecting surfaces was to continue until the demise of their trade.

With the inclusion of the backplate, and gorget plates worn over the mail tippet, by the beginning of the 15th century plate armour covered practically the entire body. Numerous brasses and monumental effigies give excellent detail of the appearance of a fully armoured knight of the period. An effigy of Edward the Black Prince, who died in 1376, shows an armour of plate that is complete except for the mail aventail to the bascinet. The lower limbs are encased all round with plate, except at the rear of the knee where mail is visible. Under the surcoat would be worn the breastplate. The arms are protected again in all-enveloping plate armour (vambraces), the spaudler (near the shoulder) made up of laminated plates for movement with a laminated elbow defence (couter) in three parts.

Leg armour now extended up the thigh under the laminated plate skirt (fauld) under which mail was often worn. The shoulder joints were also laminated and could be protected at the arm-holes with circular metal plates (besagews). The gorget now reached up to the visor of the bascinet, the visor itself closing down inside, so that it could not be accidentally opened by an opponent's blow, and the neck was fully protected with the gorget.

While the knights and armourers were undoubtedly pleased with their armour, from this first form of complete armour the defences continued to develop, alter in style and improve in efficiency and protective coverage.

Armour

The making of armour in plate form was an extension of the craft of the blacksmith. There were no sophisticated steel-making processes, few powered hammers, and so the armourer relied on his skill and his arm. His skill ensured that there was the right thickness in the right places, and that there were glancing surfaces to deflect arrows which might hit the small areas without protection, such as under the arms. Tempering ensured the metal was neither too soft nor too brittle, and also the armourer aimed at flexibility of the joints. The armour of the man on horse was not as heavy or as unwieldy as we have been led to believe by films that show hoists being used to get the armoured man into the saddle, or by the tales of fallen knights lying immobile with the weight of armour – these are pure invention. A trained man could act quite normally in all respects.

When it came to crafting plate armour, preparations were made as for a modern tailor-made suit. Exact measurements were taken and the parts tried in the raw stages to ensure a perfect fit. Iron bars were heated by the smith and roughly hammered into thick flat pieces, each piece so flattened forming one of the components of the completed suit. Each piece was then shaped by the use of heavy hammers on anvils of various shapes. The main tools were a variety of shaped hammers and "stakes" – small anvils set in a heavy trestle or block of wood – each with the indentations, ribs or raised portions required to form the part. To prevent any cracking while the metal was being worked, the iron was annealed, or heated to soften it. While working the metal for shape and fit, the armourer was also careful to ensure that the correct thickness appeared in the right places such as the front of the head, the chest and the left side of the suit. Once the sheets had been hammered to satisfaction, they were cropped with shears to the final shape of the component and the outer edges were then turned over to stiffen them. Sometimes the edge was rolled over a wire. This not only finished off the piece but, more important, acted as a stop for an opponent's blade by preventing it from glancing into a vital area.

The rough and fire-blackened pieces were now ready to be ground and polished to remove the marks of hammer and file, the final stage before assembly. The various pieces were now assembled as they would be worn, the plates attached to each other with straps, buckles and rivets, or if the components were to make up a single piece they were riveted with a reinforcing leather strap on the inside. Once this had been accomplished, the armour was fitted with

"Maximilian I in the workshop of his court armourer Konrad Seusenhofer". This print from Der Weisskönig *(Vienna, 1775) illustrates processes described in the text.*

lining of a quilted material in the helm, breastplate, backplate, upper thigh and tassets.

At this stage, any decoration of engraving or etching, the most common method, was added. Any gilding etc., was of course done before the lining or leather was fitted.

Armour

The 15th century was a busy one for helmet design and evolution. The bascinet remained very popular and came to lose the mail throat and neck protection and was fitted instead with a plate bevor. The shape had also altered, especially at the back, where it now sloped down and over the back-plate of the armour. To secure the helmet, it was usually attached to the breast- and the backplate with straps and buckles. The shape of the helmet became more rounded during the century and this form continued, albeit under pressure from other designs, until the end of the 15th and into the early 16th century.

Another design current from the early 15th century was the barbut, a pointed helmet covering the head, the back of the neck and the sides of the face in one piece with an opening for the face. During the 15th century, the tendency was for the open portion to get smaller and be more shaped for use: the eye holes were connected to the opening for the nose, which continued to the bottom of the helmet. Towards 1500 all styles of barbut disappeared.

The place of the barbut was taken by the sallet, which was really the previous design taken one step further. Early sallets were similar to barbuts but were more rounded and closer-fitting in the neck. The later sallets varied in their detail but the basic construction consisted of a rounded skull which tapered towards the back to form a neck-guard, which in the simple form was solid, although laminated neck-guards were also made. In the simple form, the rear section was riveted to the main skull; it was pointed at the back and came round the side and up at the front, covering the face to just below the nose. In the front there was a slit for vision. Other versions had hinged rear portions but more usually hinged visors. German sallets have the more pointed rear neck protection, while the Italian ones were more faithful to the lines of the barbut. The sallet without full visor was usually worn with a bevor to protect the lower portion of the face.

In the latter years of the century a new form of helmet, the armet, evolved. Owing many of its features to some of the helmets mentioned above, it had a skull and a long thin vertical ridge at the rear to help protect the neck. At each side there were hinged cheek-pieces which closed over and strapped together when the helmet was worn, and also closed over the thin rear portion. To protect the join, and the strapping at the front, a visor was fitted, pivoting at each side so that it could be raised and lowered; but for extra protection sometimes a wrapper was also strapped to the lower portion, covering the joint and also protecting

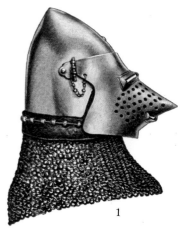

1

1. *Milanese visored bascinet,*
c. 1390–1410. The aventail is a
later addition.
2. *Italian barbut, c. 1450–70. The*
form was derived from ancient
Greek helmets.

3. *Italian sallet, c. 1480.*
4. *German sallet, c. 1450–60.*
5. *German armet, early 16th*
century.
6. *A typical kettle hat of the late*
15th century.

the lower neck. Where the strap for this wrapper fastened
at the rear, a circular piece of metal was fitted, the *rondel*,
to stop the strap being cut in action.

Italian Armour in the 15th Century

Once plate armour had become firmly established, it was the Italian armourers who took the lead in design and technology. The Italian armour that developed early in the century was noticeable for its roundness and graceful lines, while German armour developed at the same time was spiky but also elegant. The breastplate and backplate of typical Italian armour of the period were made in two parts, lower and upper portions. The upper part was overlapped by the lower part which gave not only good protection but ease of movement. Both parts were strapped together. Other important features of Italian armour were large defensive plates for each shoulder, curved to cover both part of the chest and the shoulder blades, and extra protection for both elbows, with a larger wing on the right and a plate on the left. Tassets were strapped to the lower edge of the breastplate to cover the upper thigh, and the right shoulder defences were cut away on the inner part to allow for the lance.

During the 15th century the lower portion of the breastplate increased in size, so that in the end it covered almost the entire chest and stomach area. Additional tassets were also added at the side and rear. Mail, however, remained important. It was used under plate to protect the jointed areas and also showed beneath the tassets as a skirt. For the lower regions, the armour altered little, except that the poleyn wings were sometimes increased in covering power by being enlarged and made to curve round to protect knee joints, and there was improved articulation.

Gauntlets too underwent change in Italian armour. The cuffs of the gauntlets were made longer and more pointed, while the fingers were protected by lames, the gauntlets being of "mitten" type, rather than individually fingered, from the 1430s.

One of the most noticeable features of Italian armour was in its construction. Armourers had known for some time the importance of deflecting a thrust and had produced a glancing surface, but the Italians took this a stage further. They included a rib across the defences on the shoulders, with the upper edges turned outwards to further assist in taking the thrust from the throat and shoulder. The neck and arm openings of the breastplate were also rolled outwards to prevent a blade from penetrating the joint. Every other part that would be vulnerable was dealt with – the top of the thighs, the fitting of extra metal to the forearms, in fact to any part that might be vulnerable to an assailant's weapon sliding in the wrong direction.

Milanese armour of Count Galeazzo da Arco, by Negroli dello Missaglia, c. 1445. Note the barbut helmet, the generally rounded forms, breastplate in two parts, large shoulder plates, and "mitten" type gauntlets. The turned-out deflecting edges, as on the spaudler, and the continuing importance of mail, which would have been worn under the strap-fastened tassets, are also characteristic. Part of the original right vambrace is missing.

Armour

Until the mid-15th century, German armour followed the Italian style, but it soon developed one of its own. This "Gothic" armour of Sigismund of Tyrol (second half 15th century) shows the typical Germanic style of fluted armour and spiky, elongated forms which was to become popular for a period in Europe.

German Armour in the 15th Century

In the early 15th century, German armour was still a mixture of plate and mail or scales. Any influence in developments in the first half of the century was largely due to the lead given by Italian armourers. However, the second half of the century saw the emergence of a peculiarly German style. Early 15th century German armour is extremely rare, but seems to have consisted usually of breast- and backplates, arm and leg protection in plate, and a large skirt of plates of hooped form. The headwear was the bascinet, usually with a plate gorget by this time, but on occasion the older mail aventail.

By the 1450s the whole armour started to develop a more angular look compared with the Italian suits. Fluting was beginning to appear. This style is today termed "Gothic". It was made in the important German armour centres of Innsbruck, Augsburg and Nuremburg. As in Italy, the breast- and backplates were made in two parts, upper and lower, beneath which was fitted a skirt of overlapping plates. The legs were protected with the usual pieces – cuisses and greaves. A characteristic of the style was that many surfaces carried radiating flutes, only the greaves being left plain, and there was a tendency towards a spiky, more slender form by elongating such items as the sabatons (foot defences). Another feature of the armour was the cusping of the edges where the flutes on the plate met the edge. The usual helmet worn with "Gothic" armour was the German sallet with bevor. Towards the end of the century the "Gothic" style became exaggerated with the edges of the various plates pierced with decorative emblems or edged in decorative brass strips riveted to the plates. The change also showed in the number of flutes that appeared on the various parts of the suit, and towards the end of the century the number of individual laminated plates increased, not only to give an impressive visual appearance but also to add flexibility.

The two basic forms, Italian and German, had their various followers, not just at home, for both countries had a flourishing export trade in armour, while other armourers copied and blended the two styles.

Armour

The importance of the armed man on horseback was matched by that of his horse, but it was not until the second half of the 15th century that both horse and man were fully armoured. This is not to say that horses had not previously had some form of protection – articles of horse armour such as the chanfron, a hard plate for the head, had been in widespread use for several centuries. In contemporary illustrations the armoured man's horse is usually shown wearing a *caparison* or "horse's surcoat", which makes it difficult to know what if anything was worn beneath.

In the middle of the 13th century horses were sometimes fitted with mail armour that covered the head, neck and body and was divided at the saddle into two parts. But the use of mail was limited because of the excessive weight and, of course, cost. In the course of the 14th century horse armour developed to consist of a chanfron with the addition of a crinet, to protect the top of the horse's neck.

With the advance towards complete plate armour for the mounted man and the decline of other forms such as mail, leather and quilted armour, the horse's protection too came under consideration. Complete armour for horse had one main drawback, and that again was weight, but there were a number of complete sets made. The various pieces included the chanfron (head), crinet (neck), peytral (chest), flanchards (flanks), and a shaped crupper at the back to protect the rear. In the main, however, horse armour tended to be simple, with basic plate covering the head and neck; the rest of the animal, if any protection was afforded, was covered with quilted cloth, or defended with rivets or plates sewn to cloth.

Leather also reappeared to give a cheap, light and easily constructed defence against foot soldiers. By the mid-16th century, however, with the increased importance of the gun, only a shortened chanfron and crinet were in use.

In the joust or tournament, extra items of horse protection were employed such as the *Stechkissen*, a canvas tube stuffed with straw and slung from the neck to form a fender over the chest. This was not so much a protection from the opponent as to protect the horses from collision; at the same time it gave a rudimentary form of protection to the rider's legs.

A complete armour for horse was the prerogative of the wealthy, who had the armour made to match their own suits. Perhaps the finest such example is the armour of Henry VIII, in which the entire suit and horse's armour is engraved with scenes of the martyrdom of St. Barbara and St. George.

This "Gothic" war harness for man and horse, now in the Wallace Collection in London, demonstrates the supreme craft of the armourer in making the outfit for man and beast. This is the only known instance where the armour for both man and horse have survived. The example is typical of the Germanic style of the last quarter of the 15th century. The flutes extend to all parts except for the greaves, which are plain. Note the cusped edges, the radiating flutes, and the sallet worn with visor as well as bevor.

Armour

The beginning of the century still saw the rounded Italian style much in vogue and a number of features of Italian armour had been copied and adapted by German armourers. The German influence was, however, strong in the area around Venice. The upper and lower arm protection of Italian armour (the vambrace) was usually riveted, not tied like the German armour to the leather inside joiners. This made for a flatter look and of course lacked some of the articulated movement.

The Italian armour of the period was still smooth and rounded and, despite the German influence, continued as such. While the German fluted armour of this period gained a certain favour, Italian armour was still more widely seen. A typical Italian style would have a rounded breastplate with the skirt swelling out to echo the curve. The tassets were invariably divided into three pieces and held with straps on the outside. The gauntlets were mitten-shaped and the sabatons had blunt toes. In fact, except for these few minor changes, Italian armour could be said to be behind the times as it derived its basic form from the previous century. The armet was the favoured headwear of the Italian armourers.

Lighter armours were also demanded at this time, and a large number of good quality three-quarter-length suits was produced for both mounted and foot troops. In England, as in Flanders, the Italian influence on the style of armour can be clearly seen in the plain suits used in those countries which contrast sharply with the fluted German style. That was not to say that Italian armourers did not go in for more decorative suits. There are a number of flamboyant suits showing a leaning towards civilian fashion in the making of armour. One example was made for Guidobaldo della Rovere and shown in a portrait of him. While the slashed and puffed civilian style is incorporated in metal into the suit, this is in a simple form compared with some of the German armourers' rendition of the same style.

Italian suits were still basic in their construction and the decoration, while skilled, was subdued. Etching was usually in bands with the background executed in hatching. While soon out of fashion in Germany, this form of background design continued later in England and for even longer in France and Italy.

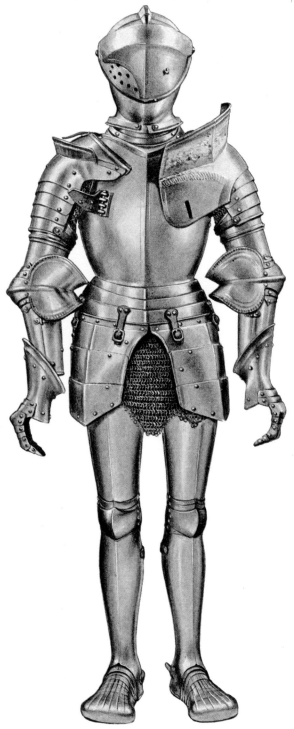

Milanese armour in the Italian style, c. 1510–15, signed with the initials N.I.

49

Armour

This German armour dates from about 1540. The rounded fluted forms of the "Maximilian" style are clearly shown, with the ridges in all parts of the armour except the greaves. The head protection is a close-helmet, with roped cauls to the visor.

Early 16-century German Armour

At the beginning of the 16th century another "arms race" took place. The forward-looking Emperor Maximilian brought in many changes in weapons and warfare; he set up a court workshop for armour at Innsbruck and from these workshops came a flow of armour which dominated armour design during the first 30 years of the century, the "Maximilian" style.

The armour was noted for the roundness and yet the intricate fluting associated with the name. These ridges, while visually pleasing, were also functional. They provided extra strength and at the same time gave many more areas of deflection for the point of a sword. The use of these ridges was not confined to the man but was also used for his horse – the usual defensive horse armour was made in the fluted style.

The making of such armours tried the skill of even the best makers. The true skill was in making an armour that was outwardly pleasing and strong. The flutes did indeed give added strength, but the armour still had to be thicker in some places than others; and correct tempering was also vital; here the Innsbruck armour-makers showed their skills. While it only remained popular for some 30 years, the Maximilian style was perhaps armour at its scientific best. Other styles may be more pleasing, others more efficient, but in Innsbruck the technology of metalworking came to the aid of the maker in a new way.

Although termed Maximilian, this armour is a posthumous result of the emperor's lavish patronage, and most surviving suits date from after Maximilian's death in 1519. The armour evolved rapidly a synthesis of Italian roundness and German spikiness, and soon every portion of the armour, with the exception of the greaves, was covered with close fluting. (Some breastplates had wolf's-teeth patterning, which may have led to the idea of fluting.)

In some harnesses, the armourer produced variations on the idea by having sets of fluting broken up with flat bands of engraving. After 1530, a style of more rounded shapes and flatter surfaces evolved.

Armour

The lead given by Emperor Maximilian in setting up an armourers' shop at Innsbruck set the fashion for other courts in Europe, notably in Scotland and later in Sweden (1551). Henry VIII of England was not to be outdone. He considered, doubtless correctly, that the state of the home armour industry was poor and lagged behind the European armourers. The king imported armourers from Italy to make the popular Italian style of armour. But fashions changed, and the German style became popular in the early 1500s. Henry then imported the required number of German armourers and in 1515 set them working at Greenwich. The task of these eleven men was to make armour for the king and favoured courtiers. Although the makers were German, with their own style, the armour they produced still owed much to the Italian influence.

Martin van Royne continued to oversee the Greenwich workshops until about 1540, when he was succeeded by the chief armourer Erasmus Kyrkenar. Permission to have an armour made at Greenwich was eagerly sought from the king, but was granted to relatively few. While the armour displayed the skill of the armourer himself it was also richly decorated with engraving and etching. Suits made at Greenwich were for both the tournament and warfare, and surviving examples have their extra pieces for adaptation to both uses. Typical armour would consist of a closed helm, back and front main plates, arm and leg protection, short tassets and cuisses made of a number of overlapping lames. Gauntlets again were made of a number of overlapping pieces for better grip. The feet were protected by mail with metal caps for the toes. The extras for the tournament would include a heavier visor, a grandguard (a plate that reinforced the whole of the left and part of the right side of the breastplate), a large gauntlet for the left hand and protection for the left elbow. Greenwich armour sometimes had the breast- and backplates made of a number of overlapping plates riveted loosely together for ease of movement, but obviously for the tournament these would be replaced by solid breast- and backplates.

Prime examples of the craftsmanship of Greenwich are the surviving suits of Henry VIII, made for him at various times. While they show the rapid increase in the size of the monarch, they also incorporate ingenious systems to make the wearing more comfortable for a man of his size. In the Greenwich suit of about 1545, the breastplate laminations at the waist and upper thigh are slotted for rivets and leathered to conform exactly to the movements of a man of considerable size.

The lead given by Maximilian gave ideas to other monarchs about setting up their own workshops. Henry VIII imported Italian and German craftsmen, and the armours made at Greenwich are among the finest made. The armour made for Henry VIII in 1540 (far right) shows his increasing size when compared with earlier garnitures. It was made for the field and the tilt. Part of the decoration was based on designs of Hans Holbein the Younger. The rear view of an earlier (1515–20) combat armour of Henry VIII (right) shows how complete encasement of the man was combined with flexibility for movement. This armour is also illustrated on p. 72.

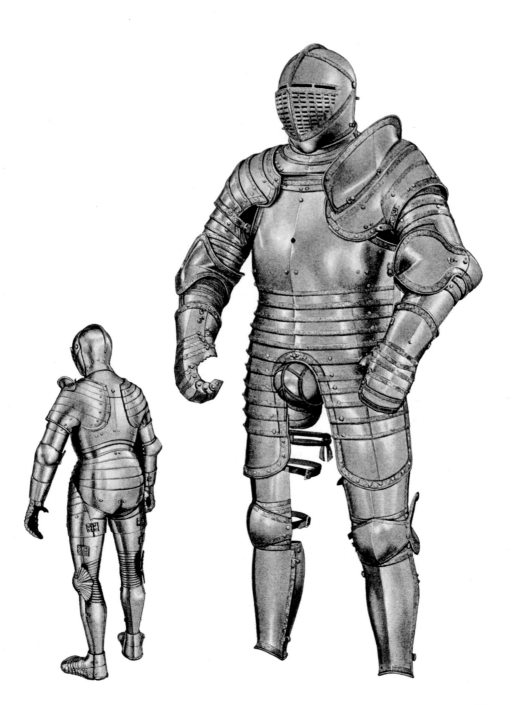

Armour

The most typical of 16th-century head protection was the close-helmet, similar in style to the armet but without the hinged cheek pieces. The close-helmet had a gorget plate attached to the lower edge which rested on the gorget of the suit of armour. The original style of close-helmet had a very low comb, but this increased in size towards the end of the century. After that once again the comb diminished in size, and the visor also became less prominent.

There was a considerable variation in the finish and style of the close-helmet. Among the prominent styles were those of the German fluted period of the 1520s and 1530s, the more pleasing style of the Greenwich armour and close-helmets, and the flamboyant, heavily etched or embossed French and Italian helmets.

Alongside the close-helmet, other forms of head protection were developing. One of the popular styles was the burgonet. This was essentially an open-fronted helmet, usually fitted with a peak. It could, however, be converted into a closed type by the addition of a falling buffe. The "1540" armour of Henry VIII (which is illustrated on p. 52) had an open burgonet, for use with the half-armour worn on foot, that could be converted by the addition of a falling buffe to a closed burgonet for use in the horseman's three-quarter suit.

Burgonets were closely modelled on the close-helmet, and most had the central comb above the peak. There are some finely embossed burgonets surviving in the classical style, a popular form of headdress in the highly decorative Italian parade armour suits.

Yet another form of head protection was also developing, but this was in a far more simple form. The morion was an open helmet with a curved brim and central comb. It was the usual headwear of the foot soldier in the second half of the 16th century. Variations again exist in the style, the two main differences being the morion with a central comb (comb morion) and the so-called Spanish morion or cabasset, without a comb but with a plain skull. Another style was the peaked morion which was similar to the morion but had up-swept peaks at the front and back.

Examples of morions show different types of workmanship from the ordinary plain versions for the troops to more decorative versions for officers and noblemen. There are many fine morions with etching and embossed work emanating from Germany and Italy. An exceptionally fine example of a morion was made for Charles IX of France; it was gilded, and had embossed scenes which were further decorated in enamels.

The 16th century saw the introduction of the closed style of helmet, but by the end of the century a more open style was adopted which, with the addition of a falling buffe, could be converted to the more protective closed form.

1. German armet, c. 1540, with plain ridged skull, hinged cheek pieces and falling visor.

2. Flemish close-helmet with the skull in two parts joined at the comb, c. 1570. The entire surface is embossed with Roman figures, cherubs, heads and strap work.

3. Burgonet by Wolf of Landshut, c. 1551. This example displays fine engraving on the typical peak and is of the open style with facial protection and front and back gorget plates. The chin piece pivots at the same points as the face guard and is locked in position with hooks each side.

4. Burgonet of Hungarian or Polish origin, c. 1630, with open facial area protected by a single sliding nasal bar, heavy earpieces and neck protection.

5. The "Spanish" morion. An example of the typical pear-shaped skulls with embossed work, c. 1575–90.

6. Italian combed morion, c. 1590. With the very high comb, highly decorated and roped, this is a prime example of the style. The plume holder is missing. The surface is heavily etched in a Roman style.

Armour

In sharp contrast to earlier fluted styles, later German armours were rather plain, yet highly functional.

Left. Nuremberg three-quarter armour, c. 1540–50. The helmet is a closed burgonet with pivoted peak and falling buffe consisting of a visor with horizontal sights.

Above. Armour for the tilt, Augsburg and Landshut, c. 1550–60. Although a composite suit, this demonstrates the clean lines of the German style.

Later 16th-century German Armour

The heyday of the Maximilian fluted style lasted but a little time and the influence exercised by it soon faded, occasionally to be revived. Even at its most popular, the Maximilian style was found side by side with plain armour. In Germany the latter years of the century produced a plainer style of armour. Although this was more clean-cut in its lines and form, it was not quite so efficient in defensive qualities. The simple lines, perhaps now embossed, or in German armour engraved, were brilliant in their effect, but the armour, while being exceptionally well produced with perfect fitting, was little match in practical terms for what had come before. The use of engraving, etching and embossing of armour had removed its one main defence apart from thickness, the deflecting surface. The surface decoration would now almost "grip" the point of the weapon, rather than turn it. The one major concession was the haute pieces to deflect from the neck, although the shape of these items was almost damaging to the wearer. The shock of a blow on these could be serious, but at least they did protect the vulnerable area, principally the throat; here they did better than the gorget because with the latter there had to be a join.

The simplicity in the armour is illustrated in the design of the breastplate with a single central ridge, and of the lower part, in which the laminated portions, or tassets, were now no longer as numerous as in Maximilian armour but limited to the simple three parts on each leg. The upper thigh was plain as it always had been, and the footwear was of simple laminated construction. The groin was usually protected by a curtain of mail, the hand by gauntlets with pointed cuffs not as high as in the Maximilian style, and the face with the closed style of helmet.

In contrast with the cleanness and plainness of this style of practical armour, there were many kings and nobles who had flamboyant suits made which followed civilian styles in clothes. One must be the Augsburg parade armour with its puffed sleeves and upper thighs in imitation of the *Landsknecht* fashion of slashed costumes.

At the end of the century, the increased desire and need for mobility made many a mounted man lighten his full armour to the three-quarter suit, doing away with lower leg protection.

Armour

In the second half of the 16th century, Italian armour was not renowned for its form so much as for its flamboyant embossing and etching. Germans favoured etching for decoration and although examples of embossed German armour have survived, the German armourers were never able to match the Italian embossed armour styles.

The Italian armourers were still hard at work producing numerous suits intended for use in the field and of course for the tournament and the tilt, although these were by now losing popularity, but the quality of the decoration was in decline. Here we must not confuse the armour for use in combat with the parade armour, that flamboyant style of purely decorative suit intended as an outward display of the wearer's wealth. (These highly decorative armours are discussed on page 64.)

The Italian style of decoration was a shadow of its former appearance at this time, the bands of etching being a rather thin and wispy version of the "trophies of arms" found earlier, so much so that one authority called it "mops and brooms" decoration.

By the middle part of the century, the German influence was creeping in and by the last decades of the 16th century, the German style appeared equally alongside the native Italian work.

The style of the armour followed the fashions in dress of the period, the breastplate becoming elongated by the middle of the century and assuming a definite peascod by the 1570s. The shape of the tassets, which were of course laminated, differed in shape according to the intended usage of the armour. For foot combat they tended to be rather square with numerous lames, while for fighting on horseback shield-shaped tassets were mostly used. Later, the laminated tassets for foot combat gave way to solid tassets engraved with lines and embossed with ridges of would-be lames.

The head protection to go with these styles usually consisted of a "Spanish" morion, a combed morion, or a burgonet, whose skull often resembled either of the two.

The couter, the all-important elbow-joint protector, was in the German style which had been popular since the beginning of the century. By the second half of the 16th century it had become smaller, and now enveloped the vital joint completely.

The basic style of decoration used in this period took the form of bands of etching with the rest of the armour plain. The bands often incorporated trophies of arms in bright steel against a background of dotting.

Compared with earlier styles, Italian armour of the late 16th century is poor in form but the quality of embossing and engraving is high. This is evident in the parade armour **Below,** *which is Milanese, c. 1590, by Lucio Piccinino. The entire surface of this rich armour (the tassets, which go under the fauld, and the backplate are not shown) is embossed, gilt and damascened in gold and silver (see description, p.64). The peaked morion is earlier, c. 1570, but also Milanese and with two broad chin-straps of three lames decorated with trophies.*

Top right. *Triple-combed morion, Italian, c. 1545, with embossed and chased fleurs de lys, ovals, rosettes, scrolling and ropework. Note the plume-holder at the rear.*
Top left. *More practical as defensive armour is this north Italian "Pisan"-style armour of c. 1570–80, with a high-combed burgonet with hinged cheek-pieces and rear plume-holder. The etching is of roping, foliage, medallions, trophies etc.*

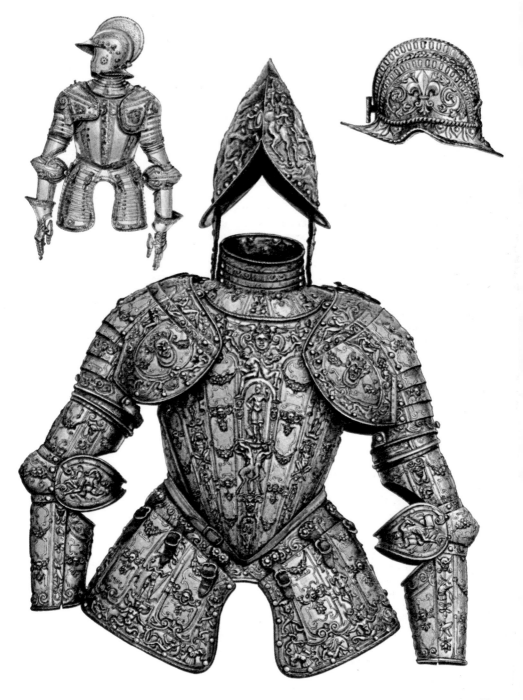

Armour

Later 16th-century Greenwich Armour

Greenwich was still producing quality armour in the late 16th century, often in a highly decorative style, usually engraved, blued and gilded. To complement the armour various extra items were also made for the tilt and foot combat. The complete armour was made for George Clifford, third Earl of Cumberland, c. 1580–90 (see text). The burgonet and breastplate were made 1590–1600 for Thomas Sackville, later Earl of Dorset.

As we have seen, Greenwich still continued to produce armour not only of fine form and quality but also of a highly decorative style. By this period, armour was being strongly influenced by contemporary civilian fashion in clothes, and the various salient features of style of dress can be seen in surviving suits in museums and collections. The peascod, for example, is reflected in the pointed lower portion of some breastplates.

By the time of Elizabeth I, Greenwich was highly reputed for its engraved suits. In the famous Jacobe Album in the Victoria and Albert Museum, named for its compiler Jacob Halder who died in 1607, many designs for armour and decoration for the favoured rich are shown in full colour detail with the names of their owners. Many of the drawings show not only the suit but also alternative headwear, horse armour and additional extra pieces for use in tournament. The decoration varies from white, i.e. polished steel, to browned or blued metal decorated with etching and gilding in bands, forming panels which sometimes bear a heraldic device, for example the ragged staff of Warwick on a suit now in the Tower of London.

A fine example of that made for George Clifford, 3rd Earl of Cumberland, in 1580 – 90. The suit and extras were made for the field and tournament or tilt and included the later style of closed helmet with central comb. The breastplate was fitted as usual on the right side with a lance-rest and was of peascod form. The tassets were short and rounded in the centre to take the codpiece. The cuisses were made from seven pieces on each upper leg for ease of movement and the lower leg was protected with greaves and fully armoured and articulated foot covering.

Later helmets appear to have been made in parts that were then joined at the comb. Although more crudely made than earlier Greenwich helmets, they were nevertheless functional.

It was not until the beginning of the 17th century that Greenwich armour too started to decline in quality and the Dymoke armour made for the Monarch's Champion is considered today by experts to be of inferior quality in both metal and workmanship. The skull of the helmet is in two pieces and joined rather poorly. The breastplate is of the peascod style already long out of fashion, but the main interest is that the armourers had still tailor-made the suit as in previous decades. This shows in that attempts have been made (and quite skilfully) to disguise the fact that the left leg is an inch shorter than the right.

Armour

During the later years of the 16th century, the armour of the ordinary foot soldier, usually a rudimentary defence, was of rather poor quality. The armour was also very much simplified. The basic armour would consist of a helmet of some sort with neck protection and perhaps a face guard, outward-jutting breastplate, a backplate, and only outside arm protection. While tassets had been popular in the opening years of the century they were soon simplified and lower leg armour was entirely abandoned. Mail collars were often worn, but there was little plate except for the protection to the shoulders and armpit. The gunners, who fired the early handguns, spurned armour altogether. It was too cumbersome, and with their type of weapon it was felt that somehow they did not need the lobster-like protection of armour. Officers, however, continued to wear more splendid and complete armours than the men.

The rounded early German style soon gave way to a different shape of breastplate with a central line dipping towards the stomach. While the pikemen continued to wear their armour, archers and those who "shot" were even forbidden to wear suits of armour. Thomas Audley, Henry VIII's one-time Provost Marshal, decreed that he ". . . wished that no shot should have armour upon him but a morion or skull upon his head, for there can be no shot, neither archer nor arquebus, serve well being Armed."

Despite such decrees, "soft armour" – jacks of sewn-in plates, or in leather or padded cloth – were still a popular form of defence. Unlike plate armour and mail, they did not impede movement and yet they gave some protection.

The *Landsknecht*, the German foot soldier who often served as a mercenary, had his own style of armour during this period. The pikemen wore breast and back armour and long leg tassets together with a gorget, a neck protection of plates with the lower edge tucked under the breast armour. Mail tippets were the accepted form of protection for the upper chest and shoulders and the headwear usually was a simple skull or, as contemporary illustrations show, a hat with feathers and band. The one original contribution made by the *Landsknecht* to fashion and also to armour was the huge puffed sleeves with slits in them, the slits extended to hose and doublet. The fashion, which spread throughout Europe, was even copied in metal, and some fashion-conscious leaders would have armour made in this puffed style.

While the "shot" often wore the jack with plates, like many other foot soldiers, the spread of firearms eventually made this form of protection obsolete. The true foot armour of plates survived with pikemen, often deployed to defend the "shot", for another century.

Above. *The ubiquitous morion, again in a typical munition version with little skill in production, but essentially good protection.*
Below. *A typical 17th-century "jack".*

Armour for the standard infantryman was not of very high quality but some troops such as the Landsknechts, *still wore distinctive armour. The "jack" and the morion were the usual form of "cheap" armour for the soldiery.*
Above. *Black and white half-armour with burgonet, gorget, tassets and front- and backplate. The armour is roughly made by earlier standards and intended for the rank and file. German, c. 1570.*

Armour

Parade armour was a phenomenon of the 16th century, when field armour was devoid of any trappings and utilitarian, and tournament armour was of a special design of its own. Pageant or parade armour was an outward display of wealth, and the more decorative or even grotesque the armour, the wealthier the wearer was shown to be. The Renaissance affected the armour of this type and armourers collaborated with artists to design armour. Many parade armours hark back to classical Roman days, with embossed panels, and even whole helmets, plates, both back and front, and shields completely embossed. Many surviving armours, such as those which depict scenes of triumph, or of an artistic or religious nature, were more or less useless as armour.

While parade or pageant armour was a version of the style either of the period or of classical antiquity, in both types it was decorated flamboyantly with blueing and gilding, precious metals, enamels and even precious stones. A typical description of an embossed parade casque or helmet of the 16th century would be: "The skull is embossed on the brow with a large acanthus leaf and on either side with a winged sphinx, seated with a spray of honeysuckle at the back."

The same sort of style would persist throughout the design. For armour, another typical description reads as follows:

"In the centre is a figure of Mars standing within an arch, supported by addorsed satyrs; below a small figure of charity, at the top the head of Medusa supported by two addorsed captives; on either side are seated the figures of Fame and Victory. The panels at the side are decorated with the figures representing Wisdom, Justice, Faith, Truth, Hope and Temperance, alternating with grotesque satyrs and chimaeras."

From the above, one can see that the true Renaissance designs so often found in other forms of art were adapted for armour. For the wearer, the better the decorative design the higher the station in life displayed. With these types of armour and headwear, the "fashions" set always seem to have been outdone by another with a yet more flamboyant style, by a better-known artist. While this still reflected the art of the armour-maker it was never the true skill of the armourer, whose fighting armour had earlier reached its peak in style, design, and craftsmanship with working armour some years before.

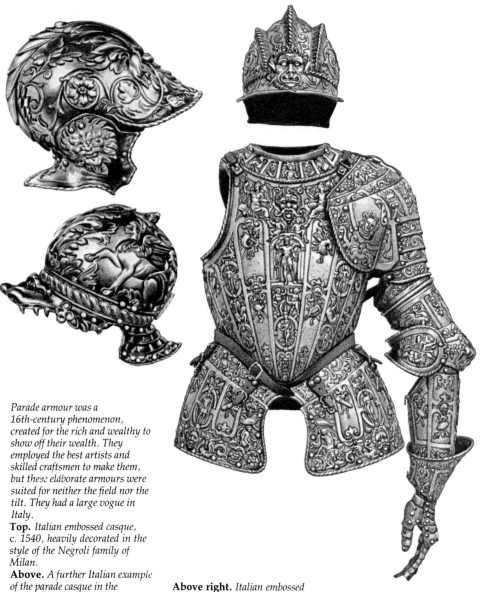

Parade armour was a
16th-century phenomenon,
created for the rich and wealthy to
show off their wealth. They
employed the best artists and
skilled craftsmen to make them,
but these elaborate armours were
suited for neither the field nor the
tilt. They had a large vogue in
Italy.

Top. *Italian embossed casque,*
c. 1540, *heavily decorated in the
style of the Negroli family of
Milan.*

Above. *A further Italian example
of the parade casque in the
burgonet style,* c. 1550, *the
decoration dominated by a winged
sphinx.*

Above right. *Italian embossed
armour of* c. 1580, *showing the
inclusion in the design of mythical
figures and symbols.*

Armour

Alongside the elaborate and often grotesque parade armour worn by men, there was the richly decorated armour made for the horse. The horse armour often followed the same style as that worn by the mounted man, and in the embossed versions the space afforded by the sheer size of horse armour allowed the artists almost unlimited scope. While Italy was the centre for embossed armour of this type, Germany held pride of place with etched styles.

A typical parade armour for horse was made in Antwerp for Eric XIV of Sweden, in 1563. The resplendent armoured man has his embossed helm topped with feather plumes which are matched by a bunch of feathers on the top of the horse's chanfron. The horse armour, divided into panels, covers the neck, face, rump and flanks, with a large upturned skirt at the front. Although destined for Eric, the armour was captured by the Danes while being delivered and it is believed to have been sold to Christian II of Saxony.

Other forms of horse armour for parade, while having the basic pieces making up the set, had many minor variations, in fact as many variations as there were in the armour of the rider. No two sets would be the same and each was individually "tailored" to suit taste, rank and wealth.

Whether or not it was embossed or etched, or inlaid with enamels, parade armour rarely presented smooth, deflecting surfaces, and it was often cumbersome; but as it was intended for pageant use, the burden was of no importance. Parade armour lingered long after the general demise of armour but it, too, went out of fashion, at least as a serious form of ceremonial wear.

Left. *Italian parade casque by Filippo Negroli of Milan, c. 1530.*

Parade Armour

Right. *Full parade armour for man and horse, German, c. 1550.*
Below. *Italian parade armour breastplate, c. 1550. The decoration and form is typical of the popular "Roman" style.*

Armour

The joust had always been a knightly pursuit and even in early days special adaptations of fighting armour were evolved. In the 13th century, jousting armour consisted of the usual field mail hauberk over which was worn a thick metal plate, fitted to the lower part of the helmet, to cover the chest; a circular plate (vamplate) was fitted to the lance to protect the hand. A robust shield was carried in the left hand and in some cases strapped to the shoulder to keep it in position. A special form of saddle with a high front meant that leg armour was seldom if ever worn.

By the late 15th century many types of jousting and tournament had been devised, especially in Germany, and armourers designed special armour for each.

In Germany the *Gestech* consisted of trying to unseat one's opponent or to smash a lance on his specially designed frog-mouth helm. In the *Rennen* sharp lances were used, and consequently heavier armour, but by the end of the 15th century only a sallet and bevor were worn with light half armour, the added protection coming from a wood shield which hung on the left side. Other variations of the tournament in Germany involved depriving the opponents of their helmets, or employing specially made shields that flew to pieces when struck in the right place.

In England, by the mid-15th century, the great helm had been adapted for foot combat by replacing the front portion with a gorget and visor. A fine example of early 16th-century armour, adaptable for both field use and for both mounted and foot combat in the tournament, is that made for Henry VIII. It was copied from the idea of the Emperor Maximilian who, with his armourer, Koloman Helmschmied, had designed an equipment known as an "armour garniture" that could be built up and adapted for various uses. The armour of Henry VIII does exactly this, converting from a horseman's complete suit to a three-quarter suit, and to half-armour for foot wear, complete armour for tournament, complete armour for joust and finally complete armour for tournament foot combat.

The horse was also armoured, usually to match the armour of the rider, but the metal was often covered with embroidered decorative cloths which could be changed at will.

The principle of added protection afforded by plates fitted over the chest and up over the lower part of the helmet continued until the demise of the tournament around the end of the 16th century. Tournaments were replaced by pageants or parades, in which elaborate copies of Roman and other armour were worn (see previous pp.).

Above. *Portion of tilt armour, Italian, c. 1580.*
Right. *German armour for the joust, made in Augsburg, c. 1500–1520.*
Far right. *Great helm for the tilt, English, c. 1515.*

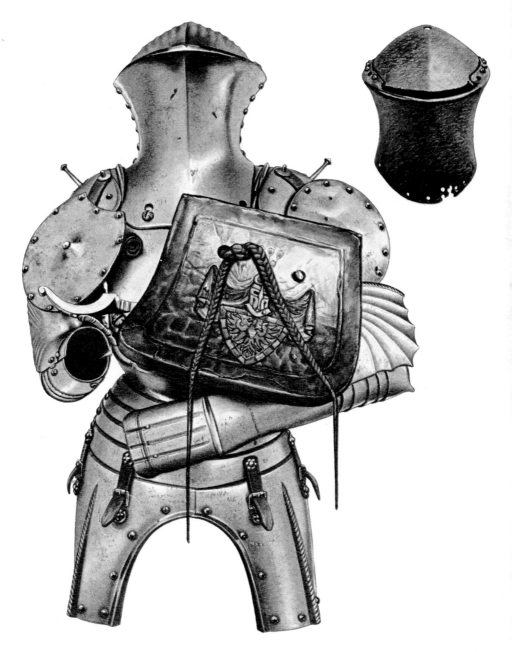

Armour

As stated previously, the armour developed under Maximilian, and emulated by Henry VIII, was the zenith of the armourer's craft and ingenuity. Additional items were evolved that converted the suit to its various uses. The adaptations that concern us here are complete armour for tournament, for the joust, and for foot combat, and the same three variations for fighting armour.

The horseman's complete armour for the field consisted of a closed helmet, breastplate with lance-rest on the right side, pauldrons and the usual arm defences and gauntlets. To the breastplate and backplate tassets were attached. The lower limbs were protected by cuisses and greaves. Beneath the armour a mail shirt or at least gussets and mail hose or "underwear" would generally be worn to protect the under-arm region and crotch. If sabatons were not worn, the feet could also be protected by mail. In the three-quarter armour the full visor of the burgonet was added in place of the field visor and wrapper and there were no additional haute-pieces on the shoulders. Longer tassets were fitted to the breastplate, reaching to the knee with no other protection for the lower leg. The half-armour for foot service was yet another adaptation of the basic harness. In this set the visor was dispensed with, and the breastplate, which bore the same tassets as the complete armour, had no lance-rest. The shoulder and arm defences in plate were dispensed with and at these points only the mail shirt, or sometimes simply mail sleeves, gave protection. Gauntlets or mail mittens were worn. The crotch was protected with a plate codpiece and a plate to protect the inner thigh. A bottom defence could also be worn for foot combat. This was a single shaped plate.

For the tilt (by the mid-15th century a barrier or "tilt" separated the two charging knights), the helmet had a heavier visor and the haute-pieces and wrapper were dispensed with. The left elbow was fitted with a large reinforced piece and a large, heavy grandguard covered the left shoulder. A special gauntlet with large cuff was worn on the left hand. The grandguard covered not only the left shoulder but also a large part of the breast and lower part of the helmet. The thighs and lower regions were protected with an extra skirt and tassets. There were other extras which could be used for the tournament, such as a special locking gauntlet which stopped the wearer losing his sword (this was disallowed in some tournament rules). Armour for foot combat in tournament comprised the field armour helmet, breastplate and tassets, full arm and shoulder protection, a codpiece, and leg protection.

With the joust being an accepted part of the noble way of life, armourers catered for it. Field armour did not require the extra protection on the left shoulder and arm needed in the joust, so the armourers designed additional pieces to be bolted or strapped to field armour. Shown here are additional heavy pieces for the tilt, including the grandguard and bevor bolted in one, heavy elbow piece, special gauntlet, extra skirt, and tassets.

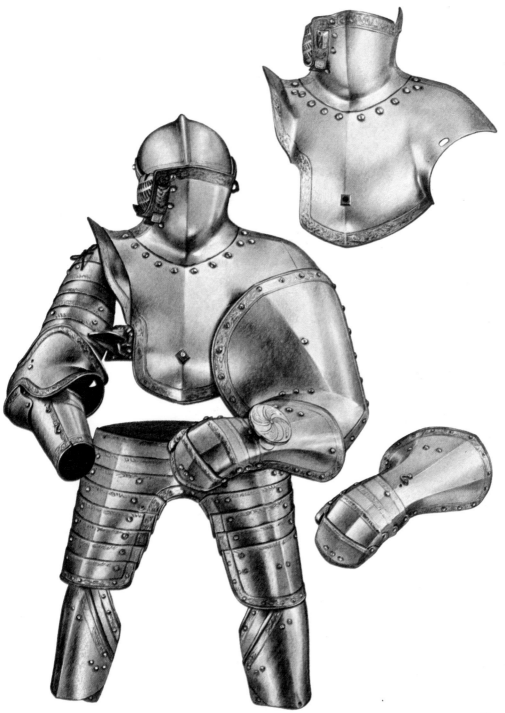

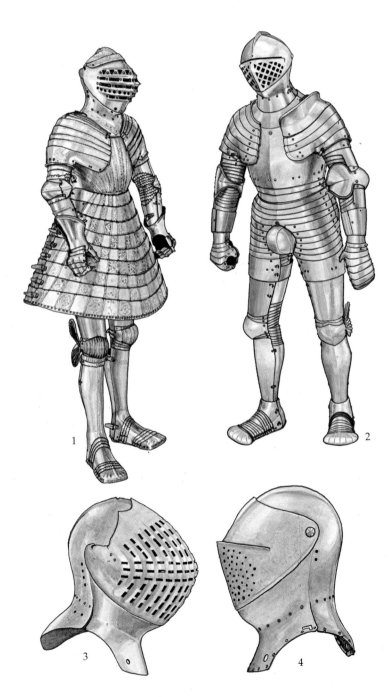

Foot Combat Armour

1. *A tonlet armour made for Henry VIII c. 1510 by Italian craftsmen in England, the helmet imported from Milan. The two halves, each of 9 lames, are fastened together by hinges (left) and straps and buckles (right) and attached to the flange of the cuirass by turning pins.*
2. *Armour made for Henry VIII at the Royal Workshops, Greenwich, c. 1515–20. Articulated splints protect the armpits, elbows and knee joints; the vambraces fasten over the cuffs of the mitten gauntlets which are free to turn on flanges. (See rear view, p. 53.)*
3. *Great bascinet, probably Dutch, c. 1500. Combines good all-round vision with complete protection for the face.*
4. *Great bascinet, probably English, c. 1515. Designed for foot combat in the lists. Vision is through holes on the left of the visor.*

In the 15th century combat on foot became an increasingly popular part of the tournament. Many types of weapons were used, including spears, swords, clubs and daggers, but perhaps most popular of all was the pole-axe. This type of combat soon proved to be very dangerous and attempts were made to reduce the risks involved, perhaps an indication that already the tournament was coming to be regarded more as a sport and less as a preparation for the rigours of war. Sometimes barriers were erected between the contestants to prevent that grappling and mauling which so often proved fatal. Another safeguard was to provide specialised armours which combined maximum mobility with maximum protection.

Until about 1500 the normal equipment for the foot combat was the ordinary field armour usually with the addition of cuisses completely encasing the thigh and, instead of the normal field helmet, a great bascinet with a globular barred visor. At first the bascinet was attached to the cuirass by straps but this was not very secure as they could easily be cut through by an opponent's weapon. On later armours the bascinet was always screwed on to the cuirass.

A new type of foot combat armour appeared in Germany at the beginning of the 16th century. This was characterised by a flared and laminated skirt known as a tonlet, which extended to the knees, symmetrical pauldrons and cuisses completely encasing the thighs. Although such armours were sometimes equipped with close-helmets, the great bascinet remained the most popular form of helmet for foot combat and two new types now appeared – one of hemispherical shape with small piercings in the visor, the other with a visor of bellows form. After the mid-16th century the tonlet armour was replaced by a foot combat harness not very different from the ordinary three-quarter field armour, the distinctive features of which were symmetrical pauldrons and special mitten gauntlets which were flanged along the inner edge to prevent an opponent's weapon glancing down one's own weapon and into the unprotected part of the hand. A practically unique type of foot combat armour, produced only in the second and third decades of the 16th century, is represented by an armour for Henry VIII which instead of a tonlet had laminated steel breeches.

Armour

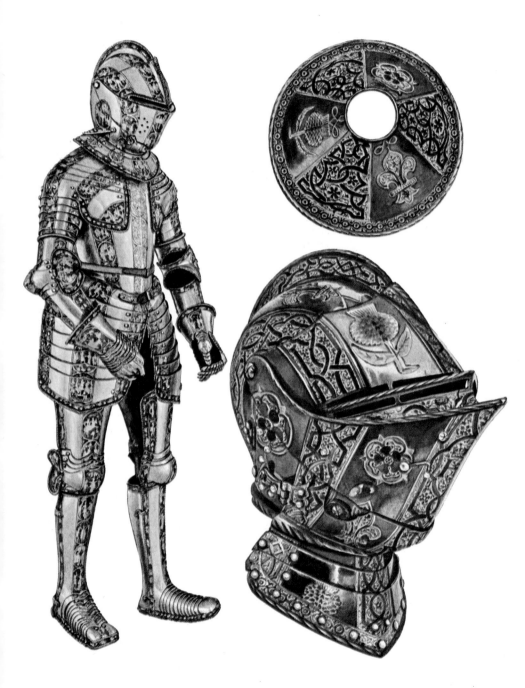

Some new forms of armour developed in the 17th century, particularly for pikemen and cavalry. In general, however, a slow decline in the use of armour was brought about after 1600 by the increased use and increased penetrating power of firearms. It was now not possible to provide "bullet"-proof armour for the mounted man to cover the whole body and yet still allow him the freedom of mobility which was one of his prime attributes. With the decline in demand for armour, the quality became noticeably poor in the average fighting armour that did still persist. There are numerous occasions on record of soldiers refusing to wear armour and of it having to be carried in the baggage carts. It even got to the stage where incentive payments had to be made to induce the men to wear their armour! All this had an effect on the makers themselves, whose munition armour now had flat breastplates, broader and shorter than the elegant peascod, symmetrical pauldrons, as the cavalry lance had fallen into disuse, and less full facial protection to a helmet, now made in two halves for ease of manufacture. Despite this, the armourers of Greenwich still produced lavishly decorated suits which combined functional use, skilled workmanship and fine form.

Those armourers still working in the noble way had diverted their attention to the often grotesque parade armour, now the fashion. These suits were an example more of the craft of the designer and artist than of the armourer. Not destined for combat, they were made with purely visual considerations in view. Such armour was sometimes worn in the carousel, the successor to the tournament, in which the participants performed equestrian manoeuvres or tried to break each others' crests with blunted swords and padded maces. The prestige of armour, however, was still strong and many military commanders still insisted on being depicted in full armour in their portraits; sometimes this was not even the sitter's own – painters could supply from their studio props, or armour was often loaned from large collections, such as that of the Tower of London, for the purpose.

Vestiges of armour still remained, even if in simple forms. The horseman still wore the breast- and backplates, the helmet, albeit with simplified face protection, and the elbow gauntlet for the bridle hand. It appears that in the Low Countries armour for foot soldiers in its true form persisted for longer, but except for the use of breast- and backplates by some European cavalry and the continued use of a metal head defence, armour was no longer viable.

After 1600 armour came to be used less and less on the battlefield. This parade armour made in France c. 1640 for Charles I of England is relatively feeble in line. The helmet and vamplate (made in the Greenwich workshops for Henry Prince of Wales to use in tilt competitions) is, however, still functional and of good form despite its lavish decoration.

Armour

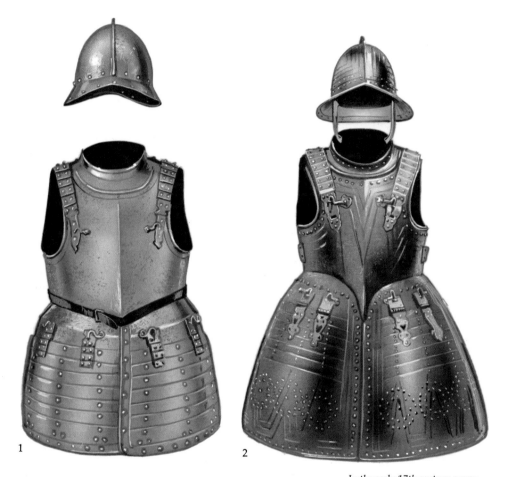

1

2

Pikemen, essential to any infantry, wore armour that did not impair their mobility yet afforded adequate protection from the weapons of the opponent. The task of the pikeman was to defend musketeers from cavalry attack and also on occasion to advance offensively. The head protection was the pikeman's pot, a rounded skull made in two halves joined at the central comb and a wide brim tilted up at the front and back and drooping down at each side. The pot had ear protectors, which are now usually missing on surviving examples as the leather securing straps have perished or been removed. These simple plates, hinged to the inside rim of the skull, fell over the ears and were secured by a thong or strap and buckle under the chin. For

In the early 17th century a new form of armour was developed for the pikemen, still a major force in European armies despite the inroads made by firearms. Despite the lines and studs, the tassets are solid, not laminated.
1. Dutch pikeman's armour with solid tassets.
2. English pikeman's armour with decorated breastplate, tassets and helmet; Greenwich (?).
3. Later English pikeman's armour for the New Model Army, with plain breastplate and tassets.

regimental distinctions, the plume-socket at the rear of the pot was sometimes decorated with a feathered plume.

Pikemen's armour was comparable throughout Europe and was even used in North America. Well known, because of the Civil Wars in England, is the English pikeman's armour, on which the following description is based. The body armour consisted of five parts. These were the collar, the breast- and the backplate, and the two tassets. The collar was hinged on one side and clipped together on the other with a keyhole and stud, and worn beneath the cuirass. Officers also wore a gorget, sometimes without a breastplate, when it was more decorative and also deeper, some coming down to almost the bottom of the breastbone. The breastplate was cut away under the arms; it had a central rib and came to a point, a survival of the 16th-century peascod, over the wearer's stomach. The backplate with a central dip between the shoulder blades, had two shoulder straps and two portions of a waist belt, riveted to the waist of the plate, one each side with a buckle on one end. The shoulder straps ended in metal-covered plate in which a keyhole shape was cut. When worn, these connected with studs on the front plate and the two halves of the belt buckled at the front. To the flange of the front of the breastplate a pair of tassets was attached, by either straps and buckles, the former covered in laminated plates, or permanently by studs, or by hinges. The tassets were square in shape and gave an all-enveloping protection to the front lower portion of the body. Although each tasset was made of one piece of metal, they were often embossed, at least in England, to give the appearance of laminated armour. In addition purely decorative studs were used, sometimes to form an initial if the armour belonged to a family armoury.

Earlier armour had often been polished bright. The armour of the pikeman was often blued or left with the black or blue colours from the forge. The colouring might also be russet.

Infantry officers wore similar armour but of better finish – this took the form of a combination of utilitarian and decorative. The more usual armour for officers was breast- and backplate with head protection only, but many officers dispensed with the breast- and backplate altogether and wore the rather large gorget described above. The use of armour at this stage combined protection with minimum weight and hindrance to movement. In fact, armour was now on the decline because of the weight required to be bullet-proof.

3

Armour

As a new style of cavalry and tactics developed, a new type of armour was produced, knee-length only and designed to be worn with heavy boots. This typical three-quarter-length suit with double gorget was made c. 1620, probably in Augsburg.

Late style Greenwich close-helmet, c. 1620.

In the latter part of the 16th century a new form of cavalry developed in the armies of Europe. The firearm had forced this on the horseman for whom the main threat was no longer the arrow but a lethal lead ball. The obvious first reply to the gun was to increase the thickness of armour, as had been the answer in the past, but this slowed man and horse and provided an even easier target, so protection with mobility became the order of the day.

The armour developed for the mounted man at this time (cuirassier armour) was in fact a three-quarter harness. During the English Civil War, a few entire regiments were dressed in these, rather than the more normal trooper's outfit of breast- and backplate, and this earned them the name of "lobsters". The three-quarter suit consisted of a breast- and a backplate (*cuirass*) and a large gorget, and on occasion a laminated culet to give added protection from behind. To the suit was added a pair of large pauldrons and vambraces to protect shoulders and arms respectively. Both hands were protected with articulated gauntlets. The lower portion was protected by knee-length tassets made up of 14 or even more curved overlapping pieces of metal (lames) to give freedom of movement, terminating in a knee guard (poleyn). These were worn above the heavy black leather riding boots, which effectively replaced the greaves. From the very articulated make-up of this armour one can easily see why the wearers earned their nickname.

There was a variety of helmets worn with this style, the most popular being the close-helmet with visored front, with a central comb to the skull and two slits in the upper bevor and perforations in the lower one for ventilation and breathing. Both bevors pivoted at each side and were held in place by hooks. Another popular style was the burgonet which had no bevors but hinged cheek-pieces tying under the chin.

A later version of the close-helmet did away with the upper bevor, replacing it with a visor and peak to which was attached a central vertical face bar.

With both the burgonet and the later version of the close-helmet there were great variations in the type and style of face bar, a most elaborate version being the armour of James II in the Tower of London which has the face bar, or more properly the protection for the face, in the form of an openwork Royal coat of arms flanked by supporters and "J" on the left and "R" on the right, for Jacobus Rex.

Armour

In the early part of the Thirty Years War (1618 – 48) and at the start of the English Civil War (1642) armour had still played a part. But in the course of those wars the three-quarter-length cuirassier's armour was largely abandoned in favour of a simpler suit or the use of small pieces of armour to protect vital areas.

The most marked changes took place in armour for the mounted man. From the cumbersome three-quarter-length harness, he had taken in the 1630s to wearing the basic essentials, the helmet, the breast- and backplate and usually a left-hand gauntlet, the bridle gauntlet which stretched up the arm giving protection from sword cuts. The cavalryman lightened his load by wearing under the plates a stiff coat of buff leather. This often, but not always, offered some protection against a glancing blow from an adversary's sword blade. The helmet with neck guard and ear flaps, coupled with the nasal bar or fretted face visor, was an ideal protection. The breast- and backplate, the latter thinner for the sake of weight, were also good basic protection. Each breastplate was "proved" by the armourers and many breastplates from this period bear a dent from a ball fired at close range to test the rigidity and strength of the plate. Such armour is sometimes known as "armour of proof". After a few years the bridle gauntlet was abandoned in favour of buff leather gauntlets.

For the foot soldier requiring increased mobility, the use

Armour for the Cavalry

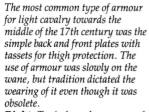

The most common type of armour for light cavalry towards the middle of the 17th century was the simple back and front plates with tassets for thigh protection. The use of armour was slowly on the wane, but tradition dictated the wearing of it even though it was obsolete.

Right. *Typical cavalry armour of the period, with upper arm defences, tassets and gorget.*

Above left. *German Zischagge with peak, neck protection and piked top.*

Above. *An officer's "pot", a burgonet style of helmet with hinged side pieces strapped over the throat.*

of armour now became a hindrance. The tassets banged against the leg, the helmet, heavy and hot, and a bullet-proof breastplate, a weight to carry. In a number of armies, the helmet for the foot soldier was replaced by either the reinforced hat or a plain hat. In the reinforced hat, the inside was fitted with either a metal skull cap or a series of metal bands (reminiscent of the early days of the 1914 – 18 war when the French soldier was said to wear his mess tin under his kepi as head protection).

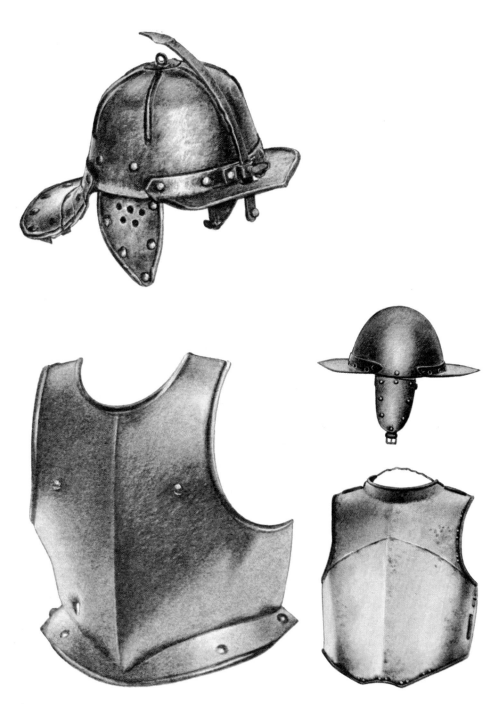

The armour of the second half of the 17th century was reduced from its former glory to a rudimentary style – breast- and backplates, and a helmet. The pikemen still continued to wear armour, if on occasion under duress, while the new musketeers shunned body armour and even armoured head protection. The cavalry still continued with a minor form of protection as did specialised troops.

Left. *Seventeenth-century trooper's armour, showing the evolved style of headwear common throughout Europe, together with the front body plate, sometimes worn without the addition of a back.*

Below left. *Siege armour. The position of a sapper was vulnerable. As ease of movement was not a priority, the extra "bullet proof" weight did not matter. This idea was resurrected during World War I for sniper's armour.*

By the later years of the 17th century, armour was very much on the decline. The cavalry contented themselves with a helmet and breast- and backplate and in some countries dispensed with the backplate altogether. The increasing use of firearms meant that the pikeman was slowly on the way out and he soon started to modify or abandon his heavy armour. The armour worn was again pared down, the tassets disappearing to leave the breastplate as the last vestige of protection.

While the infantry discarded armour with the decline and final disappearance of the pike, the cavalry, more frequent targets as shock troops, kept to their metal helmets and breast- and backplates. Towards the end of the wearing of armour, the bullet-proof qualities declined, and although armour was of a certain thickness, surviving examples show that it was no match for the more powerful musket ball. However, armour and metal helmets, as we shall see, continued to be worn by certain types of cavalry until the demise of full dress.

While armour was disappearing or being lightened, certain jobs in war still required very great protection. Sappers, whose task it was to dig saps or trenches during sieges, required heavy protection because of their nearness to the enemy. Siege armour was very heavy indeed, more so than earlier conventional armour, and was of a special design to afford maximum protection. The helmet had a thick rounded skull with a broad brim or peak at the front and back and two hinged ear protections which fastened under the chin. The breast- and backplates were of considerable thickness and usually of conventional shape.

The cavalry that did wear breast- and backplates, or just breastplates, were issued with lighter versions, which gave protection against spent bullets but were intended mainly for defence against sword or bayonet. In Britain, only the regiments of Life Guards and the Royal Horse Guards retained their cuirasses while in France, Germany and other countries regiments of cuirassiers and royal bodyguards all retained their cuirasses. While by the mid-19th century Britain had abandoned the cuirass, except for ceremonial wear, France especially and also Germany still used the cuirass in battle; France continued to do so into the first years of the 1914 – 18 war.

Armour

The demise of armour, brought about by advances in the power of firearms, was reversed during the latter years of the 19th century. Ned Kelly, the Australian bushranger who was hanged in 1880, is a celebrated, if isolated, example of one who wore armour for personal protection.

Body armour had been a part of the equipment of cavalry of some nations throughout the century and later. In the opening years of the 1914 – 18 war, the French cavalry covered their cuirasses in sacking to prevent tell-tale reflection. Metal helmets, of steel or brass, were the heavy cavalry headwear until the 1914 war, but whereas Britain reserved these for ceremonial purposes, France and Germany started the war with these items as essential protection. They soon disappeared, however, because they were ineffective and added unnecessary weight for the cavalryman.

In the 1914 – 18 war, trench armour was evolved. This was heavy enough to withstand a rifle bullet, and too heavy for general issue, although steel helmets were rapidly issued to all troops. Because the wearer of trench armour was perhaps a sniper in a fixed position the extra weight did not matter that much. For the mobile troops armour was not considered, but many British infantry officers had metal plates sewn into their service jackets to deflect spent bullets, shrapnel etc. From this developed the body armour of today.

Armoured vests made a comeback in the 1930s as personal protection for prominent people; they usually were made of plates interleaved in lobster-tail fashion and with a covering of cloth. During World War II armoured vests, helmets and sporrans were made for aircrews. Among such body defences were those manufactured by Wilkinsons for the American 8th Air Force. The vest front and back were of some considerable weight, and they were therefore provided with a quick-release mechanism in case a crew had to bail out.

After 1945, various concerns developed "bullet-proof" vests for police and other agencies. These took the form of metal (steel, aluminium or, later, titanium) plates overlapped in nylon, or of ceramic compounds, or even man-made fibre of a thickness sufficient to dissipate the impact of a bullet. The modern "flak" jacket is so composed, consisting of many layers of man-made fibre which, while not capable of stopping a direct hit at close range, will give some protection from bomb or shell fragments or from spent bullets.

In body armour, modern expertise has come to the fore,

1

2

1. *Belgian cuirassier armour, worn from the 19th century until World War I.*
2. *French "Adrien" pattern helmet, one of the many styles that evolved in World War I and were in use well into World War II.*
3. *German World War I trench*

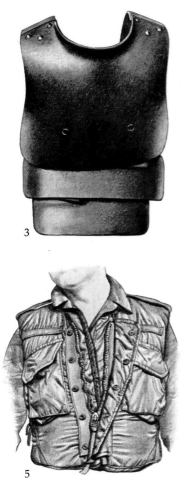

3

5

armour for snipers. Heavy in weight, with no allowance for quick movement.
4. *British trench armour. This "vest" was intended as an anti-splinter garment rather than a bullet-proof one.*
5. *Modern body armour. This U.S. personal armour, the M 1952, was essentially a "flak" jacket to absorb spent fragments and bullets.*

4

but as in the old fight of firearms against armour, the "stopping-power" of a modern firearm bullet has developed quicker than the means to halt the projectile. The armour *may* stop a point-blank shot but what of the effect of the impact on the man wearing it?

Armour

The shield, a basic and effective form of defence, continued in use for many hundreds of years, and readers undoubtedly will know that with internal security forces shields are still very much in evidence, even if modern science has come to the aid of the designers and manufacturers.

The long shields of the Normans were replaced during the 13th century by the smaller shields of flat-iron shape. Later the most common type was round and about three feet in diameter. These could be either in heavily tooled leather, or in embossed or etched steel, many having a central spike. However, smaller versions, of which many survive, were made down to the size of a saucepan lid. The use of the smaller bucklers was similar to that of the *main gauche* dagger, that is, to deflect the opponent's blade rather than directly to protect the user against blows from the opponent. When this style had died out in Europe it was still very much in use in the Indian subcontinent and continued well into the 19th century.

While the buckler was essentially the "defence" of the man fighting on foot, other shields were developed for the mounted man and the archer. The mounted man had the jousting shield, designed to let the lance pass through the cut-out between shield and body and so give maximum protection to the user. These were fashioned in wood, were usually ribbed and carried in paint either the arms of the user or one of a variety of decorative designs. The archer, on the other hand, was equipped with a pavise, a large rectangular shield of wood covered in either *cuir bouilli* (boiled hardened leather) or canvas, and again painted. The pavise (see illustration on p. 171) usually had a central rib. The shield was placed on the ground with a prop at the rear and served as a moveable barricade for 'the archer (or sometimes foot soldier), and it also provided protection for the crossbowman while he spanned his bow.

Another popular form of shield was the target. This was usually circular, of wood covered in *cuir bouilli*, the leather usually highly embossed. It could be of steel. Unlike the buckler, which was held in the hand, it was carried on the forearm and hand; the inner part was usually well padded. While this form of shield disappeared with the advance of firearms, in the Scottish Highlands the targ (target) continued in use well into the late years of the 18th century. Coupled with the broadsword, the targ, embossed with Celtic designs and heavily studded with brass domed nails, was the typical defence of the clans of the Highlands.

1

3

4

Shields

2

Shields were the fundamental
defence against any edged or early
projectile weapon and many
different styles were produced for
specific needs. While outdated by
firearms, they continued to be
used in areas outside Europe for
many years as an essential part of
the armoury.
1. Circular buckler in steel with
hook for sword or lantern
suspension. Italian, 16th century.
2. Traditional Scottish targe with
studs in brass on leather over
wood.
3. Wood buckler painted with
heraldic design. Italian (?),
c. 1600.
4. Embossed pageant shield
depicting the Tiburtine Sybil
announcing the birth of Jesus
Christ to the Emperor Augustus,
Italian, c. 1570.
5. Bouched or jousting shield
moulded in three parts with gap
for lance, covered in leather and
painted, German, c. 1500.

5

Shields

Shields were the fundamental
defence against any edged or early
projectile weapon and many
different styles were produced for
specific needs. While outdated by
firearms, they continued to be
used in areas outside Europe for
many years as an essential part of
the armoury.
1. Circular buckler in steel with
hook for sword or lantern
suspension. Italian, 16th century.
2. Traditional Scottish targe with
studs in brass on leather over
wood.
3. Wood buckler painted with
heraldic design. Italian (?),
c. 1600.
4. Embossed pageant shield
depicting the Tiburtine Sybil
announcing the birth of Jesus
Christ to the Emperor Augustus,
Italian, c. 1570.
5. Bouched or jousting shield
moulded in three parts with gap
for lance, covered in leather and
painted, German, c. 1500.

5

87

Armour

Fake, reproduction and theatrical armour sometimes appears on the market. While all of these are undoubtedly "bogus", some of the earlier-made reproduction pieces have merit of a kind, but later outright fakes, designed to deceive, have no merit whatsoever; and theatrical suits, while not strictly collectable, have a decorative quality even if they are in many cases somewhat crude or disproportionate in shape, design or workmanship.

The demand during the 19th century for armour to decorate the large houses of the new rich and to satisfy the demands of collectors caused an upsurge in the manufacture of appropriately early armour, rare even then. Much was made in the German "Gothic" style which went with the Gothic revival in taste. These suits were made in Germany and England. They are mainly examples of the tin-plate worker's art rather than that of the armourer. The plates are all the same thickness, without the added defence in vital areas which there would be in an original suit. Because the pieces of the suit were not hammered out in the old manner, there is less weight to the suit and little if any of the hammer marks that would be apparent on the inside surfaces. Many of the suits bear little resemblance to actual styles in armour and are manufactured from some crude knowledge of armour and flights of fancy. True, there are well-made suits conforming to known styles and these are of course more difficult to tell from the original.

The main things to look at in a "suspect" suit of armour are the thickness of metal, the quality of the manufacture, the edging (most good armour has well-made turned edges), and the mail, if present. But it must be emphasized that this form of knowledge is picked up with experience and although books can help determine a correct style and shape, this is not a sufficient criterion for deciding between "true" and "false".

European mail is made of riveted, not butted rings (see p. 22). Genuine plate armour has the proportions of the human body, and it is worth asking, Could this armour be worn? A complete armour may be made up of original pieces which do not belong together, giving an ill-proportioned impression. The shapes and craftsmanship of different pieces should match. Alternatively a complete harness may include some fake parts. Genuine pieces have long been the subject of modern decoration, either to raise the apparent value or to match a plain piece into an incomplete decorated armour. A "mechanical" character of engraving, perhaps shallow work, poor gilding and other inconsistencies, may betray this practice.

STAFF WEAPONS

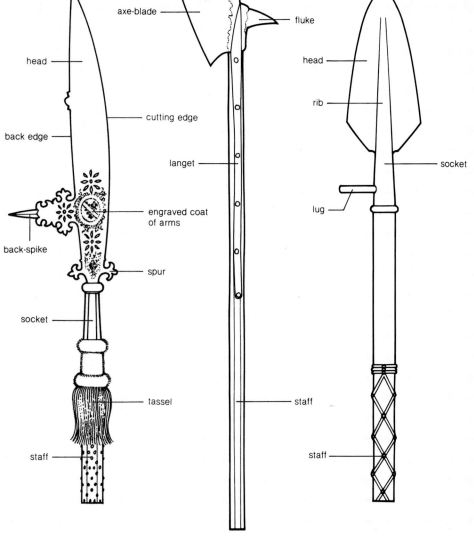

spike

axe-blade

fluke

head

head

rib

cutting edge

back edge

langet

socket

engraved coat
of arms

back-spike

lug

spur

socket

tassel

staff

staff

staff

staff

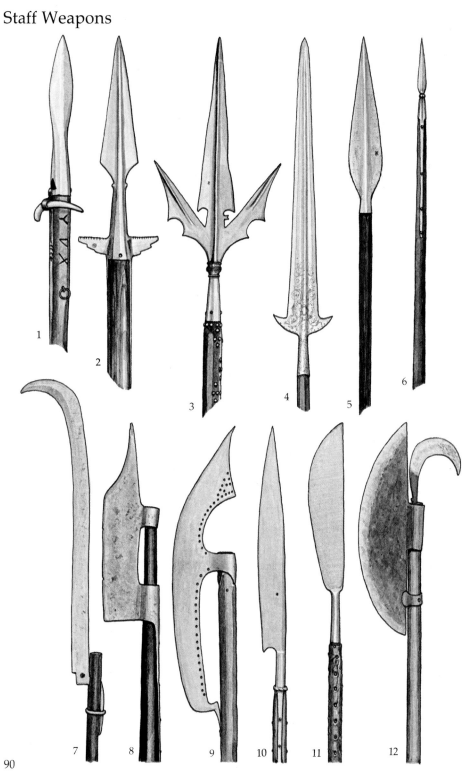

1

2

3

4

5

6

7

8

9

10

11

12

Early Staff Weapons

1. *Boar spear, German, 15th century. The bone toggle prevents excess penetration.*
2. *Lugged spear, German, late 15th century, popular for hunting and warfare. Metal lugs integral with the socket replace the toggle.*
3. *The corsèque, Italian. Possibly developed from (2). This early 16th-century example is Italian. The corsèque was also popular in France.*
4. *Partisan, Italian, early 16th century. The lugs at the base of the blade are for parrying or in later examples may be decorative.*
5. *Ceremonial weapon of boar spear type, early 16th century. This example has a hollow blade.*
6. *English pike, early 16th century. Long langets attach the head to the shaft on both sides; overall length about 16 feet.*
7. *War scythe, German, 15th century. Purely for cutting.*
8. *Early form of halberd, Swiss, late 14th century.*
9. *Bardiche, perhaps Russian, 17th century. This mediaeval, primarily cutting, weapon remained popular much later in eastern Europe.*
10. *Glaive, perhaps Italian, 16th century. A combined cutting and thrusting weapon, common throughout the mediaeval period.*
11. *Glaive, north European, late mediaeval, a more purely cutting version.*
12. *Scottish Lochaber axe, c. 1700. A simple cutting weapon of bardiche type, this version has a sharpened hook to enable the foot soldier to cut enemy cavalry's reins.*

The club and spear are probably the earliest weapons. The club increased man's hitting-power, being no more than a stone or a piece of wood. The spear, originally a sharpened sapling, perhaps hardened at the point by fire, allowed its user to inflict a wound without coming too close to his opponent. Perhaps more important was its use against large animals not affected by clubbing.

A continuous development cannot be drawn from these prehistoric weapons to those of the post-Roman period, but the principles of the club and spear – hitting and thrusting – remain two of the three main considerations which governed the design of staff weapons. The third factor is cutting. Although at most periods, including our own, there have been purely thrusting and purely hitting weapons (for example the World War II mace and pike for the British Home Guard when no rifles were available) attempts were made in the Middle Ages and later to create polearms which could be used for a combination of hitting, thrusting and cutting. Sometimes special features were provided, such as hooks to cut a horseman's reins or to pull him down, or concealed gun barrels. The introduction of the cutting blade in staff-weapon design may well have been suggested by agricultural implements, such as the scythe, which made useful emergency weapons in themselves.

The influence of these varied considerations is immediately apparent in the splendid array of shapes. The dramatic or decorative effects of massed staff arms ensured their presence in royal and town guards long after they had ceased to be used in battle.

In one respect the spear was too effective. When a heavy and fierce wild animal charged onto a spear this might well penetrate so deeply as to enable the animal to attack the now disarmed spearsman. Possibly in the Stone Age the idea had occurred of fixing a crossbar of bone or wood below the head of the spear, so preventing excessive penetration. Bronze Age spear heads have been found with projections to serve this purpose. Both types of crossbar – the attached "toggle" or integral lugs – remained in use during the Middle Ages and, in limited instances, later. Some 16th-century examples are richly decorated.

Apart from one or two exceptions staff weapons developed from the civilian tools of everyday life. Later, of course, the rudimentary staff weapons evolved in a purely military sense. The spear and the longer lance were used by the mounted man. The lance had some form of ring at the point where the hand grips, to prevent the weapon

Staff Weapons

1. *Pike, c. 1590, with spearhead and langets. These served not only to attach the head but also to protect the shaft.*
2. *Swiss halberd, early 15th century.*
3. *German halberd, c. 1500.*
4. *Halberd of the type carried by infantry serjeants c. 1740–92.*
5. *Italian halberd, c. 1550–1600.*
6. *German halberd, 1600–1620, personal guard of the elector of Saxony.*
7. *German halberd, c. 1610, with tassel.*

8. *Italian glaive, Venetian, c. 1620.*

being thrust back on impact with the adversary. While in pre-Norman days the foot soldier's spear was used as a hand weapon to defend and attack, it was also thrown. However, the staff arms that developed from the peasant's hayforks, hedging bills and the like at the same period as increasing use was being made of the bow, never were intended to be thrown.

The cavalry had their lances and half-lances, and the infantry's most common weapon was the pike, as it was easy and simple to make. Some pikes incorporated a hook below the thrusting point. Except for arms used in ceremonial, the pike outlived all the other staff weapons that developed alongside it.

In the 15th century, the halberd was a popular weapon. The head consisted of three portions (all made as one). There was a cutting edge similar to a butcher's cleaver and opposite it a spike or hook, while at the end was a double-edged spear point. The head was fitted to a long pole by langets and rivets. Another 15th-century weapon was the glaive. This had a long pole and a simple head incorporating the advantages of a sword blade for cutting and thrusting. The pole-axe, a long-handled axe, was a very lethal weapon. The staff varied from four to six feet in length and the head consisted of a sharp spike topping an axe blade opposite a hammer shaped like a miniature anvil. The head was held to the pole with langets behind which was sometimes fixed a circular hand-guard. Also called a "Ravensbill", this weapon may be found with a spike at the butt end.

The gisarme, yet another variation, was used until the mid 1400s. It was a pole with a curved halfmoon-shaped blade the top curve of which extended beyond the shaft while the lower curved portion was fitted to it by means of a round socket.

The partisan, introduced in the middle of the 14th century, became a popular weapon. The blade was long and triangular in shape; in later years, the blade was tapered more and hooks were forged each side where blade met pole. Together with the halberd it was later one of the two types of staff weapon adopted as parade arms. The ranseur was another variety of polearm with a triangular bladed head; it incorporated two shorter blades, attached one each side.

The halberd and partisan together with the spontoon, a short spear or pike, survived even the widespread use of firearms, chiefly as emblems of rank, and for dressing off the ranks.

Staff Weapons

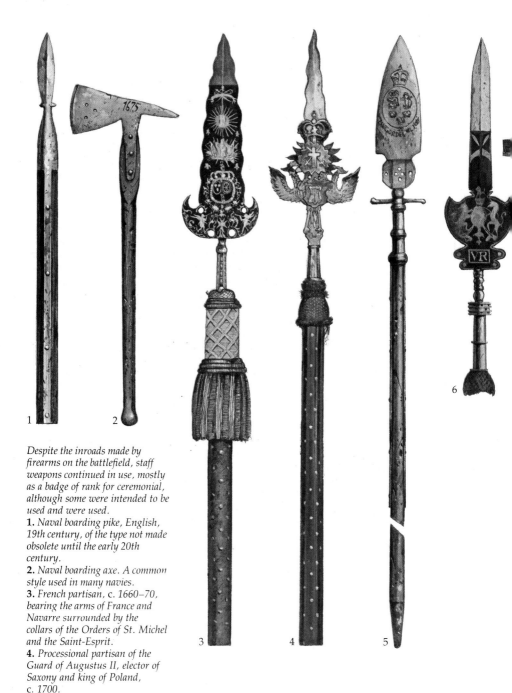

Despite the inroads made by firearms on the battlefield, staff weapons continued in use, mostly as a badge of rank for ceremonial, although some were intended to be used and were used.

1. Naval boarding pike, English, 19th century, of the type not made obsolete until the early 20th century.

2. Naval boarding axe. A common style used in many navies.

3. French partisan, c. 1660–70, bearing the arms of France and Navarre surrounded by the collars of the Orders of St. Michel and the Saint-Esprit.

4. Processional partisan of the Guard of Augustus II, elector of Saxony and king of Poland, c. 1700.

1   2   3   4   5   6

Later Staff Weapons

7

Although staff weapons as fighting implements had almost disappeared with the supremacy of gunpowder on the battlefield, the artillery still carried the linstock, a polearm with twin serpents on the head to hold the slow match from which the gunners would light their own match (see p. 187), and officers still carried spontoons. In the British army, officers' spontoons were finally abolished in 1786, but sergeants in the Royal Artillery bore spontoons until 1845.

Another staff weapon, which lingered late with navies of the world, was the boarding pike. This had a short head of a triangular section held to the shaft with langets; there was no metal butt, as this would have damaged the decks of the ships. Navies continued to use them throughout the 19th and even the 20th centuries for boarding, even though ironclads and powerful armament had long made them obsolete.

Various staff-mounted weapons, particularly halberds and partisans, continued in ceremonial use as a sign of office or status. They were frequently carried by palace guards and the personal bodyguards of emperors and princes, and some such bodies, for example the Yeoman Warders at the Tower of London and the Swiss guards at the Vatican, still bear them today. Many such later weapons were highly decorated and elaborate examples of the bladesmith's art often being etched, pierced, inlaid or engraved. Many staff weapons had gilding and blueing on them, and all had decorative staves, some covered in velvet of various colours and always bearing a decorative tassel between head and staff. The decoration would feature the arms, crown or cypher of the reigning monarch. On the death of a ruler the weapon would be sent for the cypher to be altered. Some wore so thin through successive changes that the blade had to be replaced.

While these items were made for pomp and circumstance, they were as well made as the originals would have been and they were and still are weapons that can be used. It is in these various ceremonial staff weapons that the last traces of the original weapons of the infantryman survive.

The use of staff weapons revived as part of the 19th-century movement of Romanticism. Sheriffs in England, for example, formed guards of "Javelinmen" with specially made "javelins" that were a form of halberd. These and similar weapons are not uncommonly found today and can be acquired by the collector. Even the prices of earlier staff weapons are generally lower than those of contemporary swords.

5. *Danish officer's spontoon pattern 1734 with the arms of Denmark and name of regiment etched on the blade. The spontoon was abandoned in Denmark in 1784.*
6. *Partisan of Yeomen of the Guard and Yeomen Warders, Tower of London. This style, here bearing the cypher of Queen Victoria, has been in use since the 16th century.*
7. *Artillery linstock, used to hold burning slowmatch and placed between guns as a convenient source of fire. English, 18th or early 19th century.*

Staff Weapons

The lance was perhaps one of man's oldest weapons, developed from the spear when he became mobile on horseback. The heavier and longer lance was carried by heavy cavalry and the lighter half-lance by faster, less armoured troops. The lances for jousting and the tilt should not be confused with the fighting lance. The jousting lance often had a rebated head or coronel, and was sometimes hollowed to break easily. Many were richly painted or even gilded.

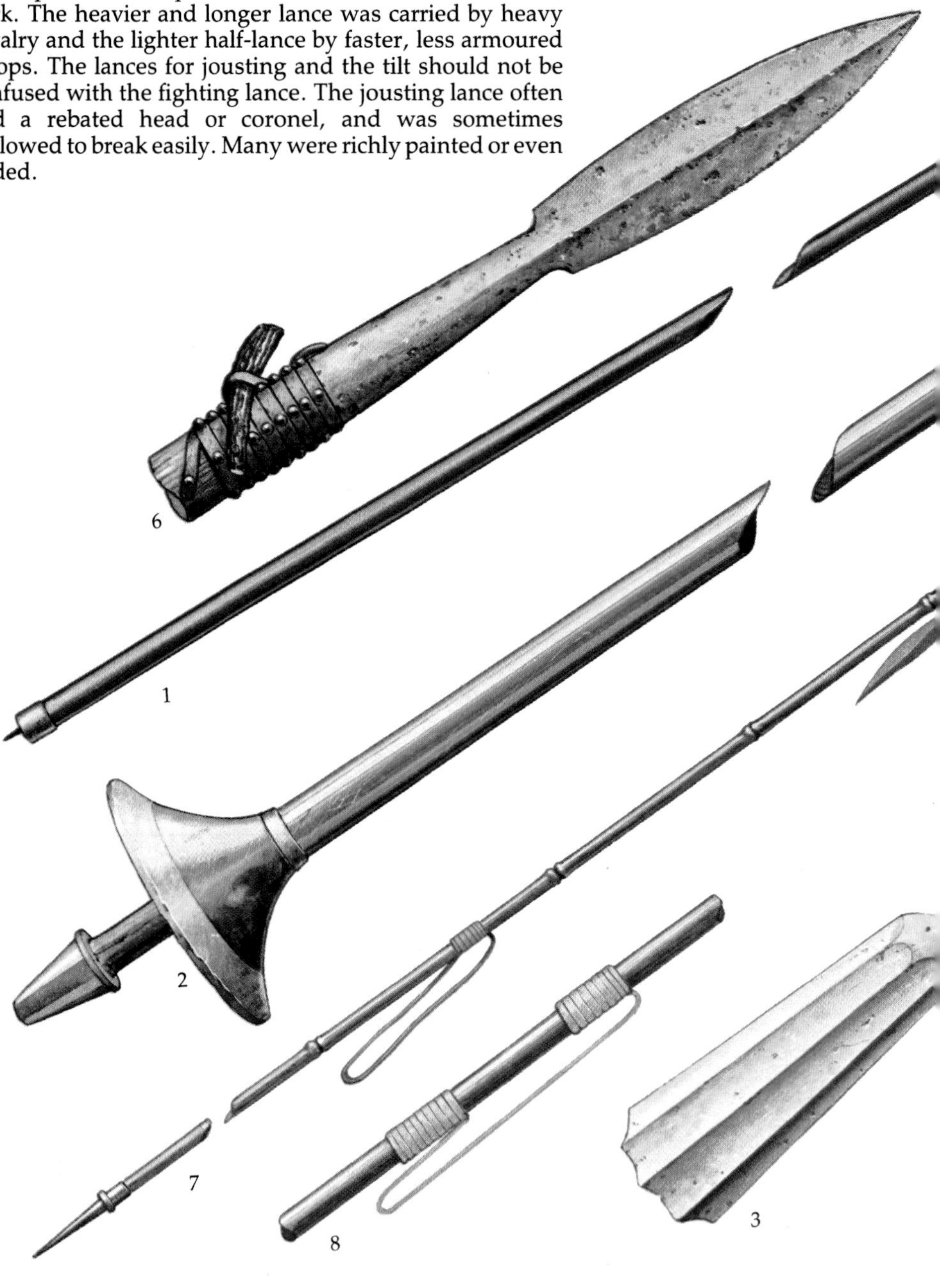

6

1

2

7

8

3

1. *Mediaevai lance, 11 feet in length, the standard weapon of the mounted man.*
2. *Tilting lance with the usual hand shield (vamplate) and decorated pole.*
3. *Rebated (blunt) head and* (4) *"coronet" head, used in the tilt.*
5. *Head of a 16-century Spanish lance.*
6. *Boar spear, 19th century.*
7. *British pattern 1868 cavalry lance with triangular head and bamboo pole.*
8. *Sling on 1860 pattern (the lance point was attached with langets).*
9. *Head detail of (7).*

The half-lance or *demi-lance* was prominent in the late 15th and the 16th centuries, but when the changing tactics of warfare placed more reliance on firearms, the lance declined and was replaced with pistol, carbine and sword.

During the Napoleonic wars, the lance was revived in the French cavalry. It was adopted in Britain in 1816 and by other European countries. The French lance had a blade of triangular section secured by two langets and rivets to the long wooden shaft 16 feet in length. The bottom of the shaft was protected with a metal shoe or butt.

The first lance adopted in Britain was a copy of the French *gendarmerie* pattern, although the length was soon reduced to a more manageable nine feet. It was during the 19th century that the military lance came into its own in the armies of Europe (but not America). Various patterns were adopted, and as late as 1889 Germany converted the last of its cavalry regiments into lancers. After the British experiences of the Boer War, when the rifle was established as the supreme weapon, the lance was discontinued by Britain in 1903. However it was revived again in 1909 and used as by other European countries during World War I, when it was employed in some notable old-style cavalry charges. In Britain the lance was finally abolished in 1927.

In India lances with specially designed heads were used for hunting, particularly for boar hunting, or "pig sticking" as it was termed.

97

Staff Weapons

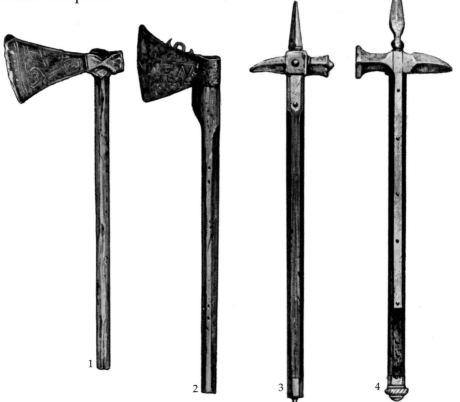

1

2

3

4

The axe was one of the favoured weapons of the Danes. This weapon had a six-foot handle for double-handed use and a fearsome head with a curved blade. This axe also proved a popular arm with the Saxons, as did the later battle-axe with the Norman knights. The battle-axe had the usual large head but the shaft was three to four feet long. It was a weapon still very much used in the 13th to 15th centuries, mainly for the soldier fighting on foot, but also for the knight, and with its pole length and weight the pole-axe (the name derives from "poll" meaning head, not from "pole") could be swung double-handed about the head. A smaller one-hand version was used by mounted men. This was fitted not only with a cutting edge but had a spike on the opposite side of the socket to which the shaft fitted.

The early mounted fighting man also equipped himself with a rudimentary form of club, and there were many later variations. In effect, these maces and war clubs were to oust the axe as a weapon for the mounted man. The later war-hammer was to all intents and purposes a scaled-down version of the pole-axe. With a shorter shaft that made it more versatile for a single-handed blow, the weapon had a weighty head consisting of a flat or studded

The axe was a natural tool or fighting weapon made in its early forms from flint and staghorn. With the use of metals it became a formidable weapon. From the axe evolved the mace and the hammer, both capable of inflicting terrible wounds. The mace, or club, was one of man's earliest weapons and still survives today in the police truncheon, the night stick and the pick handle.

1. *Danish axe with decorated head and wood shaft.*

2. *European axe, 15th century.*

3. *French (?) war hammer, c. 1450.*

4. *Italian war hammer, c. 1490.*

5

6

7

8

9

5. *Indian or Persian war hammer, 19th century, an example of the late survival in the East of weapons superseded in Europe.*
6. *South German mace, c. 1470.*
7. *Italian (?) mace, c. 1540.*
8. *Milanese mace of the morning star type, c. 1560.*
9. *European morning star with grip, chain and head, c. 1500.*

"hammer-like" head at the front, a rear spike, always called the "backspike", sometimes slightly curved, or a blade instead, and for good measure a thick spike at the top of the shaft.

Alongside the war-hammers developed the maces, the evolved club of earlier days. These usually had metal shafts which had a leather or twine-bound grip with an oval or round disc at each end of the grip to prevent slipping. The heads were usually what is termed flanged, that is, with separate triangular-shaped metal "fins" originating from the central shaft. These could, like some of the hammers, pierce armour on occasion.

A further variation on the basic theme was the holy-water sprinkler or morning star, an awesome shafted weapon with a round head studded with armour-piercing spikes. Again, as in all these single-handed weapons, the weight was in the head, which was sometimes attached by a chain to the shaft. The flail was another club weapon, with the weighted portions attached to chains from a central pole. It had a double advantage, that of weight and of striking at various points, and also offered the possibility of entangling the opponent's person or equipment, so enabling the bearer to unhorse him.

Staff Weapons

Throughout the history of arms there have been attempts to unite one type of weapon with another with the intention of combining their best features in an effective dual-purpose weapon. In the majority of cases, the idea failed, and with staff weapons combined with firearms the failure rate was high. Because of the gun's ignition system, usually either matchlock or wheel-lock, the combined weapons were clumsy and not as effective as had been hoped.

As late as the 19th century, both in mainland Europe and in Britain, the idea was revived again when efforts were made to combine the cavalry lance with a firearm. This too was never a success. The most recently issued gun lance, really a gun with a very long bayonet, was adopted in France under Napoleon III by the Cent Garde. This took the form of a carbine with a full-length cavalry sword; the latter, when fitted to the muzzle, gave a reach of lance proportions. It was only ever issued to the Cent Garde and, like them, it no longer saw service after 1870.

Many experiments in increasing the effectiveness of staff weapons by a firearm combination took place during the 16th century. One well-known example of the earlier combined weapon was the halberd fitted with a wheel-lock, a monster weapon some eight feet long, with the head of the halberd of necessity split into a two-pronged fork. The head was mounted on the staff in the usual way. The gun barrel was housed at the upper end of the staff and the wheel-lock mechanism itself was placed on the right side. This would have been a clumsy weapon, difficult to aim as a gun and difficult to load. Most examples of this type of combination weapon suffered from similar drawbacks.

Unlike the smaller combination weapons, pistol and dagger or sword, and pistol combined with axe or mace, the combined polearm and gun had little following. However, the idea reappeared, for example in the modern cartridge era, in a pig-sticking lance made with a pin-fire barrel in the head, fired when the blade was thrust home into the prey.

1. *Combined wheel-lock gun, halberd, and fork. German (?), 1580.*
2. *Combined halberd and linstock to hold slowmatch.*
3. *Wheel-lock and barrel combined with axe. German, c. 1570.*
4. *Spear with wheel-lock and barrel. European, c. 1600.*

1

2   3   4

Staff Weapons

3

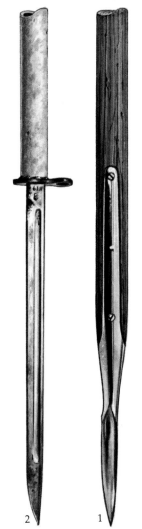

Surprising as it may seem, staff weapons have been made, and used, in modern times. The naval boarding pike was still a standard issue in many navies in the years before World War I, while the continued use or re-introduction of staff weapons, however lethal, in ceremonial guards this century is quite a different matter from the valuable contribution made by various such weapons in various fighting forces.

The weapon mounted on a pole has always been an easy way for the population to protect itself, and in spite of machine guns and modern rifles the pike-and-shot mentality in Europe rightly still saw the staff weapon as an easy and cheap method to arm the people. In the Balkans, in Greece and Turkey, and other sensitive areas of Europe before World War I these were the only weapons that the peasants could wield against cavalry. Like the billhooks and other polearms of earlier days, skilfully used they could unseat a cavalryman with sword.

In World War I staff weapons also found a use in trench warfare, as well as being used by guards on camps for internees and prisoners. During the trench warfare, raiding parties used various shafted weapons, usually made at local level, including maces with nails knocked into the head, coshes with long handles, and pole implements for lifting, cutting and breaking barbed wire.

Perhaps the most organized issue of staff weapons in the 20th century occurred in World War II in Britain with the formation at short notice of the Local Defence Volunteers (later the Home Guard). This force, which involved large numbers, required weapons that were in short supply because the withdrawal of the British Expeditionary Force from France involved the loss of much valuable weaponry and equipment. Before those rifles that could be spared were issued, the Home Guards were issued with pikes. They were made from nine-foot lances; by cutting these in half, it was possible to issue one man with a spear or short pike, and another, using the heavy butt-end portion, with a lethal war hammer. Later surplus P13 and American P17 bayonets were welded to lengths of gas piping to provide rudimentary pikes. They were heavy and primitive, but at least they were some form of offensive arm, and in hand-to-hand combat their reach was good. Despite modern weaponry the staff-mounted weapon, such as the pike, will always be a part of man's armoury in such circumstances of dire need.

Staff weapons have still been used, in earnest, in the 20th century. The British Royal Navy boarding pike (1) was not declared obsolete until 1904. Another pike issued to the Home Guard (2) in 1940 was a hasty marriage of the No. 3 bayonet and a length of gas piping.
3. World War I trench club, made from a length of threaded pipe and a heavy hexagonal nut from machinery or artillery.

SWORDS, DAGGERS AND BAYONETS

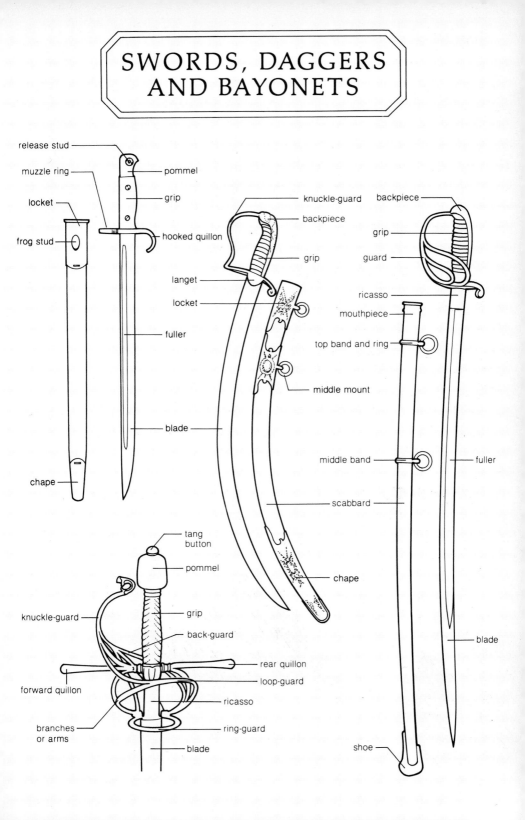

release stud
muzzle ring
pommel
locket
grip
frog stud
hooked quillon
fuller
blade
chape

knuckle-guard
backpiece
grip
langet
locket
middle mount
blade
chape

backpiece
grip
guard
ricasso
mouthpiece
top band and ring
middle band
scabbard
fuller
blade

tang button
pommel
grip
knuckle-guard
back-guard
rear quillon
loop-guard
forward quillon
ricasso
branches or arms
ring-guard
blade

shoe

Swords

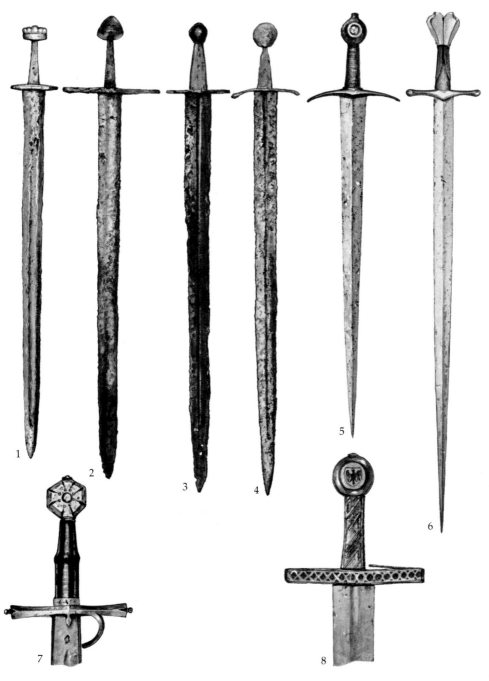

The Viking sword, like the earlier Saxon sword, was of the most simple design. It had a double-edged blade, plain straight cross-guard, straight-sided grip and a rounded pommel that helped the hand to keep its hold and to balance the weapon. The tang was also riveted through the pommel which thus also helped to hold the components together. It was essentially a cutting and hacking weapon whose weight was in the blade. The construction of the blade was ingenious, on the pattern-welded principle. Because the component portions of iron or steel were of varying degrees of hardness, the strips of iron were twisted together and hammered under heat to form the desired shape. As the blade tapered to the point, the weight was further back, making a blow from the centre of the blade extremely dangerous. For fittings, the Vikings used bronze or iron for the cross-guards, which were either straight or sometimes curved at the extremities towards the point of the blade. The pommel was a "Brazil nut" shape or semicircular, although many other variations on these themes are known.

Swords changed little in the 12th and 13th centuries, and conformed to the basic shape described above, although pattern welding became less necessary with better metallurgical techniques. The most popular pommel-shape was another, new variation, in the form of a disc, either plain or chamfered, sometimes decorated or inlaid with ancient coins or relics. While the swords of the Vikings and the 12th century look similar, the design had altered by the use of heavier pommels, bringing the balance of the weapon nearer the cross-guard and making the grip sit well back in the hand.

The advance in the use and design of armour meant that by the 14th century thrusting as well as cutting swords were important. A move in this direction had been made in the 13th century, when because of armour blades were not only lengthened and fullered for strength but made heavier, with elongated grips so that two hands could be used. Towards the end of the century, diamond-sectioned blades came into use, the idea being to thrust at the mail and break the links, thus piercing the suit; they could also be used to thrust between plate armour joints. The blade of the thrusting sword was wide at the cross-guard and tapered to a sharp point, and was not very suited to cutting. The cross-guard was generally longer, and curved towards the blade, but the practice of hooking the first finger over the guard for better grip required a short blunt portion at the top of the blade (the "ricasso").

Swords

As armour design progressed, so did the design of swords. While outwardly similar, they had been refined. In order to maintain the length and strength of the sword in the face of opposing plate armour, and at the same time to make best use of the weight, the blade was hollow-ground, or in some cases made with a central rib with thinner flat portions each side. Blades varied between the short and wide to long and more slender. Cross-guards were long and either straight, curved, or in a shallow S-shape.

The use of two hands in wielding swords was now a common practice and to this end the top six or so inches were left unsharpened so that the right hand held the grip and the left the top portion of the blade.

At this time, the foot soldier started to wear a sword. This was shorter than that carried by the mounted man, and the style soon came to incorporate a cross-guard bent upwards over the grip on the side of the leading edge to form a rudimentary knuckle-guard. There appears to have been more preoccupation with hand protection, and loops were incorporated into the cross-guard. Some swords had as many as three loops giving extra hand protection, but the idea was not popular in England until the 16th century was well advanced.

In Germany a large fighting sword was popular, the so-called hand-and-a-half sword, which was not as large as the two-handers (see following pages). This had a broad tapering blade and an elongated grip for holding with either one or two hands, or with one hand on the grip and the other hand half on the grip and half on the ricasso. The hand-and-a-half sword continued to be carried and used with deadly effect well into the 16th century.

The simple cross-guard of the normal fighting sword had now generally developed beyond the simple cross, as we have seen, and a typical example of this evolved style was carried by the *Landsknechts*, the German mercenaries who were recruited to fight for Austria under Maximilian I, Holy Roman Emperor from 1493 to 1519. The blade was double-edged and the grip tapered towards the blade from the wider pommel. The cross-guard was a combination of bars and rings, the more usual type however, incorporating the typical S-shape. These were the last vestiges of the old-style Viking sword before the science of swordplay dictated another form of blade and guard. The lingering effects of the use of larger and larger swords to combat armour will be seen in the following pages discussing two-hand weapons.

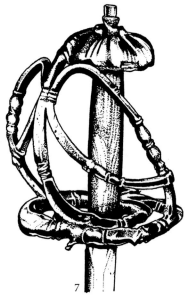

7

During the 14th century the straight sword with simple cross-guard had given way to more adventurous shapes, the curved blade and the slightly more elaborate cross-guard. In the confrontation between sword and plate armour the cutting power of the hand-and-a-half sword was called into action, especially in Germany.

1. *German hand-and-a-half sword with straight quillons, 15th century.*

2. *Venetian sword with double-edged blade, short fuller and curiously shaped pommel, 15th century.*

3. *Hand-and-a-half sword, with twisted guard with bars, German, early 16th century.*

4. *Curved German sword of the 16th century with open guard, deep pommel, and rings to the cross-guard.*

5. *Falchion of the mid-16th century, an example with the arms of the Medici and elaborate cast bronze lion head and cross-guard.*

6. *Earlier pattern of Landsknecht sword with simple "S" cross-guard and widening grip, c. 1500.*

7. *Landsknecht sword with typical late curved hand-guard c. 1530.*

1

2

3

4

5

6

Swords

As armour maintained its lead over the sword, sword design yet again surged forward to combat the new techniques in armour construction. The last throes of the heavy fighting sword were the two-hand swords of Germany, the *Zweihander* of mammoth proportions with heâvy pommel, elongated grip and a simple cross-guard incorporating loops and bars for extra protection. Some of these

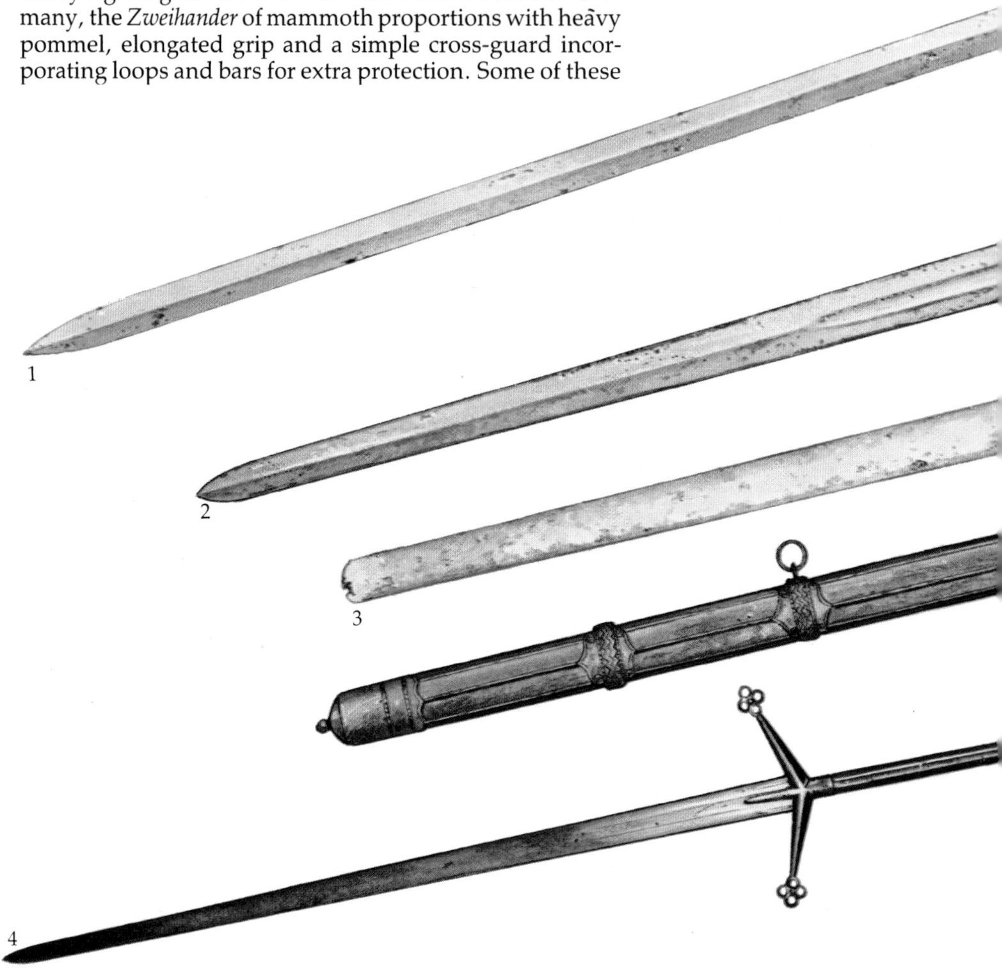

1

2

3

4

The last development of the
"giant" sword was the
two-hander, a fearsome weapon
designed to cut men and armour
alike. The supremacy of the
firearm rendered it obsolete.
1. German two-handed sword,
mid-16th century.
2. German bearing-sword,
mid-14th century.
3. Executioner style sword with
blunted point, and upturned
cross-guard to protect the hand.
4. Scottish claymore, 16th
century.

swords went to strange lengths, examples being known of wavy-edged blades and leather-covered ricassos for extra grip with projecting spikes each side to stop the adversary's blade. Swung by a large man, the two-hand sword must have been a most terrifying weapon to combat.

Although Germany seems to have been the main area where this style of sword was found, it also appears in Scotland where the legendary early claymore or *claideamhmer* was in active use for many years before having its name given to the basket-hilted sword that has long, if erroneously, been known as a claymore. The original claymore was a two-hand weapon with down-pointing crossguard ending in characteristic quatrefoil terminals, and a large pommel. The grip, providing room for two hands, was in wood, and the blade long with a sharp double edge and a spear point. The Scottish claymore lasted longer than its German counterpart and was still used in the late 16th and the 17th centuries.

At the same time as these monster weapons were in use, two other styles of sword were derived from them. The first was the executioner's sword, a double-edged weapon with enough room on the grip for two hands but with a truncated end to the blade. Favoured in Germany, France and central Europe, this style of sword with its clipped point was the last survivor of the large sword-against-armour edged blade.

From the two-hand weapon also developed the processional sword which many countries used, and still use today. These swords, carried blade uppermost, represent the symbol of the might and power of the ruler or rulers. Many of those that are still carried today date from the 16th century, when they were derived directly from weapons of war.

Swords

While the military still preferred the cut-and-thrust swords (mainly the cutting-only version, because of cheapness of manufacture and the lesser skill required to use it), the art of swordplay was developing fast. From Spain came a new form of fighting with the *arme blanche*, utilising only the thrust. First references to this style of sword are found in a French document of 1474 which refers to an *epée rapière*, but it was also termed the *espada ropera*, the Spanish for dress sword.

By 1530, these words had come to mean a light civilian style of sword with a slender thrusting blade and a hilt of a number of loops and bars forming a hand-guard. The main causes of the upsurge in the use of this style of weapon were the increase in the wearing of swords by civilians and also the influence of Italy, which spread throughout Europe with the Renaissance. With this came the Italian art of the "fence" taught by the masters, where the thrust and the point were the most important elements of swordplay. The rapiers used had slender double-edged blades, some as long as five feet, and with the decline of the

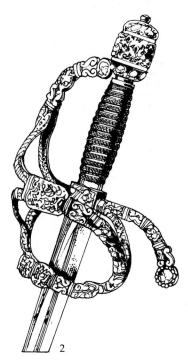

2

1

The science of swordplay demanded a more sophisticated weapon than the cut-and-thrust sword and the art of "the fence" came to be synonymous with the long, slender rapier.

1. *Swept-hilt rapier, German, c. 1590.*

2. *Italian swept-hilt rapier with chiselled hilt, c. 1580.*

3. *German rapier and companion dagger, c. 1600.*

4. *"Pappenheimer" sword, German, c. 1620–30.*

tournament, differences came to be settled by duelling with the sword. Because armour was not part of civilian attire, there was no thick protection for the large, weighty cutting sword to penetrate and so the rapier was ideal. Worn as an everyday part of civilian attire, the rapier was carried slung on a belt, always ready for use. In the art of the fence, thrusts were parried with the left hand, at first wrapped in a cloak but later carrying the left-hand or *main gauche* dagger, produced to act as an instrument for parry and on occasion to break the opponent's blade. These daggers were made to match the sword in hilt design and decoration. (See pp.142–3.)

With the rapier and *main gauche* dagger, hand protection was all-important – the civilian's hand and arm were not protected by armour. To this end, numerous styles and types of hilt-guard evolved. There were rapiers with ring-guards, bars, the swept-hilt rapier and rapiers with plate hand-guard, simple cross-guards and those incorporating both bars and rings. The choice of style of combination of bars and rings depended not only on the purchaser but also on the form recommended by the fencing master to suit the techniques he was teaching.

3   3   4

Swords

In the 17th century, as the rapier evolved, better and more practical hand-guards were designed and produced. Together with the desire for more efficient hand protection came an increased emphasis on the decorative aspect of the sword. The Italian Renaissance had earlier brought with it a decorative repertoire which was now applied to swords; decorative chiselling, casting and engraving continued throughout the life of the rapier and the small sword that evolved from it.

The use of plates for the hand-guard has been mentioned. In this period the plates grew in size and altered in shape to produce the cup-hilt rapier, the so-called "Pappenheimer", with a combination of a swept hilt and a shell-guard. There were cup-hilt rapiers with elongated quillons above the cup and the Flemish style with swept hilt and an outer perforated shell-guard.

Later rapiers tended to be lighter in the blade and more elongated and tapered in shape. The guard was simplified, and the shell and cup guards led to lighter and more manageable swords.

1. *Cup-hilt rapier of German origin, in the Spanish style, c. 1650.*

2. *The so-called "pillow sword", a transitional weapon between rapier and small sword. French, c. 1650.*

3. *Elaborate sword rapier with chiselled guard, cross-guard/shell-guard and quillon. German, c. 1660.*

1   2   3

Late Rapiers

4. *Chiselled cup-hilt. Spanish (Toledo), late 17th century.*
5. *Dish-hilt rapier with pierced guard. German, mid-17th century.*
6. *A "transitional" small sword with silver hilt. French (?), c. 1660.*

But even as the new rapier styles appeared, mostly in the 17th century, there was a decline in the use of these long swords, although in Spain they persisted in use with the *main gauche* daggers until the early 18th century. The emphasis on the use of the thrust and the point meant that it was possible to have a lighter sword with a shorter yet still effective blade. In France and England the new style – the small sword – had been adopted by the 1660s; but before this there had been a transitional weapon, with a diamond-sectioned blade, or sometimes one of square section, and a very simple hilt without knuckle-bow and, if a shell-guard was present, with only two short quillons above it.

The small sword in its early form was based on the rapier, but soon the large guards with numerous rings and bars gave way to a simpler hilt with shell-guard, knuckle-bow, rings called "arms of the hilt", and a slender blade.

4   5   6

Swords

Although the term "court sword" may refer to the small swords of the 18th century, the description strictly applies to the later swords designed to be worn only at court. They derived their style and shape from the so-called "town sword" or "small sword", the direct descendant of the rapier. With the changes in dress fashions, the small sword was far easier to wear as personal protection than the larger rapier and by this time the sword had been supplemented by the pocket pistol for defence against footpads.

The small sword that evolved from the 17th-century *flamberge* (see previous pages) had a pommel, usually round and sometimes pierced, a grip, knuckle-guard, and two down-turned quillons which touched the shell-guard between hilt and blade. The blade shape was that of the rapier's, although a new style called the *colichemarde* had some popularity in the second half of the 18th century, only to fall from favour in the early 19th century. In this the *forte*, or part of the blade nearest the hilt, was about 1¾ inches wide; the blade then suddenly narrowed after some eight inches to a width of about ¾ inches. The blade was triangular in section throughout its length and hollow-ground on all three sides.

Most small swords after the early years of the 18th century were fitted with an evenly tapering hollow-ground blade.

The hilt of the small sword, however, was the portion on which the craftsmen lavished most care and attention. Hilts were often in steel, russeted and gilded, pierced, or with embossed scenes raised in the metal; sometimes the hilt could be removed, so that in mourning a black hilt could be fitted, though mourning swords were also made specially. By the early 18th century, silver hilts were in vogue rather than russeted steel, and these in turn gave way to cut-steel hilts, popularised by Matthew Boulton of Birmingham, inlaid with faceted studs and sometimes guards of chain in place of the solid bar. Although plain, they have a beauty of their own, being in highly polished steel, and are still in use today by some court officials and sheriffs.

By the 1760s the dishing of the shell had disappeared and the arms of the hilt forming two finger-loops, and going back directly to rapier design, had decreased in size and become purely ornamental. By the 1780s the small or town sword was becoming outmoded and it was soon abandoned for everyday wear. It continued as a popular sword for presentation, there being many elaborate versions in existence.

There were many variations of the town or small sword, for both civilian and military users, as well as finer and more decorative presentation pieces.

1. *Gilt and cut-steel court sword with faceted cut-steel chain hand-guard, c. 1810.*

2. *Scottish archer's dress sword, c. 1910.*

3. *Small sword, with pierced hilt in silver. French, c. 1730.*

4. *Military sword modelled on the lines of the small sword. Russian c. 1790.*

5. *Military style court sword, for an officer of the Duke of Manchester's Light Horse, England, c. 1860.*

6. *French small sword with hilt gilded and russeted, c. 1720.*

7. *Gold, jewel and enamel-hilted small sword, a presentation to Admiral Lord St. Vincent in 1797, English.*

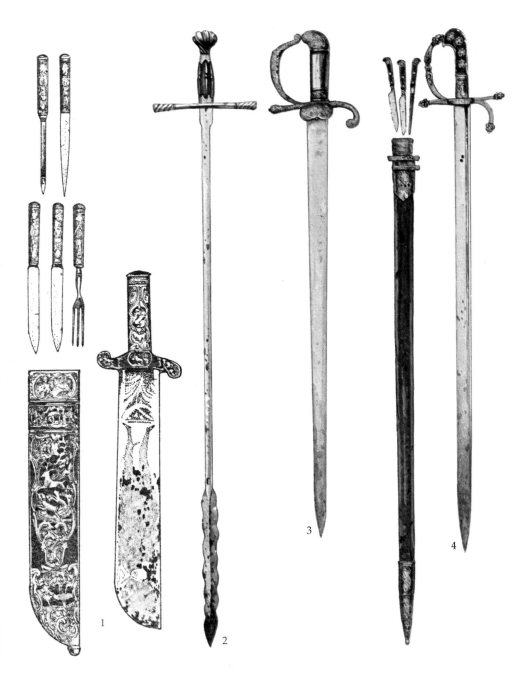

1

2

3

4

Hunting Swords

By the 15th century various forms of sword had been developed for hunting. These were true swords with added items such as small knives etc. in the scabbard.

1. Set of eviscerating instruments, a trousse de chasse, *including all the necessary items to skin, cut and eat the prey. German, c. 1740*

2. *Boar sword of German origin, c. 1530, with simple cross-guard, grip and twisted pommel, and slender blade with flame-shaped point. Note the slot in the blade for a bar to stop deep penetration.*

3. *Hunting hanger with gilt chiselled work by Caspar Spät of Munich, made by Peter Munsten of Solingen, c. 1640.*

4. *A perfect example of the hunting sword with long curved blade, with the file, knives etc. in small sheaths at the top of the scabbard. This sword belonged to Maximilian I, Holy Roman Emperor 1493–1519.*

By the 15th century, with hunting now for the nobility a sport rather than a necessity, various weapons had been developed for this activity. The hunting sword was perhaps the most common – in the 15th and 16th centuries no gentleman was "dressed" without some form of sidearm and these varied with his clothes. For the hunt, a conventional long sword was too unwieldy for use on horseback and the weapon required would have to fulfil more than one purpose. The hunting sword sometimes included a saw-back to the blade; some were of special design, such as the boar sword, in which the point was spear-like and the rest of the blade provided the support for this thrusting point. The length enabled a mounted horseman to use the weapon.

Most hunting swords (not to be confused with hangers later carried for self-defence) had a long thin blade with a spear point, a widened, or a wavy-edged point, the hilts being a simple cross-guard, although many were fitted with rings for the fingers. The prototype of this style of sword was that of Emperor Maximilian (1459–1519). The sheaths of such swords were usually fitted with additional implements, such as a knife with the back edge bevelled and roughened, a long skewer, a skewer with a hook, etc., all intended for the cutting up of the animal after the kill. Many of these swords also had a cross-bar or toggle lower down the blade away from the hilt cross-guard, towards the point. This cross-bar was usually fitted with a spring and was intended to prevent the sword from entering the boar too deeply, so that the blade could easily be removed.

Another very decorative part of the hunter's equipment was the *trousse de chasse*, which consisted of a large broad-bladed knife with a scabbard fitted with useful instruments. Many of the surviving *trousses de chasse* are richly ornamented with chased mounts on the scabbard and elaborate designs on the grips of the main knives and instruments. The tools sheathed in the scabbard of the *trousse* usually consisted of knives, bodkin, file, fork – in fact everything needed to cut up the animal, and in some cases even to eat it! All *trousses* are distinguished by the large chopper-like blade of the main knife, used to cut up and joint the animal, while the smaller knives were for more delicate work. (See pp. 144–5.)

By the 17th century, with the wide introduction of firearms, especially the wheel-lock, for use on horseback, the hunting sword slowly fell into disuse and was replaced by the hanger, carried for defensive purposes. The boar spear, however, continued in use. (See pp. 96–7).

Swords

In the 17th century the short *hanger popular with the military as well as huntsmen was considered the sidearm to be worn. Usually utilitarian as well as decorative, these swords survive in many fine examples with horn or mother-of-pearl grips, and brass or silver mounts. The blades, with or without saw-backs, came in a variety of styles, mostly curved.*

1. *English or German falchion with quillons and shell-guard. The hilt is in carved boxwood, c. 1600–1620.*
2. *Hanger with a cap-shaped pommel, and grip and blade in the typical hunting style, c. 1630.*
3. *German forester's sword, a popular style still in use today and worn by huntsmen, c. 1900.*
4. *Stylised hunting hanger with carved grip and silver mounts, c. 1720.*
5. *Hunting hanger with staghorn grip and pommel, the knuckle bow and shell-guard depicting hunting scenes. German, c. 1780.*
6. *Hanger with silver mounts and ivory grip. English, c. 1775.*
7. *Hunting hanger with staghorn grip, silver mounts and saw-back. English, c. 1750.*

The hanger, a short, usually curved, sword, was most popular with both huntsmen and the military. It was a good secondary defence weapon when ammunition had been expended, or musket and bayonet lost. For the 17th-century huntsman, the hanger was generally a short, curved single-edged weapon with a knuckle-guard in brass or iron and the grip in either stag's horn, or wood bound with leather or wire.

While the blade shape (sometimes with a saw-back) changed little – except perhaps for the shape of the fuller and the point, which was with or without an additional cutting edge on the back – the shape of the hilt altered with fashion. The earlier hangers had a robust hilt in metal with a knuckle-guard, while later weapons had hilts that were simpler in form, often without a knuckle-guard, yet more highly decorated, sometimes mounted in silver. In some cases there was a chain knuckle-guard which was purely decorative. The scabbards were mounted with locket and chape to match the hilt mountings, and in some of the more elaborate weapons the body of the scabbard was covered with shagreen.

By the 18th century the hanger had also found popularity as a civilian weapon for self-defence. (Until the late 18th century every gentleman wore a sword as part of normal dress.) Well-ornamented hilts in enamels were made, as well as cut-steel ones, but in these cases the weapons, although undoubtedly weapons they were, were more examples of the outward show of wealth. Many of the swords of this civilian style would have the down-pointing shell-guard, not as a protection for the hand but intended to snag the blade of an adversary. Military hangers, or sidearms of related style, continued in use well into the late 19th century in many armies. The hanger of most armies was a simple affair, cheap yet efficient. Most had cast brass hilts; in some cases this was in one piece, as in the hanger of the Land Transport Corps, or the Roman hilt (the French type) with cross-guard and simple ribbed hilt copied by Prussia, Russia, and even South American countries well into the 20th century. Other brass hilts were in three pieces – hilt, grip-pommel and knuckle-guard. This style found popularity in Britain until the end of the 18th century; hangers issued in Britain after that date were for police, prison warders and revenue and customs officers. The brass-hilted police hanger lingered in Britain until the 1860s, but by that time most police forces were armed, if they were armed, with sword bayonets left over from the military.

Swords

From the simple cross-hilted weapons used by the Romans, Vikings and Normans through to the bowl-and-bar hilted rapiers which afforded some protection against the opponent's slender blade, it was the style of fighting which dictated design. As the thrusting style of "fencing" was abandoned in military (not civilian) use during the 16th century in favour of the cut, with heavier-bladed weapons, hilts had to give more protection, especially as armour decreased in popularity. The number of intricate bars increased, and rings came to be added. The "basket" style often associated with Scotland and with Highland regiments was not an exclusively Scottish design, nor was such a sword in Scotland called a claymore as it is today. The basket-hilt was not essentially a cavalry sword, but it became very largely used as such. The large protective hilt was pierced for lightness, the openings often small enough to stop the sword of an opponent; the hilt was usually lined with buff leather. There are hilts of many designs in this style, but all envelop the hand in such a manner that, while the weapon is excellent for cutting, it makes a poor thrusting sword because of the cramped guard shape. This is reflected in the type of blade fitted – generally wide and heavy.

In the 16th century, before the basket-hilt fully evolved, the first of these extra-protective hand-guards was that used by German mercenaries, the *Landsknechts*, whose swords had a cross-guard that included bars and rings for hand grip and protection. The basket-hilt which developed from this rudimentary beginning had by the 17th century been almost universally adopted as a cavalry sword. It was in use with the British army well into the latter years of the 18th century and, for Highland regiments, the 19th. In other countries it remained in use with many armies even some years later, although with a less constricting guard. In Britain one of the well-known types of basket-hilted cavalry sword was the so-called "mortuary" sword (see overleaf).

For the civilian the small sword replaced the rapier, but in the military sphere, the broadsword with its basket-hilt was favoured in Britain, America, Germany, France and Scandinavia, as well as being used in Italy, where the characteristic *schiavona* hilt evolved, and Austria.

By the 1790s, however, the basket-hilted sword had lost favour with most countries. It had been adapted in a way that lessened the hand protection, in the form of "three-quarter-basket" and "half-basket" hilts, which later decreased in size and became bar-hilted swords.

Swords

European armies, formed on a firm and permanent footing during the 17th century, adopted swords with national characteristics. Most if not all these weapons, while cruder in construction, owe their styling to civilian swords. The broadsword was perhaps the only exclusively military sword for the mounted man.

1. *Spanish officer's sword. The shape and blade owe everything to the rapier, which continued to be carried in Spain long after it had been superseded in other countries.*

2. *Late Landsknecht sword, still with the characteristic hilt and blade, although devoid of some bars.*

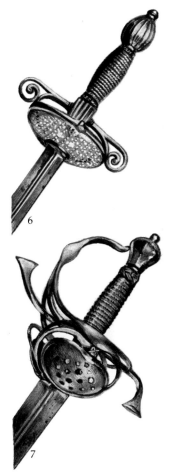

6

7

When European armies were put on a more permanent footing during the 17th century, both cavalry and infantry were armed with swords. The style varied from country to country but all were cut-and-thrust weapons with broad blades and a good protective hand-guard. The form of the cavalry sword used during the first three-quarters of the century had of course developed from the civilian style, but it also met the military need for a strong and heavier sword. The blade was usually straight and double-edged and the hilt a bowl-guard from which the knuckle-guard extended to reach the pommel. The guard was often pierced out to give the impression and the protection of bars. A prime example from the early and middle part of the century is the "mortuary" sword, so called because the head incorporated into the design of the guard of typical examples was said to represent that of Charles I of England. However, examples of this style of sword are known dating from long before the date of the king's execution in 1649. Many of these swords have the bowl and three-bar guard; others have as many as five or six bars.

In Austria and the Low Countries a favoured style was the so-called "Walloon" sword. This had a broad double-edged blade with a hilt consisting of a large round pommel with single knuckle-guard and two lower kidney-shaped bars in place of a solid shell. The space enclosed by these bars was fitted with a perforated plate. In the Austrian version, the hilt had additional bars and a thumb-ring on the inner side of the guard. At the turn of the century, the Austrian light cavalry sword had a curved blade with a simple knuckle-bow that did not reach the pommel. Russia preferred the straight-bladed sword with the simple pommel and shell-guard, while Spain clung to the rapier style of the previous decades.

Small swords (mattrosses, cutlasses etc.) with simple hilts and curved blades were probably in common use for infantry and artillery, though few survive. The term hanger covers these weapons, which often had a cast brass hilt. As firearms continued to take over on the battlefield, the traditional fighting foot soldiers, such as the *Landsknechts*, adopted simplified swords as second-line defence. In swords used by the cavalry, the trend was to the double-edged blade and the iron basket-hilt with bowl-and-bar protection, but personal choice allowed variations to flourish. During the following century, the use of bars combined with a bowl (often diminished in size) continued. For the infantry this trend was reversed with the hand protection on the hanger being simpler in general.

3. *Broadsword for cavalry, with fully enveloping basket-hilt.*
4. *Seventeenth-century English "mortuary" sword with full basket-hilt and bars screwed to the pommel. Again, a popular style of sword for the mounted man.*
5. *The "Walloon" sword, with single bow and pierced shell-guard, which was extremely popular in many armies.*
6. *A transitional weapon that found favour in some armies.*
7. *Another form of rapier-style hilt, but with broad double-edged blade.*

Swords

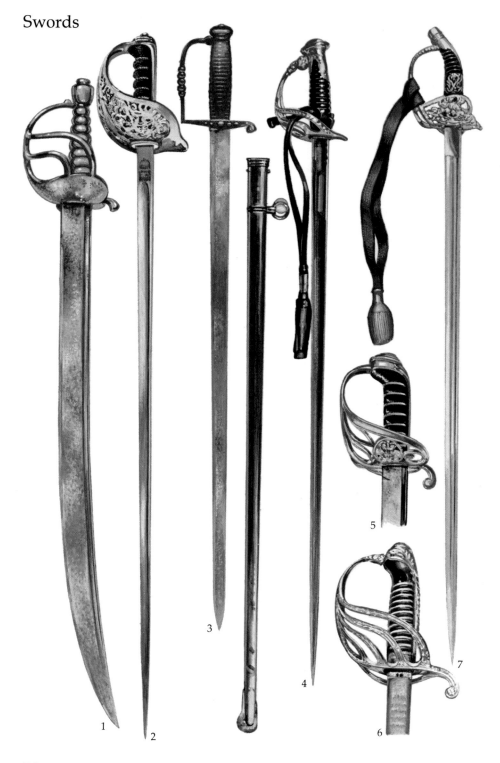

1

2

3

4

5

6

7

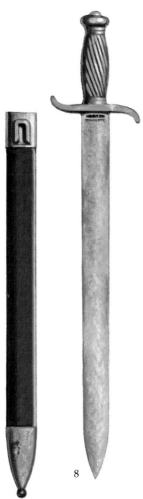

8

1. Mid 18th-century British infantry private's hanger.
2. British 1895 pattern infantry officer's sword, still in service today.
3. United States model 1810 infantry officer's sword, with solid brass grip and guard.
4. Belgian infantry officer's sword, pattern 1889.
5. British 1822 pattern infantry officer's sword.
6. French infantry officer's sword, model 1882.
7. German infantry officer's sword, pattern 1911.
8. Prussian infantry private's hanger, 19th century.

While the infantry officer did carry a fusil (usually a lighter version of the ranks' musket) or a staff weapon such as a halbard or a spontoon, he also carried a sword, and this eventually became his main armament and weapon of rank before the advent of the revolver, which first complemented and finally ousted it.

The first regulation styles of sword carried by infantry officers in Europe were generally based on the civilian swords of the period, and it must be remembered that officers bought their own swords, and until about 1800 those for their regiment also. Thus it is no surprise to see the typical shape of pommel, knuckle-bow, shell-guard and blade based on the small sword. A variant, and a popular one, was the "five-ball" or beaded-hilted spadroon with ivory or ebonised grip. Yet another version that was popular, especially with militia and volunteers, was the ivory-grip sword with pommel and knuckle-bow; the grip, which could be of wood, was bisected by a strap and cartouche in metal usually bearing the badge of the regiment.

All these in Britain became obsolete in 1796 with the new regulation sword, which again was based on the small sword. This had a brass hilt with pommel, knuckle-bow and two shell-guards; it was gilt for more senior officers.

Other nations, especially Russia and the Germanic states, followed this style with a number of variations, mainly in the shape of the pommel but also in blade shapes and in single and double edges. At the beginning of the 19th century officers were armed simply with a sword, and more care was taken with its design (although most officers generally also had a pistol, even if this was not official wear). In Britain in 1822 a sword was adopted that was to last most of the century. In France patterns were adopted in 1845 and 1889. In Prussia and the Germanic states there were nearly as many patterns as states until 1871, when a near-universal pattern was adopted. In the United States the French pattern was followed, to remain with little if any change until 1903, when a universal sword was adopted for all the army.

In 1892 British officers of infantry, except for Highland regiments and the foot guards, were armed with a steel-hilted sword with a protective bowl-guard bearing the royal cypher and a straight, purely thrusting blade. This has remained, with minor modifications, the infantry officer's sword to this day. In France the 1889 pattern still lingers, and in the United States their universal pattern. No new basic designs have been adopted this century.

Swords

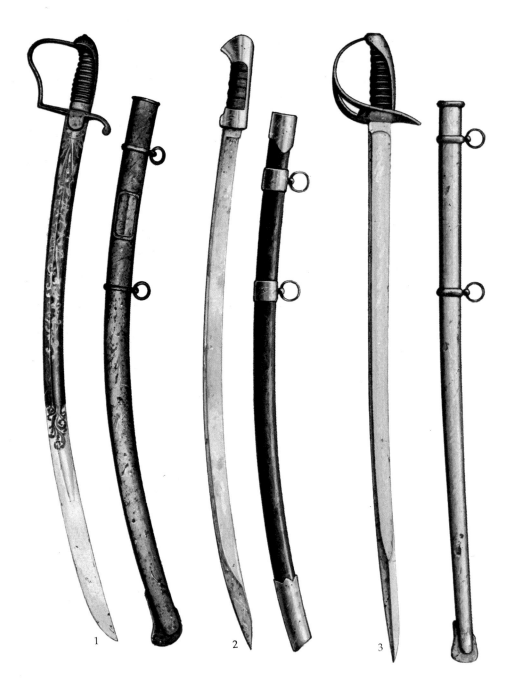

1

2

3

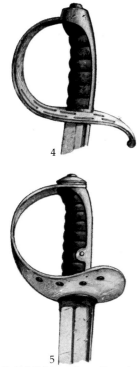

1. *British light cavalry pattern of 1796, presentation version.*
2. *Russian "Asiatic" pattern 1838 issued to all Cossack regiments and influential on other Russian sword styles.*
3. *Danish pattern 1843, one of the first universal swords for all arms of cavalry, and for both officers and men. The sheet steel guard was cut out in the shape of bars. It was superseded in 1848 by an improved version.*
4. *United States 1803 model cavalry sword hilt. This style owes a little to Austrian and Prussian influence.*
5. *Austrian 1845 pattern cavalry sword hilt with pierced guard. This style dominated in Austria from the late 18th century and was the model for the British 1796 heavy cavalry pattern and for swords of other nations.*

The light cavalry has always had a distinctive dashing air about it, and rightly so up to the late 19th century, when all cavalry, although still described as either light or heavy, came to act in almost the same manner.

Traditional light cavalry, by the nature of its role, comprised lighter men and lighter horses moving at a faster pace. Their action was surprise attack and scouting and their sword was usually the cutting-only pattern with curved single-edged blades copied from Eastern models. Hilt protection was almost non-existent, just a simple knuckle-bow or "stirrup-hilt", or a few extra bars.

In Britain the light cavalry adopted in 1796 a pattern with a curved single-edged blade which widened towards the tip. It was an excellent weapon whose loss was bemoaned in 1821 when it was replaced by a three-bar hilted pattern of inferior design, which was nevertheless much copied in Europe. This lasted in Great Britain until 1853 when a universal pattern for all cavalry was adopted, but the three-bar hilt was retained by the dashing Royal Horse Artillery.

In France, light cavalry had a single-edged brass-hilted sword with three bars. This continued with minor modifications as the main sword for light cavalry and eventually became the universal pattern. In America, this pattern of sword was issued until 1913, when a weapon based on the universal British 1908 pattern was adopted.

In Germany, Hungary and Russia, the light cavalry favoured the curved cutting blade, which continued in use until in the mid-19th century the trend towards universal pattern swords decided its fate. In Russia, the curved blade and the distinction between heavy and light cavalry continued many years after other countries, while the Scandinavian countries were some of the first to adopt a universal sword and abandon the curved light cavalry sabre. In Austria, the light cavalry had a variety of superb curved-bladed weapons with either single knuckle-bow guard or a hilt composed of bars.

In light cavalry, the pattern carried by officers continued much later and most light cavalry officers retained a distinctive pattern until the end of the 19th century. In the United States, Britain and in France, the standard cavalry sword was carried by officers and men, but in Russia, Scandinavia and in certain cases in Austria and Germany, the special officers' patterns were retained and many continued in use until the sword ceased to be a part of an officer's dress.

The distinction between light and heavy cavalry in relation to swords eventually disappeared. (See pp. 128–31.)

Swords

Heavy cavalry troopers were armed with a more fearsome style of sword than their light cavalry counterparts. The weapon naturally tended to be heavier, with a wider single-edged blade which was usually straight. Austria adopted a straight-bladed weapon with a disc-hilt pierced with holes. This served as the pattern for the British pattern, that of 1796, which lasted until 1821 when, although a new pattern was adopted, the original pattern was modified by losing the langets and reshaping the blade point. The 1821 pattern British sword had a solid bowl-guard and a curved blade with a single cutting edge, along the lines of the light cavalry weapon of the same period but with a heavier blade.

The heavy cavalry of France were armed with a straight-bladed sword with a half-basket guard which later evolved into the three-bar pattern carried by the French until the end of the 19th century. In Prussia, too, the brass-hilted sword developed into a four-bar hilted sword, as did the patterns of Russia. Denmark also supplied a straight-bladed sword with an intricate arrangement of brass bars on the hilt, as well as more elaborate straight-bladed swords with shields or ovals on the guards which had developed from the old style basket-hilted heavy cavalry sword.

In the United States, a variety of heavy cavalry swords was carried, mainly of the full-basket style inherited from the British and the later swords of the 1780s, with elaborate bars in steel and straight grip and blade. By 1840, however, the United States had adopted as its cavalry sword a brass three-bar hilted weapon with a curved single-edged blade based on the contemporary French pattern.

The discussion of heavy cavalry sword patterns is often complicated by the nature of the establishment of armies. In Britain there were just two categories of use, heavy and light, but in other countries cuirassiers, dragoons, and bodyguards were treated differently and each had a different pattern of sword. The Germanic states, some bound together by treaty but each independent, had many differing patterns but tended to copy the pre-eminent states, e.g. Prussia and Bavaria. This continued even after 1871 and the creation of the German Empire.

By the closing years of the 19th century there was very little distinction anywhere between the swords of heavy or light cavalry, only royal household troops and bodyguard cavalry retaining individual weapons. Russia persisted with different issues even with their rationalisation and the adoption of the "System 1881".

4

Until the time of universal swords, heavy cavalry used a wide, chopping blade and a heavy guard. The basic basket-hilt design was popular until Austria introduced the disc hilt, after which designs became less cumbersome and more functional. Blade shapes varied with countries, but most at this period still owed their origin to earlier days.

1. Prussian heavy cavalry model 1732.
2. French heavy cavalry model 1790.
3. Spanish heavy cavalry, c. 1750.
4. American cavalry, 1780.
5. Austrian heavy cavalry model 1769.
6. British heavy cavalry pattern 1821.
7. British Household Cavalry, c. 1808–18.

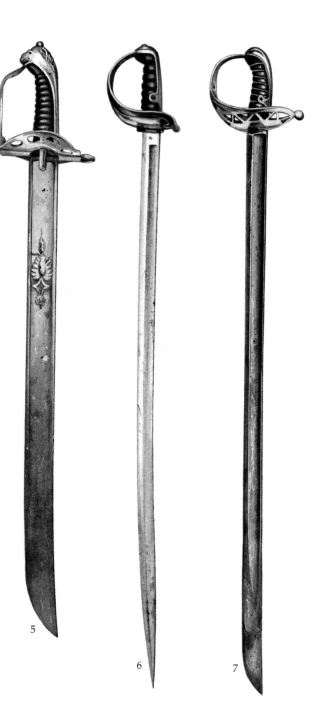

5

6

7

129

Swords

In the middle and late 19th century the distinction between light and heavy cavalry types was in many cases eroded, but the search for the perfect sword continued until the opening decade of the 20th century.
1. Polish light cavalry, c. 1840.
2. Russian dragoons, system of 1881.
3. Prussian officer's model 1889.
4. British cavalry trooper's sword, universal pattern of 1864.
5. British cavalry trooper's sword, universal pattern of 1908 - the "perfect sword".
6. United States 1913 pattern cavalry enlisted man's sword, based on the previous British pattern.

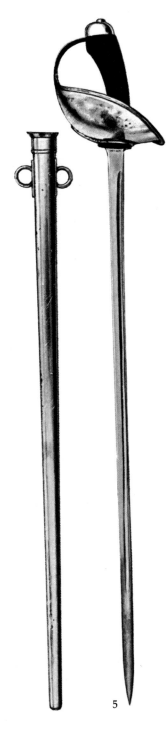

5

By the mid-19th century the sword of the cavalryman had taken on a design less distinctive from those of other corps. Heavy cavalry and light cavalry tended with some exceptions to be armed with the same weapon and this was the popular cut-and-thrust type. In Britain the first universal pattern had been that of 1853, with three-bar hilt and slightly curved cut-and-thrust blade. This style of blade continued in the 1864 sword, with a solid guard pierced with a Maltese cross, through the 1882, 1885 and 1890 patterns which were basically the same, and with a new guard the blade shape appeared again with the 1899 pattern – all intended for both heavy and light cavalry. After many experiments cut-and-thrust was abandoned and a perfectly designed purely thrusting weapon (many if not all agree this was the perfect cavalry sword) was adopted in 1908.

Other countries also had adopted universal pattern swords, Germany adopting one in 1889, Austria adopting one before Britain in 1845, and Russia, except for the Cossacks, adopting a system of regularity in 1881. But the Indian Army came late to universal patterns, with a copy of the British 1908, in 1918. Denmark became an early user of a universal pattern, adopting one in 1843, with an improved version in 1899. In Sweden it was 1854 which saw the introduction of a universal pattern while the U.S.A., having no distinction between light and heavy cavalry in the mid-19th century, adopted the three-bar brass-hilted version, copied from the French. The French were one of the few nations still to distinguish heavy and light cavalry in the issue of swords. In South American countries the distinction between light and heavy cavalry also remained late, but universal patterns were adopted during the late 19th century.

In the final design of a universal cavalry sword, Britain undoubtedly led the field, and the 1908 pattern still to be seen today on ceremonial with other than the Household Cavalry was considered, at least by one nation, worthy of copy. Troopers' swords were plain, officers' engraved on guard and blade, and Indian versions slightly smaller. In 1913 the U.S.A. introduced their own version of this sword. With a bowl-guard, grip cast in one piece and straight thrusting blade, this sword was made by a different process from those in Britain. With machine-set factories, the blades were milled from solid, the grips cast with little need for finish, and the whole assembled with ease. While the sword was inspired by the British 1908, it was never as good, as the metal grip was less natural in shape for the hand coming down to the charge position.

Swords

The tradition of every armed man carrying a sword carried on well into the 20th century, with bandsmen and buglers for example often having their own style. Short swords were issued to corps such as artillery and engineers; in the first place this was because the swords performed a useful function. One prime example is the 1856 British pattern Pioneer sword carried until 1903. With its saw-back and cutting blade it was cumbersome in either function; the hilt had a knuckle-guard that protected little of the hand and made it difficult to reverse the weapon and use the saw-back.

Originally the swords used were designed for the needs of that particular corps, being for either pioneers, engineers, medical personnel (for dress or self-defence only, one hopes!) or gunners. Soon many of these corps found little time for hand-to-hand fighting and in a number of instances they were issued with obsolete bayonets as side arms for dress only. In France brass-hilted sidearms had always been issued to corps and from these and the Prussian variants, other armies copied theirs, such as the British for the Land Transport Corps and the United States for the artillery. Other armies tended to arm their corps with full-length swords, especially if they were mounted, but it was perhaps in France and Prussia that the individual corps weapon lasted longest. In Britain, while the short side arm of the Pioneer lasted into this century, the artillery abandoned their "Dundas" pattern driver's sword in favour of the bayonet in the late 1850s, while the Army Hospital Corps had a sword similar to if not the same as that issued to Coast Guards. The sergeants of the Medical Staff Corps in 1888 were ordered in place of swords to carry the obsolete 1856 pattern Lancaster brass-hilted bayonet.

Police also carried swords, perhaps for longer in France, where the obsolete brass-hilted 1842 bayonet was used, and in Germany, where a specially designed side arm was provided. In Britain, police were armed with a brass-hilted sword as were prison warders, although theirs was all in steel until after the 1850s. The swords were again short in the blade, slightly curved, with a solid brass grip and three-bar hilt, and a black leather brass-mounted scabbard.

In Germany the carrying of side arms, often in the form of a bayonet, lasted well into the World War II, and in other countries also the side arm of the early years of the century had given way to the dress bayonet, an elaborate copy of a bayonet, with stag-horn grips, and badge, but no locking device to attach it to a rifle. It was thus largely a "weapon of rank" rather than a fighting arm.

1. British prison warder's hanger.
2. Spanish artillery hanger with broad double-edged blade.
3. French style popular in Germany (e.g. mounted artillery) and other countries; used by police in South American countries.
4. American artillery sword copied from French and Prussian styles.
5. British Land Transport Corps sword of the "Roman" style much in vogue in the 1850s.
6. British 1856 pattern Pioneer sword with saw-back; this was issued until 1903.

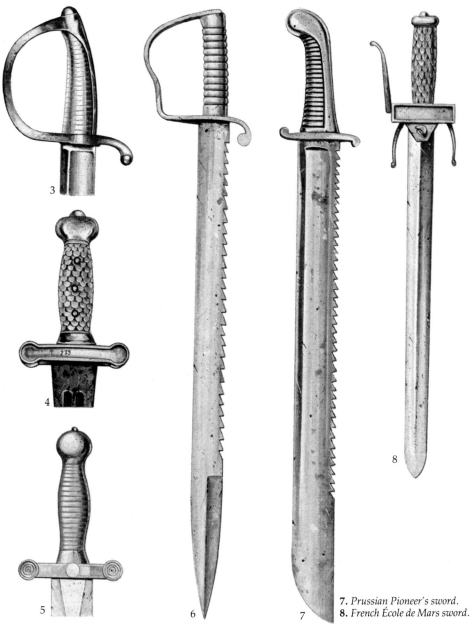

7. *Prussian Pioneer's sword.*
8. *French École de Mars sword.*

Swords

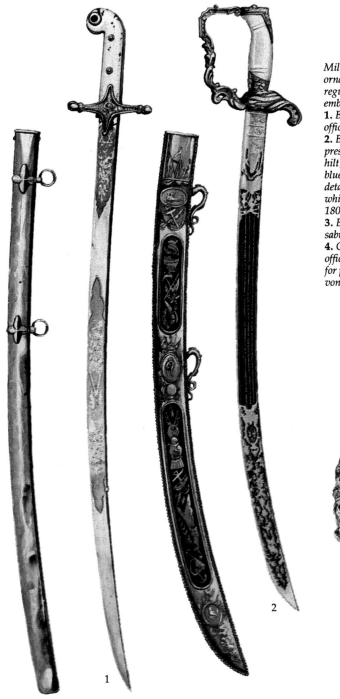

Military swords were not only ornate for high-ranking officers; regulation patterns were often embellished for presentation.
1. British 1831 pattern general officer's sword with ivory grips.
2. British Lloyd's-style presentation sabre with richly gilt hilt, mounts and scabbard, with blued and gilt blade bearing a detailed inscription of the deed for which the weapon was presented; 1807.
3. British 1803 general officer's sabre with gilt hilt and ivory grip.
4. German regulation infantry officer's sword richly ornamented for presentation to Field Marshal von Hindenburg, 1916.

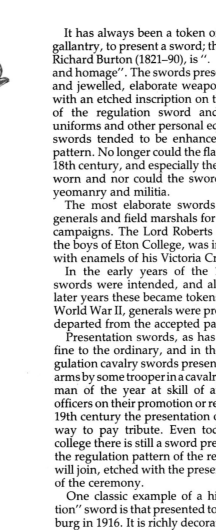

It has always been a token of esteem, and a reward for gallantry, to present a sword; the sword, as was said by Sir Richard Burton (1821–90), is ". . . the highest form of oath and homage". The swords presented ranged from the gold and jewelled, elaborate weapons to the ordinary pattern with an etched inscription on the blade. With the coming of the regulation sword and the tight regulating of uniforms and other personal equipment, the presentation swords tended to be enhanced versions of the original pattern. No longer could the flamboyant swords of the late 18th century, and especially the Lloyds patriotic sword, be worn and nor could the swords presented to officers of yeomanry and militia.

The most elaborate swords were those presented to generals and field marshals for exploits in various wars or campaigns. The Lord Roberts Eton sword, presented by the boys of Eton College, was in silver and gold decorated with enamels of his Victoria Cross and other medals.

In the early years of the 19th century presentation swords were intended, and allowed, to be worn, but in later years these became tokens only; as late as the end of World War II, generals were presented with swords which departed from the accepted patterns.

Presentation swords, as has been said, range from the fine to the ordinary, and in the ordinary category are regulation cavalry swords presented for example for a feat of arms by some trooper in a cavalry regiment, for best swordsman of the year at skill of arms, swords presented to officers on their promotion or retirement. Indeed in the late 19th century the presentation of a sword was an accepted way to pay tribute. Even today, at Sandhurst military college there is still a sword presentation, albeit a sword of the regulation pattern of the regiment which the recipient will join, etched with the presentation legend and the date of the ceremony.

One classic example of a highly embellished "regulation" sword is that presented to Field Marshal von Hindenburg in 1916. It is richly decorated and etched and a prime example of this style of regulation presentation weapon. Another, non-regulation, type is represented by the swords given by the Prince of Wales on his Indian tour of 1876. The swords were based on a regulation style of simple form, with the addition of a brased-on oval depicting the prince's head within the collar of the Star of India and perhaps an ivory grip, and non-regulation scabbard. As these were intended for Indian princes, the slight deviation from the "regulation" pattern did not matter.

Swords

Naval swords and daggers were regularised later than equivalent military weapons, and almost all adopted a distraction of gilt hilts, white grips and an anchor incorporated in the design.

1. *British midshipman's dirk, pattern 1879.*

2. *German officer's dirk, c. 1900.*

3. *Austria officer's dirk, c. 1910.*

4. *British officer's spadroon, c. 1790.*

5. *British officer's regulation pattern of 1827 with blade form used until 1846.*

6. *British officer's small sword with colichemarde blade, c. 1740.*

7. *French cutlass, c. 1840. The style was copied by many, including the United States.*

8. *British cutlass, c. 1820.*

9. *French officer's sword, 1848.*

10. *Dutch officer's sword, model 1889.*

11. *Russian cutlass, c. 1860.*

The navies of the world were latecomers to a regulation pattern of swords and it was not until the late 18th and early 19th century that efforts were made to establish uniform swords, dirks and cutlasses. Prior to 1805, British Royal Navy officers carried a number of styles, the most popular being the "five ball" guard spadroon or the slot-hilted sword, usually decorated with suitable devices such as an anchor. In that year a standard pattern was ordered to replace the previous dress and fighting swords. This pattern endured until 1827, when a sword with a solid version of the infantry "Gothic" pattern hilt was adopted. The sword also had a lion-head pommel and back-strap, and the crown and anchor badge instead of the royal cypher in the cartouche. With changes in blade shape, this has remained the pattern to the present day. For the dirk, carried by midshipmen at various periods, there was no regulation pattern until 1856. Early examples have curved blades, straight blades, elaborate hilts or just a plain cross-guard. The new pattern had a lion-head pommel and back-strap, white grip and cross-guard with acorn finials. A later addition was a cartouche on the side with the crown-and-anchor device.

Cutlasses were about 1800 crude affairs made for ease of use and cheapness, the earliest pattern having a "figure-8" guard. Various patterns were adopted and the cutlass finally bowed out as a serious weapon in 1936.

In other countries, various styles of naval sword appeared, many with brass or gilt brass hilts. The French pattern with its pierced guard was adopted by other countries such as the United States and the Netherlands, while the German pattern closely resembled that of Britain. Other countries modelled their swords on the British or French patterns and many of the South American countries copied one of these patterns, depending usually on where their ships were purchased or who helped train their navy. Dirks were used by nearly every navy, some not confining their use to midshipmen, the most notable in this style being Germany. Cutlasses, while varying between countries, are recognizable from their basic short, heavy blade and well-protected hand-guard. The French pattern was copied by the United States and a number of European countries.

Swords

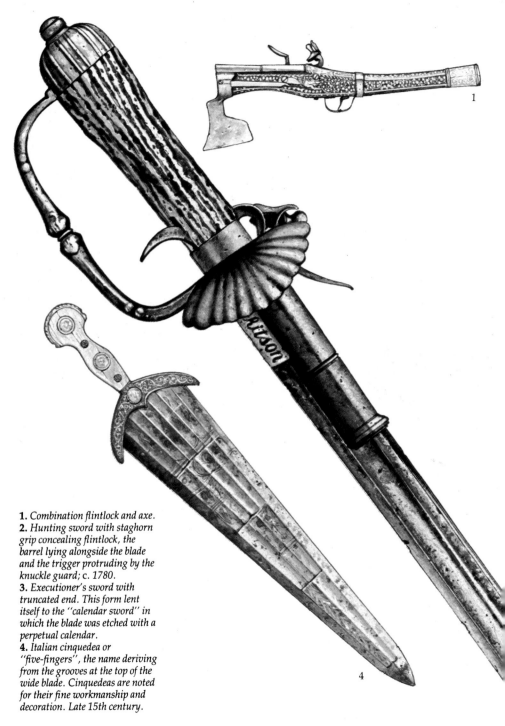

1. *Combination flintlock and axe.*
2. *Hunting sword with staghorn grip concealing flintlock, the barrel lying alongside the blade and the trigger protruding by the knuckle guard; c. 1780.*
3. *Executioner's sword with truncated end. This form lent itself to the "calendar sword" in which the blade was etched with a perpetual calendar.*
4. *Italian cinquedea or "five-fingers", the name deriving from the grooves at the top of the wide blade. Cinquedeas are noted for their fine workmanship and decoration. Late 15th century.*

3

As with firearms, there are unusual swords as well. Some were designed for a particular purpose, others as a result of the search for increased defensive or offensive power, for example the combination weapon. Among the unusual blade shapes is the Italian *cinquedea* (meaning five fingers), the blade at the top being fullered and the width of five fingers. Another unusual form of blade is the calendar sword which bears an eternal calendar engraved or etched into the blade.

A rarer blade shape is that of the executioner's sword. This needed and has no point, its blade being abruptly rounded off at the end, and has straight edges intended for beheading. A more modern but nevertheless unusual blade form is that made in the 1930s for Abyssinia, the flame blade. Shaped like a naked flame, the blade is etched, plated, and coloured to represent the colours of flame – red copper, gilt etc.

The combination of firearm and *arme blanche* is an old one. The piece known as "Henry VIII's Tuck" with concealed gun is an early example of the combination idea, but most of the sword-with-gun systems that survive today are from the 17th and 18th centuries and are mainly hunting swords or hangers with the hilt worked to house a flintlock pistol. In these cases, the barrel either protrudes from the right side of the blade and lies along it or it aligns over the top of the blade. The flint-lock cock, pan and frizzen are mounted in the centre at the point where blade joins the hilt and the distinctive shell-guard of the hanger is retained to "protect" the pan and frizzen. The mechanism and spring are housed inside the grip with the trigger protruding. In most designs there is no trigger-guard, as the knuckle-bow of the sword protects the hand and trigger; but in some, usually later, instances where the hilt has no guard, a trigger-guard of the conventional type was fitted to the weapon.

While some of these weapons were originally designed as combination weapons, others have been converted. There are a number of long- and short-bladed weapons whose "hilt" is no more than a conventional pocket pistol with one or two barrels, the blade being fitted to the frame. (See pp. 242–3.)

As swords in civilian circles lost popularity to the gun, fewer and fewer combination weapons were made. However, the pocket pistol in the 18th century assumed another role when, as in many cases, it adopted a spring bayonet, making the gun the first and the blade the secondary weapon.

Daggers and Knives

From earliest times the dagger and the knife have been an essential weapon and an essential tool. During the 5th century, the Saxon all-purpose knife was the scramasax, seax, or sax. This was a single-edged knife, but of no fixed blade-length, and considerable variations have been noted. The main characteristic of the scramasax, despite the difference in local manufacture and of course length, was the shape. The back of the blade did not run parallel to the cutting edge but broadened out from the hilt for just over half its length and then turned inwards to meet the cutting edge at the point, almost giving the appearance of the clipped point of the Bowie knife and some later knife bayonets.

During the 12th and 13th centuries, a knife or dagger became an indispensible part of the fighting man's equipment. The knights now carried along with their swords a short double-edged dagger, shaped like the full-size sword. By the 15th century there were a number of popular styles of daggers in use but the one most favoured by the knights was the rondel dagger. The blade was double edged and tapered, and diamond or triangular in cross-section. The hilt consists of a circle of metal where the blade joins the rounded grip, with the same style of disc as a pommel. Some rondel daggers have conical pommels. In the same period a popular knife was the ballock knife, so called owing to the hilt shape. Called a kidney dagger by the Victorians, this form was popular from the 14th to 17th centuries in northern Europe, especially in the Low Countries, England and Scotland. The blade was usually double-edged but it was the grip that was unusual. This was normally made from carved wood and was wide at the top where the grip was usually covered by a metal plate where the tang was riveted over and tapered towards the blade. Where grip joined blade, the grip swelled out each side into two lobes. These acted as a hand-stop. It was from this style of dagger that the Scottish highland dirk evolved.

Other distinctive styles of dagger included that carried by the *Landsknechts* in the 16th century. This had a narrow double-edged blade and a steel grip that tapered out from the cross-guard to the wide oval pommel. The metal sheath is often distinctive for its raised bands. The 15th-century Italian eared dagger was yet another distinctive type. This had the pommel formed by a pair of discs inclined outwards from the slender grip to its narrow blade. The Baselard had pommel, grip and guard in the form of an "H". It was often used by "civilians" and could have a relatively large blade.

1   2

Evolving from the Saxon all-purpose knife the scramasax, knives and daggers came to have different hilts, grips and blade forms. After a period of disuse, in the 14th century the knife and

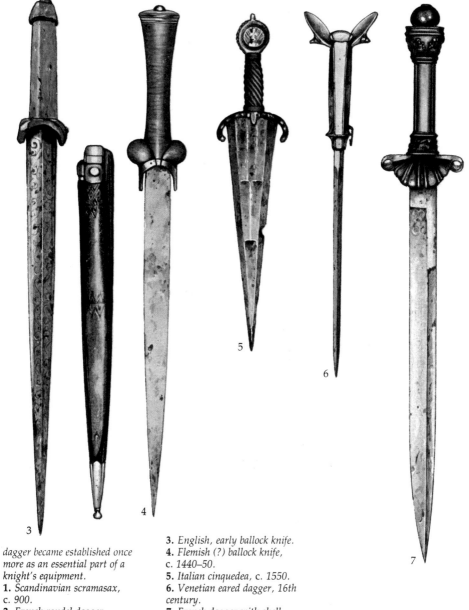

3

4

5

6

7

dagger became established once more as an essential part of a knight's equipment.
1. *Scandinavian scramasax, c. 900.*
2. *French rondel dagger, c. 1440–50.*

3. *English, early ballock knife.*
4. *Flemish (?) ballock knife, c. 1440–50.*
5. *Italian cinquedea, c. 1550.*
6. *Venetian eared dagger, 16th century.*
7. *French dagger with shell-guards, c. 1500.*

Daggers and Knives

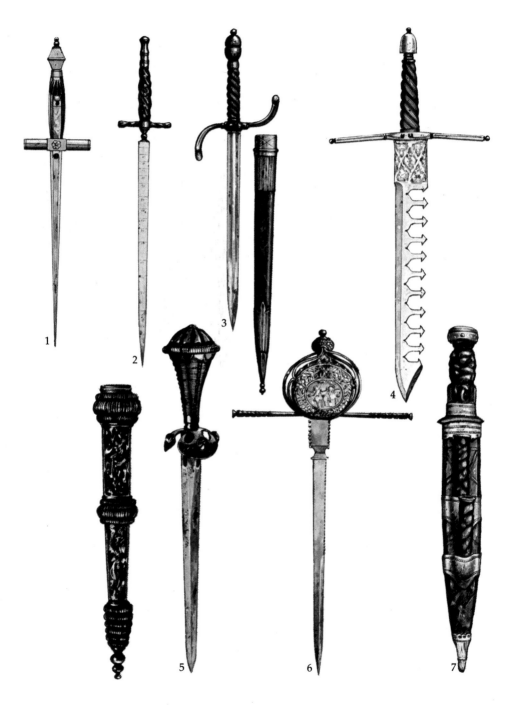

Later Daggers

In the 16th century and onwards various specialised forms of knife and dagger developed.
1. *German combined stiletto and primer, c. 1660. The grip is hollow, to allow it to be used for holding priming powder.*
2. *Gunner's stiletto, Italian, c. 1650. The triangular sectioned blade is marked with graduations.*
3. *German dagger, c. 1610, with a table knife fitted in the top of the scabbard.*
4. *Italian sword-breaker dagger, c. 1600. The deep, barbed teeth on the blade work on springs; they allow the opponent's sword to enter but not to be withdrawn. The blade could then be twisted and the opponent's blade broken.*
5. *Landsknecht dagger and sheath, German, c. 1550. This shows the typical style carried by these German mercenaries.*
6. *Spanish left-hand dagger, c. 1640–50; the companion rapier bears the same decoration.*
7. *Highland dirk. This shows the later evolved style, with knife and fork.*

Within the categories of the dagger carried for self-protection and the knife used when hunting, specialised forms evolved. The Italians favoured the thin-bladed stiletto as a weapon, because it could be thrust between the joints in armour to kill, while the Spanish with their rapier favoured the left-hand dagger used in swordplay. The dagger or *main gauche* was usually decorated to match the rapier it accompanied and its double-edged blade was essential in warding off the adversary's thrusts (See pp. 110–13.)

The left-hand dagger was also popular in Germany, but never in Britain. In Italy, the left-hand dagger was used with the sword, although the style of fighting varied from that practised in Spain. All these left-hand daggers have blades that are reasonably heavy in proportion to their length as they had, like a shield, to withstand severe blows and needed to be capable of breaking an opponent's blade. To this end, so-called "sword breakers" were manufactured. They come in varying types but usually have a thick pointed blade with a series of cuts or notches in the top edge to snag the opponent's blade and then with a wrist movement hopefully snap it.

Another specialised dagger was the gunner's stiletto. This had calibrations engraved on the blade to aid the gunner in his "art". The German *main gauche* was a three-pronged affair; when the outer blades were folded flat against the central one, it was, for all intents and purposes a stiletto, but with these branched out, it was an effective left-hand dagger, a sword-breaker and a deadly thrusting weapon. Another unusual style of dagger could be used as a pair of dividers, but once the two arms were closed the result was a deadly stiletto.

The dagger that was both a hunting and a fighting weapon, used as a *main gauche* with broadsword, was the Scottish dirk. This evolved in the 17th century from the "ballock" knife and over the years acquired Celtic interlacing and carving on the wooden grip. The dirk is a single-edged blade (a number were made from broken broadsword blades). The scabbard, initially simple, acquired sometimes elaborate mounts. With the revival of things Scottish brought about by the novels of Sir Walter Scott, the dirk became fashionable again years after the Jacobite rebellions of 1715 and 1745. It was further embellished, to it were added a knife and fork – although some early examples do have an extra knife – and it was adopted by Highland regiments. The dirk is still with us today in both Highland civilian and in military dress.

Daggers and Knives

Knives have always been one of the sidearms carried by hunters, usually for cutting up the prey, skinning, and also for eating and for cutting firewood. Hunting knives, as opposed to daggers and stilettos for fighting, usually had a broad single- or double-edged blade.

The earliest "style" of hunting knife that was copied by other countries, and had a revival with the Nazi regime, was the Swiss style, with the scabbard chased with Holbein's "Dance of Death". One of the other favourite styles was the "ballock" knife or kidney knife, the name deriving from the shape of the grip with two round protuberances where hilt meets blade.

There also evolved during the 17th and 18th centuries the *trousse de chasse*, a set of eviscerating instruments with large-bladed knife-cum-cleaver, and smaller instruments housed in the scabbard for the various tasks of cutting, skinning, jointing and eating the prey. (See pp.116–17).

Other huntsmen, however, contented themselves with useful knives with simple cross-guards which could also be used for defence if required. So popular was the knife and dagger during the 16th and 17th centuries that it formed part of the everyday wear and most certainly part of the equipment for the hunt with hanger, boar sword and firearm.

During the 19th century, many types of knives appeared from the workshops of London, Sheffield and Solingen, many designed by well-known sportsmen such as Colonel Shakespear of the Indian Army whose knife was made by Wilkinsons, others designed by eminent sporting firms such as Dixons, whose knife-cum-bayonet could be attached to a pole and used as a boar spear. But perhaps the most famous was the Bowie, from which many other types of knives evolved in America. The Bowie can be called the "father" of the modern hunting knife.

Named after the designer, Colonel James Bowie, the knife had a broad wide blade with a clipped back to the point, and a simple cross-guard and grip. The style was spread in the United States and elsewhere due to the sales efforts of George Wolstenholme & Sons of Sheffield. They produced a variety of blade shapes based on the Bowie design with a host of differing scabbards, cross-guards and hilts. Many of the blades were etched with patriotic legends and the blades or scabbards marked with their famous trademark "IXL". The Sheffield cutlers enjoyed 50 years of lucrative selling in the United States, but by the 1880s Solingen knives were cheaper and America produced their own. The Bowie is still popular today.

Hunting knives have always formed part of the equipment of the hunter, to accompany spear, bow or firearm. Some have combined other functions.

1. Swiss dagger with scabbard representing Holbein's "Dance of Death", 1573.
*2. I*XL Bowie-style knife with German silver hilt and pearl grips, c. 1850.*
3. Victorian copy of a German late 16th-century hunting knife with companion knife and fork.
4. Wilkinson-manufactured Shakespear knife, c. 1890.
5. German hunting knife, one of numerous variations offered, c. 1905.
6. Hunting knife with staghorn grip and spring clip to hold blade in scabbard. German, 1900.
7. Bowie-style knife with tortoiseshell grip, inlaid with mother-of-pearl. Sheffield, 1880.

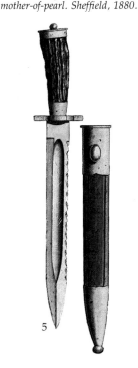

5

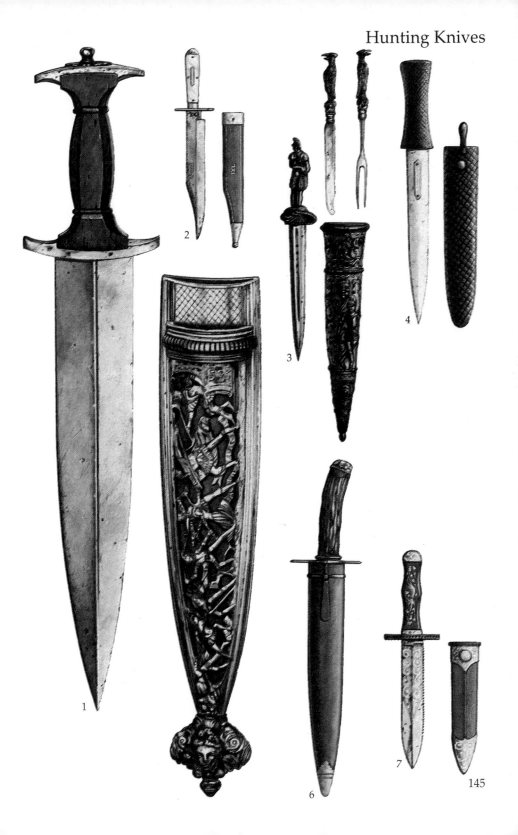

1

2

3

4

6

7

145

1

2

3

4

6

7

8

146

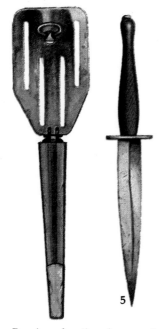

5

Even in modern times daggers and knives have still been retained in many armies as combat and survival weapons. The large variety of even recent knives testifies to the military interest in this field.
1. Germany, Weimar Republic police dress bayonet, c. 1930.
2. Scotland. Civilian dress dirk, silver mounted, c. 1870.
3. Scotland. Military officer's dress dirk, c. 1890.
4. France. Bayonet cut down to a trench dagger, 1914–18.
5. Britain and Allies. Fairbairn and Sykes commando/fighting knife c. 1943, in scabbard with webbing attachment.
6. Foraging and jungle machete, of a type still made today after over 100 years.
7. Germany. Huntsman's or forester's sidearm, of a type carried since c. 1840.
8. Germany. Nazi SA dagger, c. 1938.

Daggers as such survived for many years until the firearm combined with bayonet became the important weapon of the fighting man. But bayonet design itself, as can be seen, tried to integrate the use of a bayonet with that of a knife and so in time there evolved the dual-purpose weapon. By the time of the standing armies, the dagger, except for hunting, had ceased to exist and it was perhaps the close combat of World War I with its stagnant trench warfare that brought the dagger back into the armoury of the fighting man.

The oldest, or at least one of the oldest, regulation fighting knives has been the Scottish dirk. Although by the beginning of the 19th century a purely regimental decoration, in earlier times it had been a close-combat knife. Other knives had been developed in the late 19th century to provide defence and to serve some other purpose, such as entrenching knives doubling for shovels, or the Elcho bayonet which was a bayonet and a brush cutter.

World War I saw an increased demand for the issue of knives to troops. These were at the beginning crude efforts, or at best cut-down bayonets, but as the war moved to its final phase, designed knives were issued. During the interwar years, the idea of a fighting knife disappeared amidst the modernisation of horse-mounted troops, the development of aircraft, and the increase in power of the artillery piece. However, in the early years of World War II there was a need for a fighting knife for the commando-type raids like those made on the French coast, and here the expertise of two former officers of the Shanghai Police, Fairbairn and Sykes, and of the Wilkinson Sword Company produced a fighting knife second to none, and known as the FS after its originators.

Even though firearms are perhaps more powerful today, the fighting knife is an integral part of the equipment of the commando, ranger or marine, as silent killing today is just as important as it was before. The designs of knives take many forms. Some, such as the FS knife, are for killing alone, some others are combined survival and killing knives, whereas some are purely survival knives issued to aircrews and naval personnel for use in cutting down trees, opening tins, etc.

While modern warfare to the outsider seems to be nuclear, the ordinary soldier will have to hold ground in any conflict and in this he will need rifle, bayonet and above all the fighting knife for survival. There are new patterns of fighting knife, but the one thing all have in common is a slim, double-edged blade, the best edged killing weapon in the world.

Bayonets

The youngest of the edged weapons in this book is perhaps the bayonet, which originated with the expansion of the use of firearms. The vulnerability of the new musketeer was his lack of defence when, having discharged his musket, he was engaged in the lengthy act of reloading and was at the mercy of the enemy's cavalry. Most armies deployed their musketeers with a protective covering of pikemen behind whom they could retire. This tactic, however, meant that musket and pike were deployed together and no tactical advantage could be taken by using muskets in a surprise attack.

How the knife or dagger came to be used as a bayonet and how it got that name is still the subject of much conjecture. It may be true to say that the bayonet came into being by chance when a musketeer found himself alone and defenceless and to give himself a better chance thrust the handle of his dagger into the barrel of his musket.

Neither of these theories explains why the weapon is called a bayonet. Early references in drill manuals such as the *Abridgement of the English Military Discipline* (1686) term the weapon as a dagger, yet mention is made in the memoirs of a French officer, in a 1642 campaign, of his men being armed with "bayonettes with handles one foot long and the blades of the bayonettes were as long as the handles, the ends of which were adapted" (i.e. tapered) "for putting into the barrels of the fusils to defend themselves, when attached having fired". A 1611 dictionary gives *"Bayonnier"* as a crossbowman. A further possible explanation of the name is that crossbowmen were renowned for their shortswords, from which the bayonet could have developed following the adoption of the musket. One more claimant is the town of Bayonne, well known for its ironworks and cutlery trade; a dictionary of 1694 describes "bayonette" as "a type of dagger, called thus from the town of Bayonne".

The French and a number of other European countries employed bayonets before their introduction in England in 1660, and Louis XIV issued a proclamation forbidding the use of bayonets because of accidents.

The plug bayonet was also used in sporting and hunting and continued to be popular as such for many years after the military had discarded it. Examples are known with ornate fittings which were still being made and used in Spain in the middle of the 19th century. However, although certainly made in the form of a plug bayonet these cannot have been intended for insertion into the gunmuzzle, such is the richness of the hilt decoration.

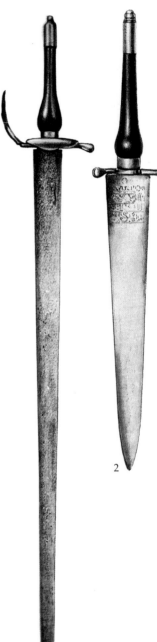

1

2

The plug was the first of the many bayonet forms used by the armies of the world. The design of new styles continues today, although the practical use of the bayonet is now more limited.

1. British plug bayonet with long sword blade and shell-guard from an infantry hanger.

2. Typical British plug bayonet of the 1660 period with polished wood grip, brass fittings and dagger-shaped blade.

3. British. The same grip as (2) but with a broader, shorter blade.

4. English. Ivory hilt with silver inlay bayonet. Many of this style were produced, with different blade designs.

5. Sweden produced a number of innovative bayonet designs. This longer-bladed Swedish weapon has a spring attachment.

6. Ornate late Spanish hunting plug bayonet. The Spanish were the last to abandon the plug bayonet, in the 19th century.

7. English plug bayonet, with a bulbous lower grip, c. 1686.

8. English plug bayonet with ornate fittings but a wood grip.

Bayonets

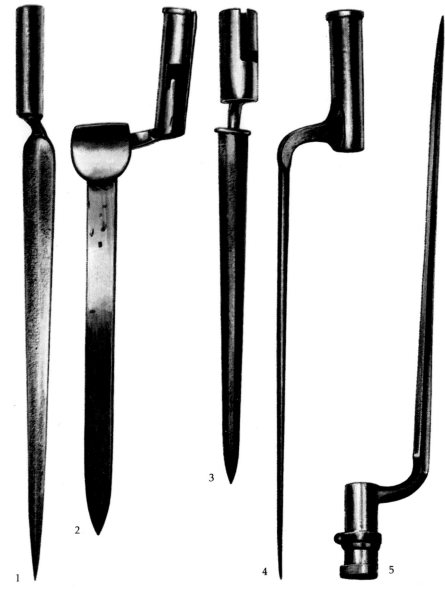

The greatest step forward in
bayonet design was the
substitution for the plug of a
socket to fit over the barrel.
1. *Closed-socket bayonet, the
socket without a slot.*
2. *Open-socket bayonet designed
to fit barrels of different diameters,
c. 1690s.*

3. *Early British bayonet without
collar to the socket, c. 1720.*
4. *United States late 18th-century
socket bayonet with blade welded
to socket.*
5. *French model 1777 socket
bayonet with locking ring.*

6. *Austrian specialised socket
bayonet with shaft bearing spear
point.*
7. *Swedish all-steel socket
bayonet, with solid socket and
fixing nut.*

An early attempt to find an easier method of attaching and detaching a bayonet was to fit rings to the bayonet which were slipped over the barrel. The socket bayonet soon evolved, in the earliest examples being of the split-socket type in which the socket or tube is split along its length. This allowed the bayonet to fit all types of muskets, which in those days were not standardised. The socket bayonet also avoided the chief dangers of the plug – too tight a fit, or the bayonet being broken off when inserted in the muzzle.

At the beginning of the 18th century there was a wide range of bayonets in existence. One officer wrote to the Board of Ordnance in London that ". . . all regiments raised since the disuse of pikes have provided Bayonets as they do swords and belts at their own charge . . . few of the officers agree to the sort of Bayonets fit to be used and in the manner of fitting them to the Musquets as may appear by the various sorts of them in ye Army."

By 1720, a closed-socket bayonet of a standard pattern with a flat blade was in use in Britain; the later 18th-century type with a triangular section blade remained in use in the British army until 1853. In Britain fitting depended on the inside diameter of the socket and the outer diameter of the barrel being exactly right: what actually secured the bayonet was a "zig-zag" slot that fitted over the sight. In other countries various methods of fitting the bayonet securely were tried.

In Sweden, early patterns of bayonets were secured by a wing-nut. In France the locking ring was favoured. In other countries a plain socket was preferred, as in America, where a home-produced musket and bayonet were manufactured in the 1790s. Prior to that in America a variety of mainly French muskets and bayonets were used as well as captured British and German weapons.

The main advantage of the split-socket and later the closed-socket bayonet over the plug is obvious: now the soldier could fire his musket with bayonet fixed. This meant that military tactics changed and the armed soldier could now fight as a self-contained unit without the extra protection of pikemen. It was now feasible to have bayonet charges (at the time, a surprise volley swiftly followed by a charging line was not an accepted part of warfare).

The universal introduction of the socket bayonet in its various forms made the pike obsolete and it soon disappeared from the battlefield. Mounted as well as foot soldiers could be now armed with bayonets, and many were.

6   7

Bayonets

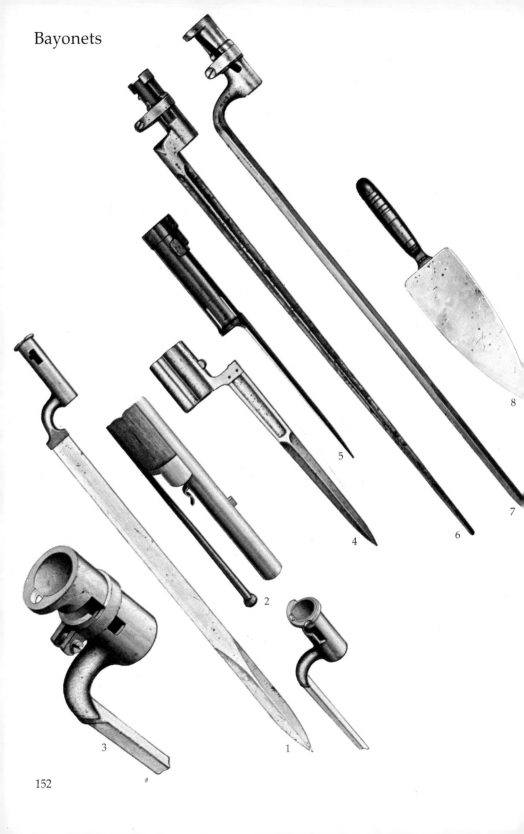

Later Socket Bayonets

Despite the onslaught of the sword bayonet during the 19th century (see pp. 154 – 5), its use remained restricted to the specialist regiments and corps, and to NCOs, the bulk of the rank and file being armed with the cheaper and shorter socket bayonet that was easier to use. With the general developments in arms during the mid 19th century, ordinary bayonets too improved, developing from the basic socket with slot, already described, to models of similar form but with more complex and effective locking devices. The Hanoverian spring catch was adopted by Britain in 1843. This had a catch on the muzzle of the musket which engaged a collar on the bayonet. France and other countries, however, had long preferred to have a locking ring on the socket to keep the bayonet firmly in place, and this form was adopted eventually by Britain.

Although socket bayonets for the majority of the troops had blades of triangular section, a number were manufactured with sword-style blades or for specialist tasks. In Britain these included the Sappers and Miners' bayonet for carbine, with saw-back blade, the socket acting as grip, and with a light cavalry-style three-bar guard. In the final issued model this was simplified to a blade with a socket which could act as a grip if required. This provided a heavy and rather impractical side arm and bayonet. The East India Company also issued such a weapon for its sappers, but this had as an integral part of the socket a knuckle-bow, and also the added advantage of a slot in the collar to engage the spring on the fore-end.

The Austrian Lorenz socket bayonet of 1854 had a graduated sloping slot in the socket, locked by a ring, while the American Springfield of 1873 had the regular slot with ring but also the sharp horizontal arm joining blade and socket, as in the French pattern and many other European versions. By the 1880s in many armies the socket bayonet had given way to the knife bayonet, although many countries continued to supply specialist troops with the long-bladed sword bayonet until World War I. The last bastion of the socket bayonet was undoubtedly Russia, where with the adoption of the Mosin-Nagent rifle in 1891 they continued the use of this form of bayonet for the infantry following on the Berdan series.

The socket bayonet, however, seems to refuse to die and various patterns were made during World War II. Even today the Belgian company Fabrique Nationale (FN) supply or have supplied a socket bayonet for an automatic carbine. Similar to that patented by BSA in 1948, the weapon is of tubular construction with a locking device.

Bayonets

With the formation of rifle corps in a number of armies at the beginning of the 19th century, the adopted style was that of Germany, and *Jaegers* (hunters), as they were termed, wore distinctive uniforms and carried a rifle and bayonet. This was a sword bayonet suited to the needs of the *Jaegers* who acted, unlike the line battalions, as skirmishers and specialist troops. The bayonet adopted by most if not all rifle corps was based on the German *Jaeger* pattern with its broad, straight blade and brass hilt with knuckle-guard. Most early sword bayonets for rifles followed this pattern but there were of course variations. Denmark converted its 1791 cavalry sword into a bayonet by cutting down the blade and fitting a block and spring to fit into a rectangular box brazed to the side of the muzzle.

In Britain, the brass-hilted Baker pattern adopted in 1800 continued with minor modifications until 1815, when it was decided that the bayonet was too heavy on the muzzle when the rifle was fired. A sword was issued in its place and the rifles were converted to take a socket bayonet. A shorter knife bayonet for the Baker was also issued, but when the Brunswick percussion rifle was adopted in 1836 a heavy brass-hilted sword bayonet was again chosen.

The Danish style of sword bayonet, or *Hirschfänger*, had a brass hilt with small cross-guard and a box brazed to the flat left side of the grip which was fitted with a spring. The bar on the muzzle slid into the box and was held by the spring clip. This pattern survived until the 1860s, when other countries had adopted the French style.

The French style, which dominated sword bayonet design (with minor modifications in the metals used for the hilt), was introduced in 1842. It had a brass hilt with beak pommel, a leaf spring set in and a recurved yataghan-shaped blade of Turkish inspiration. This form continued with the Chassepot rifle of 1866 and was finally replaced in 1874 by the straight-bladed Gras bayonet. Elsewhere in Europe, nearly every country had adopted the yataghan blade-shape.

In Britain the 1853 artillery bayonet was an almost exact copy of the French 1842, complete with brass grips, but by 1856 the brass hilt had been abandoned in favour of a steel one with leather grips. In America various brass-hilted yataghan-blade bayonets were adopted, such as the 1855 pattern with less recurved blade than the European bayonets, and the 1861 U.S. Navy rifle with a brass-hilted bayonet. There were numerous others for privately made rifles, and many unidentified ones were imported during the Civil War.

Sword bayonets, popular at the beginning of the 19th century, were modelled mainly on German lines, and issued to rifle and other light infantry troops. By mid-century, the French influence predominated, to last until the general adoption of the knife bayonet in the last decades of the century.
1. Volunteer sword bayonet based on the light cavalry style with locking ring in the hilt. British, 1800.
2. Baker bayonet, 2nd pattern 1801.
3. Austrian, 1867.
4. Danish, 1860s.
5. Brunswick rifle bayonet, 1836.
6. French model 1842 with yataghan blade, beaked brass pommel and leaf spring, the most influential design in the later 19th century.
7. British artillery pattern 1856, with steel hilt and leather grip.
8. American sword bayonet with typical less recurved yataghan blade, 1865.

155

1

2

3

4

5

6

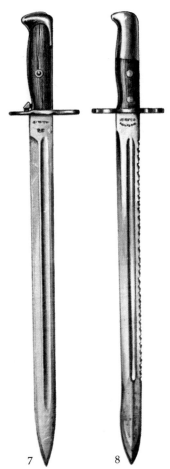

7   8

In the later years of the 19th century, dual-purpose bayonets abounded and the straight-bladed style slowly ousted the predominant French yataghan.

1. *Italian Vetterli model 1870.*
2. *British cutlass pattern 1871.*
3. *German model 1871.*
4. *British Elcho pattern 1871.*
5. *French Gras model 1874.*
6. *Spanish model 1893.*
7. *American Springfield model 1905.*
8. *Swiss Schmidt-Rubin saw-back model 1911.*

From the middle to the end of the 19th century was the heyday of the sword bayonet. In this field Britain was perhaps the front runner. Up until the introduction of the Enfield rifle, the sword bayonet had been used with rifle regiments on the Baker and later Brunswick rifle and also for double- and single-barrelled arms for special units such as the Irish Constabulary and Cape Carbines. With the number of varying patterns of the 1853 Enfield rifle and its derivatives such as carbines, short rifles, etc. intended for various arms of the service, a multitude of sword bayonets appeared.

The most popular shape world-wide was the yataghan blade which saw service in France, Britain, the United States, Austria, in Scandinavian and many other countries. That it was so popular as a blade shape is surprising, as the original yataghan was a cutting weapon whereas a bayonet by its very nature is a thrusting one.

In France, the yataghan-shaped blade, first introduced in 1842, continued until 1874, when a straight cruciform-section blade was introduced. But in Britain, the yataghan sword bayonet continued with rifle regiments and sergeants of the line until 1888, when all specialist bayonets were withdrawn in favour of a single knife pattern. In the meantime, bayonets with saw-back blades were introduced or proposed (Elcho and Constabulary, as well as those for New Zealand and artillery); bayonets for the Navy, cutlass in shape with fixings; bayonets for gunners, with knuckle-guards – the number and variety of designs were bewildering. In Europe, sanity in bayonet design seems to have reigned, although alongside the socket bayonet various countries produced special bayonets, as did the German states with their "individualised" saw-back versions and models for *Jaegers*, and Switzerland as late as 1911 produced a saw-back bayonet of a considerable weight. The drawback to all these dual-purpose bayonets was their weight; in battle, and with tiring limbs, this adverse affect on aim could be all-important. In the United States they produced a trowel bayonet intended to double as an entrenching tool, but it was short-lived and many of the bayonets of this specialised nature hardly ever saw action. Britain, engaged in colonial wars, was never to know how useless these designs were. In the 1880s most countries had plumped for the knife bayonet, and although there are certain variations today, such as the Russian wire-cutter (insulated!), they remain a knife as a bayonet, perhaps a full circle to the original bayonet as a knife thrust in the muzzle.

Bayonets

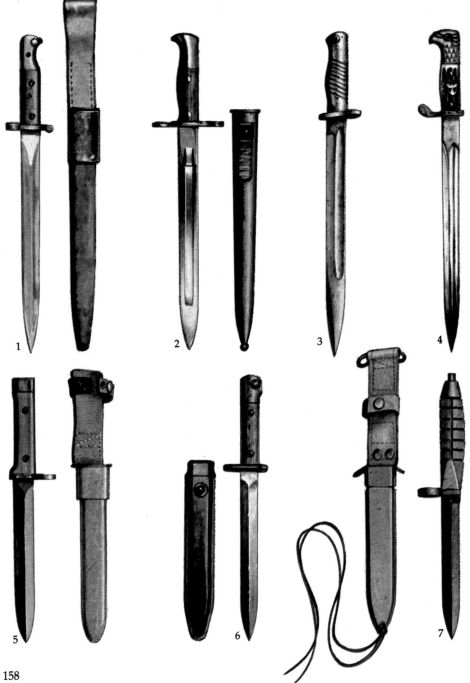

1

2

3

4

5

6

7

The spirit of the pike still influenced bayonet design until the closing years of the 19th century. Bayonets, whether sword or socket, had an impressive blade length designed to give the foot soldier extra reach for use against cavalry. While that might have been necessary when square formations for fighting against cavalry were in vogue, the pattern of warfare in the latter years of the 19th century had changed. Artillery and firepower had seen to that.

With the introduction of the magazine rifle in the armies of the world, hand-to-hand fighting decreased. The bayonet, however, still survived. In most cases the knife bayonet was adopted, but some countries, such as Switzerland and some Scandinavian states, still preferred a bayonet with a good blade length. Britain adopted the knife bayonet in 1888 and followed with another pattern in 1903, but in 1907 adopted a bayonet with a 17-inch blade. At this time many countries had adopted bayonets of differing designs with about this blade length, while others had chosen a shorter true knife blade. Italy still retained a good blade length, while Austria and Germany had, except for some corps bayonets, adopted the knife form. There was also a vogue in many countries, for economy, of shortening existing bayonets and regrinding the blades to bring them to the new shape and length.

The knife bayonet was a handier weapon on and off the rifle, as it could be used as a utility knife as well as a bayonet. Like sword bayonets, knife bayonets came in a variety of shapes and sizes, with differing blade designs, hilts and a host of fastening systems. By the beginning of the 20th century the knife bayonet was gaining ground. During World War I it was in use with Germany and Austria and, with unprecedented numbers of troops, bayonet production in all countries rose at an astronomical rate. In Britain alone, Wilkinsons, the main bayonet contractor, produced 2.5 million pattern 1907 bayonets. In Germany the economic situation and naval blockade resulted in a variety of bayonets. Some were converted from captured stocks, others crudely made with a minimum of skill and metal. These *Ersatz* bayonets exist in a great number of variations, and much has been written about them alone. Since World War I the general trend has been towards the knife bayonet and all countries of the world now have knife bayonets in their arsenals. The knife bayonet gives a better balance to the rifle, it is useful for survival and close combat, but how long will the bayonet survive? Is it another outdated piece of military hardware?

8

Bayonets

1. *Russian survival knife-cum-bayonet. This weapon (now copied in the Federal German Republic – see previous pages) is also a tool for cutting electricity cables, the scabbard and handle both being insulated.*
2. *A late World War II German development, the cumbersome grip incorporating a tool kit. Since the 1960s many copies have become available, of inferior quality.*

7

3. *British experimental bayonet of an old style patented by BSA in the late 1940s. A superb weapon, easy to make, and cheap. The "shoot through" system of attachment has not won acceptance.*
4. *Ornamental Spanish bayonet for bodyguard troops.*
5. *German FG 42, late experimental ramrod-style bayonet, similar to the French MAS 36.*
6. *United States ramrod bayonet for the U.S. model 1901 rifle. None of the ramrod bayonets tried between 1833 and 1903 was adopted.*
7. *British Webley-Greener, a private venture in World War I providing a bayonet for officers to fix to their Webley revolver. The blade and scabbard were cut down from French Gras bayonets.*

Almost as soon as the first bayonets were designed, inventors and swordmakers tried to improve on the basic bayonet and these adaptations usually combined the bayonet with another weapon to provide a dual-purpose implement. The earliest such forms were, of course, those combining swords and bayonets, i.e. swords with fittings for attachment to a musket or carbine.

The unusual also took the form of the ordinary. In this light we look at "ramrod" bayonets. Each musket or rifle had a ramrod or often, in later times of metallic cartridges, a cleaning or clearing rod. Why not employ this as a bayonet? Many did, including the Americans with their Springfield pattern '03. Later, the French issued their MAS 36 with its reversible ramrod-type spike bayonet.

Other unusual bayonets include a spike style made for the Sten gun during World War II. By modern standards this is very much a Heath Robinson idea, and few were made. Other unusual types include the 1948 pattern patented by BSA, which is very much akin to a 19th-century customs officer's probe for grain, having a tube cut away to form a point. The Russians have produced a bayonet which combined with its scabbard forms a good insulated wire-cutter, while the Germans during World War II produced a bayonet with a miniature toolkit in the handle. This style was revived during the 1950s and produced in Germany for the Sudan.

Perhaps the most unusual of bayonets was the pistol bayonet manufactured by Greeners for the Webley. The brainchild of Lieutenant Arthur Pritchard (3rd Royal Berkshire Regiment), this weapon combined a cut-down Gras (French) T-section bayonet and a cast brass hilt which was so designed as to clip over the muzzle and around the body of the Webley Mark VI revolver, the standard issue for officers and for other ranks who carried revolvers. Pritchard obtained a patent for his bayonet in November 1916.

There has always been a desire among arms manufacturers to combine two weapons in one, in bayonets as in other weapons. The author has himself been party to the development of a number of experimental bayonets, including some that could clip to a Browning 9mm pistol, and one designed for the Sterling sub-machine gun utilising the standard bayonet with its grip enclosed in a larger grip with compartments for matches, pills, salt tablets etc. None of these appeared in public, because the overburdening of the bayonet with extra uses made its use as a bayonet impractical, and as a dual-purpose knife its performance was indifferent.

Blade Weapon Fakes

In the field of edged weapons there will be found a number of complete fakes and altered or repaired items. Some repairs were done within the weapon's own lifetime as "honest working repairs". Quite different are those weapons adapted to deceive, and others badly repaired through lack of knowledge. While those repaired in their working life and others honestly repaired with mis-spent enthusiasm may be acceptable, depending on condition, those altered to deceive are not.

Sword fakes are often of weapons from the early days before standing armies or, more often, they are of later military swords. One of the favoured fields for faking is the inclusion of spurious markings. On early swords this mark can be the symbol and name of a well-known swordmaker, while in later military swords faking runs to presentation inscriptions and the inclusion of a simple engraved military marking to assign a certain weapon to a certain regiment. Favourites for the regimental markings are the 17th Lancers at the time of the Charge of the Light Brigade in the Crimea in 1854, or the Royal North British Dragoons, later the Royal Scots Greys, of the time of Waterloo (1815). Other celebrated actions of this type immediately spring to mind.

The other form of faking is to take an ordinary regimental pattern sword of the officer's type and then to etch or engrave on the blade, or perhaps the scabbard mounts, a spurious inscription to a famous person or to honour a famous deed. With acid etching on the blade, various pointers stand out to tell the right from the wrong. The different colour of the background of the etching left grey by the attack of acid should be apparent to the naked eye and the different depth of the faked etching should show that it was done later than the overall blade etching. The engraving of an inscription on the steel or gilt brass locket will again have tell-tale signs of age if genuinely contemporary. The portion of brass where the engraving tool cut will be dulled, the minute lines filled with the dirt of ages, and in the steel locket rust has probably played its part in darkening the area. The style of engraving is all-important as well. The obvious, but sometimes ignored, step is to check whether the recipient would have worn a sword of the type, i.e. was it a sword of the right regiment, or even was he alive and serving when the pattern was adopted.

It is of course possible these days to have recourse to metal tests, and on old and very expensive weapons, this is advisable.

There are a number of newly manufactured "antique" bayonets of rare patterns available today.

Example of a "suspect" sword. It appears to be a Royal Engineers sword of c. 1856–97 with a gun-metal guard pieced out in the heavy cavalry pattern style which was regulation. However, certain points are false. The grip is the "modern" infantry pattern of the 1897 sword which appeared about 1937. The backpiece is in the same modern style, cast in brass and copper plated. The wire binding is again modern and the blade bears modern proof marks and embossing. The fuller on the blade is the wrong style. The only original part of the sword is the guard.

BOWS

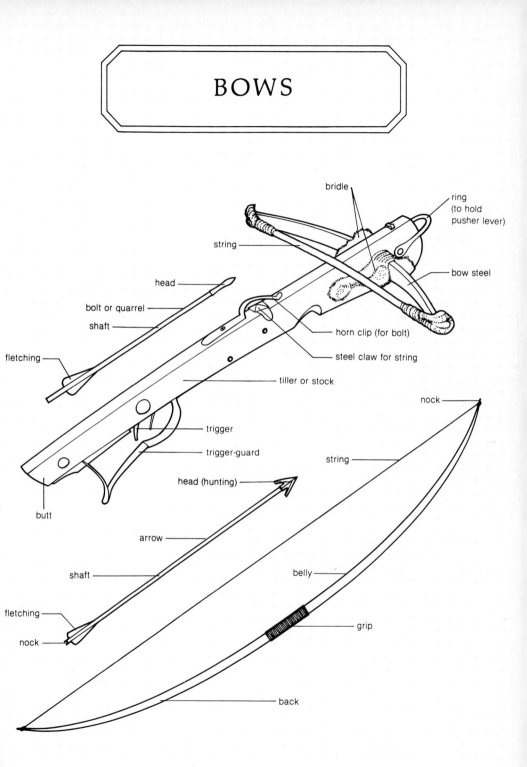

bridle

ring
(to hold
pusher lever)

string

bow steel

head

bolt or quarrel

shaft

horn clip (for bolt)

steel claw for string

fletching

tiller or stock

nock

trigger

string

trigger-guard

head (hunting)

butt

arrow

shaft

belly

fletching

grip

nock

back

Bows

Together with the sling (used regularly, sometimes attached to a pole, by European warriors up to the late 14th century) the bow ranks as the oldest projectile weapon used by man. It combines simple components and simple manufacture with ease of supply of the materials. In the early Viking period, the bow was already well established. As in earlier versions, the bow used in Scandinavia was shorter than the well-known but later English longbow. The short bow's construction was simple, and yet the weapon was so effective that it was a major contribution to Viking success. The outer side (away from the user) is termed the back and the inner side the belly. The short bow was shaped to give thickness in the middle for a hand grip and to taper towards the ends. These bows, averaging some four to five feet in length, were used by the Saxons, for both hunting and fishing. The arrows were also simple with well-wrought iron heads.

The Normans also employed the short bow at the time of their invasion of England in 1066. The short bow was used differently from the longbow with which we are more familiar, as the arrow was not drawn back to the lips for aiming but to the centre of the chest.

The development of the "English" longbow owes much to the Welsh. It was noted that the Welsh bows were made from elm whereas the bows of the English or Normans were made from ash or yew. The Welsh bows were also renowned for their stiffness and size and it was said that not only could their arrows pierce an oak door four inches thick (siege of Abergavenny Castle, 1182) but that they were more than a match for existing armour. It was Henry II who laid the foundation for the fame of the English long-bowmen when in 1242 it was decreed in the Assize of Arms that all with annual incomes of between £2 and £5 should be armed with bows. Throughout the 14th and 15th centuries the English longbow prevailed over the new firearms by reason of its reliability, its rate of shooting and its cheapness of manufacture.

The longbow, traditionally of yew, could be made of various woods, in fact at one time it was ordered that to preserve yew, witch-hazel, ash or elm be used. The longbow usually had horn ends – "nocks" – where the string was hooked and was made the same height as the bowman. Continual practice is what made the English bowman so deadly and it was ordered that every Sunday and holiday, the art of archery should be a compulsory activity.

For the arrows, ash or birch was used. They measured three feet in length with their goose-feather flights. The

The bow came in many shapes and sizes depending on the country of use and some of the primitive bows from the east show a remarkable versatility in shapes. In the Dark Ages a shorter bow was used but by the 14th and 15th centuries the English longbow had established its supremacy.

Below. *Cross-section of an English longbow, showing the lighter sapwood and darker heartwood. The sapwood always formed the back of the bow.*

Below. *The longbow in action, from the* Chroniques de Froissart. *This shows the battle of Crécy (1346) with French crossbowmen pitted against the English longbow. Froissart executed his book in the 15th century, and the figures are dressed in armour of his period.*

heads varied from broad-pointed to needle-sharp "bodkin" heads for armour-piercing. Also common were triangular- or square-section pyramid heads. As armour was designed to combat the arrow, so the heads became less leaf-shaped and more acutely pointed to pierce armour or to penetrate the target between the joints.

Once used in their thousands, few mediaeval longbows survive, although the few from the wreck of the *Mary Rose* (1540s) are of the correct type. Arrow heads, however, are more common.

Bows

While various military thinkers of the late 18th and even the early 19th century, when faced with the inaccuracy of the infantry flintlock musket, advocated the re-introduction of the longbow, there was no serious attempt to bring it back for military use once the musket was established. Apart from anything else, it was no longer possible to enforce the long practice required for longbow shooting.

For sporting use, however, the contest between bow and gun was another matter. In hunting the bow had the advantage over the gun in that it was silent. Nor was there the warning to the quarry of the flash of a gun's priming powder, or the brief delay before the main charge was ignited. The bow also had immense penetrating power, it could be swiftly "re-loaded", and it was more available than the expensive firearms.

Despite being declared obsolete in Europe's armies during the 16th century (though in England not until 1595), the longbow therefore still retained a following. But it was the revival of "toxophily" – the love of archery – at the beginning of the 18th century which heralded a new lease of life for the weapon. Hunting was by then accomplished almost entirely with other weapons. For the bow, the main area of use which was developed was that of target shooting and distance shooting.

In 1789, a certain Mr Tower fired an arrow 340 yards, while in America Ingo Simon, the collector and archer, attained a distance of 462 yards 9 inches in June 1914. The secretary to the Turkish ambassador in London, it is claimed, shot an arrow 482 yards, but he said that the bow was stiff and he was out of condition!

During the 20th century, and especially in the past 30 years, archery in competition has become a very exact science. Modern materials have come to the aid of the archer, and fibreglass and other substances now replace or supplement the natural wood. Man-made laminated bows, balance weights, sights and other equipment supplement the strong arm and eye of the archer. Anyone who has witnessed modern archery contests, either live or on television, will have noted the lengths to which steps have been taken to develop the longbow so that it performs with even greater accuracy, and one wonders what the archers of Crécy would have made of the modern target bow.

The longbow has come a long way since the simple early styles used on the battlefield before being ousted by firearms. The modern bow is now a sophisticated and highly accurate weapon.
Right. *A fine example of a 19th-century bow set, cased in the same way as many shotguns or rifles of the period.*
Above. *A modern longbow, showing the complex sighting arrangements and the use of modern techniques in construction.*
Below. *A cross-section of a modern composite bow showing the central wood core with laminations of fibreglass on both sides.*

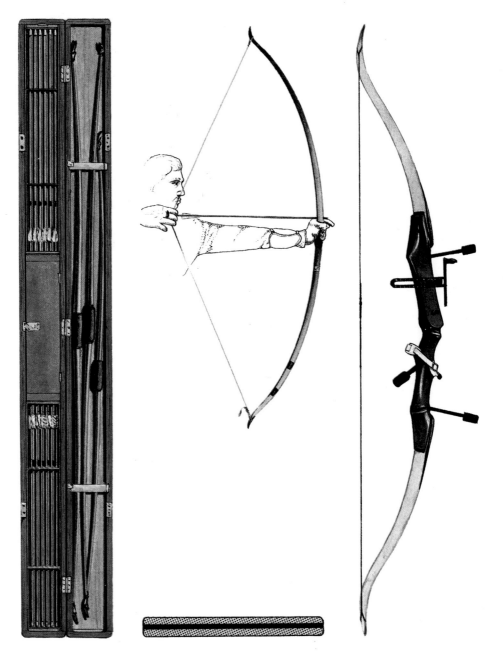

Bows

The crossbow was a scaled-down version of the ordinary bow laid crosswise on a stock, or tiller, to give a better and steadier aim. It was highly favoured in mainland Europe, and many of the armies had bands of crossbowmen, often mercenaries. (Contrary to traditional belief, crossbows were used on a fair scale in England also.) The crossbow seems to have originated in Han dynasty China, many years before Christ, and to have been brought to Europe at the time of the Roman empire. The Romans used the system in a much larger form as a siege engine, the arcuballista. After the break-up of the Roman empire, little is heard about this weapon but records of its use appear in 985 and later from written works and illuminated manuscripts. By the middle of the 12th century the crossbow had spread across Europe.

The crossbow was the ideal weapon for defence of fortresses and castles and on board ship, where space was all-important, but it also enjoyed a large following for its use in the hunting of game. As a hunter's weapon and for target shooting the crossbow survived the introduction of the gun and was used well into the 19th and 20th centuries. But as a military weapon, the crossbow became less widespread in the armies of Europe around the end of the 15th century; its military use rapidly died out, although in Sweden, the crossbow survived as a military weapon until 1570.

The early crossbows are constructed entirely of wood with the bow bound to the end of the stock by cords. The

The crossbow found its way from China to mediaeval Europe. Not so popular in England, where the longbow reigned supreme, the crossbow enjoyed immense popularity in other countries.
1. Spanning the crossbow was accomplished by a variety of means at different times, but in the most basic the archer placed his foot in a stirrup and used a claw attached to his leather belt to pull back the string.
2. Detail from a miniature of the siege of Mortagne-sur-Sèvre in 1377. The figure spanning the crossbow is using an early windlass for pulling back the string.

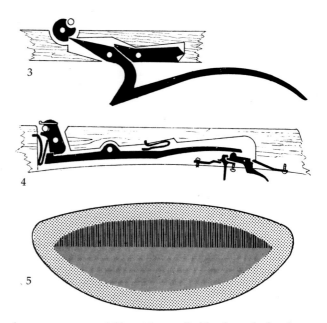

3. *The basic crossbow release mechanism comprised a trigger, a spring and a horn release nut. Although superseded by more complex systems, this remained popular for many years.*
4. *A more advanced mechanism with double-set trigger and a claw to hold the string in place.*
5. *A cross-section of a composite bow with a central core of wood and bone covered in layers of shredded sinew.*

bow was spanned (the string pulled back ready for shooting) by hand, then hooked over a staghorn "nut" with a large and a shallow notch cut in it. The stock or tiller was fitted with a sear which allowed the bow to remain in the shooting position by locking the nut. When the sear was depressed, it allowed the nut to turn, thus releasing the bow-string and shooting the quarrel – a crossbow arrow is always called a quarrel or bolt. The quarrel rested in a groove or guide. As the weapon developed, more attention was paid to the gutter, and in some cases it was covered over to form a kind of barrel. The nut also received attention to make it more efficient; at the same time a clip was fitted over the nut to hold the quarrel in position.

The drawback of the crossbow in this form was that it was never as powerful as the longbow. The next step in the crossbow's evolution was the manufacture of what are termed composite bows, in which the bow is laminated from various materials, such as horn and sinew. These provided a great improvement in penetrating power, but the much stiffer bow had now to be provided with an aid to spanning. The earliest device (known from the early 13th century) was a stirrup at the end of the stock, which was rested on the ground and the foot of the bowman placed in it to give him a better pull on the string. A variation on this was the bowman's leather belt, having a hook attached, to which the bow-string was fitted. With his foot in the stirrup, the bowman could span the bow by straightening his body, leaning back if necessary.

Bows

One answer to the increasing strength of the bow as steel replaced the composite bow in the 15th century was an adaptation of the previous belt with a hook, this time fitted with a rope and pulley with a metal hook at the end. For spanning, the metal pulley hook was placed on the bow-string; one end of the rope fitted onto a peg on the shaft of the bow, the other being attached to the belt. The strength of the man's back was then used to pull the bow-string to the nut.

The most common method, and the cheapest, was the gaffle. The gaffle, introduced in the 16th century, was a forked lever of which the ends were curved to locate behind two pegs on the stock. Between the arms of the fork were two bent pieces to engage the string. To span the bow, the gaffle was positioned with the fork over the tiller, the ends of the fork behind the pegs and the two shorter bent pieces engaging the string. When the top of the fork was pulled to the rear, the lower ends of the fork engaged behind the pegs and acted in a pivot movement, so that the string held by the two shorter pieces was pulled towards the rear, so spanning the bow.

Another more efficient method was the windlass, necessary on the most powerful bows. This involved fitting to the butt end of the tiller a device with two crank handles fitted on a central bar to which was attached a cord passing through a series of pulleys with claws at its end. With the mechanical advantage of a series of pulleys, the bow could be spanned quite easily. The bowman placed his foot in the stirrup, fitted the windlass over the butt, engaged the claws in the bow-string and then wound up, using the handles.

The stock of the crossbow was from the 11th century or earlier grooved at the top to guide the bolt or quarrel. The bolt was of course the active part of the weapon; the most common type had a short shaft of ash or yew, two or four fletchings often of wood or leather, and an iron head. According to contemporary illustrations, there was a variety of heads, some with two or three prongs, others barbed, but the quadrangular-sectioned head of spear- or leaf-shape was among the most common in use.

1

The crossbow continued to be used in war, and with the increased power of the steel bow and faster spanning by new systems it was still a formidable weapon.
1. *A mid-17th-century windlass, a spanning system never popular for hunting first used on military and target bows.*
2. *A pavise, the defence for the largely stationary archers as they spanned, aimed and fired their bows. This one dates from c. 1480.*
3. *Steel bow with covering in parchment, and veneered tiller with polished staghorn relief, c. 1450.*
4. *Three typical bolts for the crossbow, the shafts thick and the heads diamond in section.*

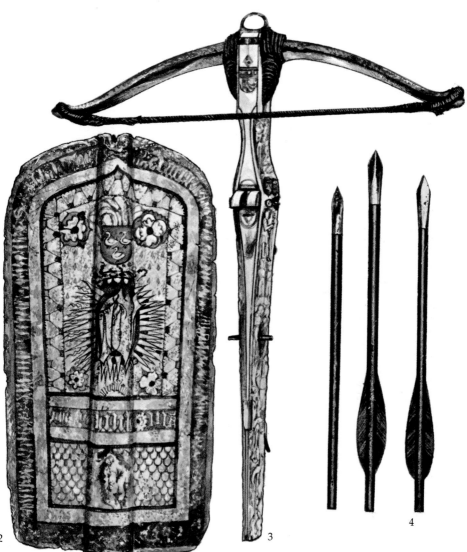

2   3

4

As with all weapons, there was at first little if any difference between the crossbow for military use and its counterpart for civilian use such as hunting. The weapon performed both services. Because of its accuracy and hitting-power, coupled with its ease of use and near-silence, the crossbow was always popular for hunting, especially amongst the upper classes, even when the matchlock was in common use.

These bows were usually finished in a highly decorative manner, with carved and inlaid stocks. Special attention was given by the maker to the mechanism, so that when the trigger was pulled, the whole action functioned smoothly.

A few years after the introduction of the windlass (see previous pp.) another, far more efficient, piece of spanning machinery appeared in Germany. First documented in the first half of the 15th century, the cranequin was an ingenious rack-and-pinion device employing a toothed rack and cogs of two sizes. The cranequin had a rope loop attached to the metal body which was slipped over the tiller until it rested on two projecting pegs. The claws of the rack were hooked onto the bow-string and the crank-handle on top of the cranequin was turned. This rotated a small cog working on a larger one which in turn engaged the toothed bar known as the rack, thus drawing the rack and bow-string back until the string caught in the release-nut of the crossbow. The cranequin was then removed, and the crossbow could be held safely until required to shoot.

Many hunting bows were richly decorated as they were in wide use during the period of the wheel-lock and the same style of inlay is common to them both. (See wheel-lock illustrations, pp. 190–95.)

There were various types of bolt or quarrel used for hunting. To facilitate carrying, they were placed in a quiver which was either carried by a belt across the shoulder or hung from the waist-belt. The various quarrels differed only in the head. The shaft was straight and stout and the flights, instead of the feather ones of the longbow arrow, were usually made from leather, wood or thin brass, although they were similar in their intention to impart a revolving motion to the quarrel in flight, to improve accuracy. The heads were spear-pointed, or broad, or crescent-shaped with forward-curving wings; there was also a blunt stunning bolt for smaller birds and game so that the meat would not be damaged by penetration from a large sharp bolt-head.

In popularity the crossbow rivalled the gun for hunting, and in various forms it was produced and developed for this particular pursuit. The use of steel for the bow greatly improved the range and power of the weapon, and the introduction of sophisticated spanning tools and differing types of heads for the bolts made it a popular and widely used weapon.
1. *Composite crossbow with foot-ring and a peg on the stock for using as a lever fulcrum in spanning. Italian, 16th century.*
2. *Steel crossbow with inlaid stock and long trigger arm. German, 16th century.*
3. *Cranequin for spanning a crossbow. This version is elaborately pierced and engraved. French, 16th century.*
4, 5, 6. *Bolt heads, broad, blunt and spear-shaped.*
7. *Quiver and arrows, the quiver made of deerskin. 16th century.*

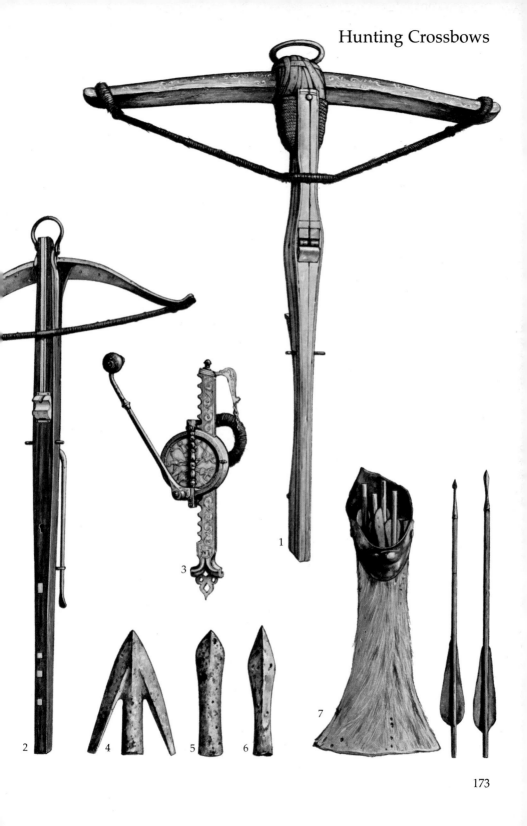

1

2

3

4

5

6

7

Bows

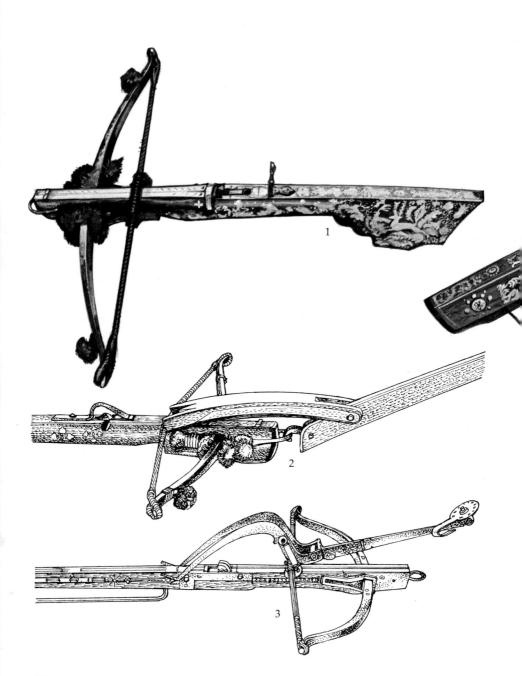

4

Crossbows remained a popular hunting weapon long after they had ceased to be a serious weapon of war. The various styles were elaborately decorated, as befitted their often noble users. A variety of types of lever were used for spanning the bow.
1. German, c. 1650. This steel bow has a walnut stock and folding backsight.
2. German sporting bow of c. 1700 being spanned by a wooden lever of the "pusher" type.
3. Spanish crossbow of c. 1550 being spanned by a typical "puller" lever, the gaffle or pied de chèvre.
4. German crossbow of 1623, with double trigger mechanism, and inlaid in the style popular with gunmakers of the period.

While the crossbow as a hunting weapon declined in various countries, it remained exceedingly popular in German states and neighbouring countries, and in Spain. It developed further, despite the inroads made by firearms, especially the wheel-lock and later the flintlock. In line with the improvements in firearms, the crossbow-makers adopted a more suitable stock for aiming, a trigger-guard, and more sophisticated and easier ways of spanning the bow (see previous pp.). Decoration still continued to be important and the tillers were inlaid with bone and engraved with spirited hunting scenes. The bow was by now all-steel and this gave the increased power that made it an effective hunting weapon.

The most popular means of spanning the bow and one which is still in limited use today, was the goat's foot lever (*pied de chèvre* or *pied de biche*). This was in fact the gaffle mentioned previously (p. 170). Spanning tools work on one of two principles – pushing or pulling the string back to the nut – but many are engraved with a variety of borders.

By the 18th century, however, a more convenient spanning device was introduced. This also took the form of a bending lever but was made integral with the weapon. The bending lever was hinged through the tiller and when not in use was recessed into the top of the butt. When the bending lever was required it was raised from the butt end towards the bow until the pivoted claws engaged the string. The lever was then returned to its recess with sufficient force to span the bow. This method is still in use today.

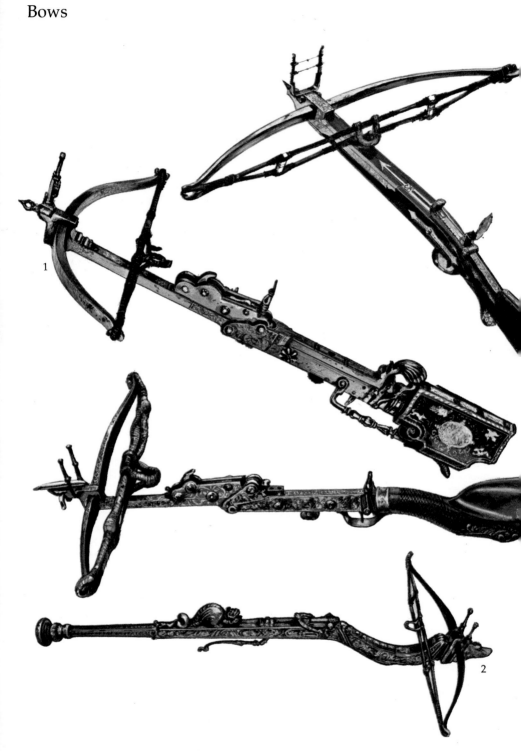

1

2

Stone-bows

1. *Italian stonebow or prod,
c. 1580. The bow bears the arms of
the grand chancellor of Bohemia.*
2. *Italian stonebow with elaborate
stock and fore-sight, c. 1570.*
3. *French, early 18th century but
with stock c. 1820. The butt also
is a later addition similar in style to
a gun butt of later form.*
4. *English bullet crossbow by the
famous gunmaker Joseph Egg,
1818–19.*

4

3

At the beginning of the 16th century the popularity of the use of round projectiles of stone or other materials in crossbows had already increased. Known during the Middle Ages, this round projectile was effective against birds and other small game. The stone-bow, otherwise often similar in every way to the crossbow that fired a quarrel, had a double string with a leather pouch in its centre to hold the projectile.

Some of the earlier specially made stone-bows have a slender tiller that dips in an almost half-circle between the point where the string is attached at the ready-to-shoot position and the bow itself. These are associated with Italy. From contemporary illustrations, such as one by Pietro Olina dated 1622, a lot of enjoyable sport seems to have taken place with these bows. The engraving shows men with stone-bows bagging wood pigeon as they roost at night, while another man dazzles the birds with a lantern.

During the late 17th and in the 18th century, the stone-bow was greatly improved in shape and power, and many incorporated a spanning device. By the middle of the 19th century, the weapon had taken on a more sophisticated look. The stock was often fashioned like that of a target rifle, and a mid-19th-century Belgian model had a barrel with a slot cut in the breech-end for the single cord.

Besides game shooting, target shooting with the stone-bow became popular. One of the most popular sports was shooting at a dummy wooden bird called a "popinjay". These bows were fitted with rifle sights, shaped stocks and refined trigger mechanisms.

The stone-bow, or more properly the bullet-bow (the clay or lead bullet had now long replaced the pebble), was popular in England by the mid-18th century and in the next 100 years some fine examples were made by the leading sporting gunmakers of the day. They were every bit as well-finished as the flintlock fowling pieces and rifles. By the 1840s the popularity of the stone-bow was on the wane in Britain; however, in some European countries, especially Belgium, the weapon still had many devotees.

The demise of the stone-bow came suddenly when, in 1854, there appeared on the market in America the .22 rimfire cartridge, which allowed those who could afford the gun to shoot small birds and game at very little cost.

Yet the idea of the stone-bow still refused to die: in 1900 a country gunmaker in Somerset in southwestern England produced a variation which dispensed with the bow and substituted the catapult. These items finally went off the market in the 1930s.

Bows

Throughout the Middle Ages target shooting with crossbows was actively encouraged by the governing classes, who required trained and proficient bowmen for their armies. However, the crossbows used for this target shooting were not especially made for the purpose – they were weapons produced primarily for warfare and hunting. It was not until the 16th century, when the crossbow was declining in popularity as a military weapon, that special types of target bow began to appear. It was at this time, too, that the guilds of crossbowmen, which had been formed throughout northern Europe in the later Middle Ages for the protection of individual towns, changed from being essentially military organisations to sporting clubs dedicated to the art of crossbow shooting. The most popular target for crossbow shooting had always been the popinjay – a brightly coloured wooden, cardboard or leather bird which was either raised on a tall pole or positioned high in a tree. Many of the crossbow guilds adopted their own variation of the bird target. For instance, the Dresden society shot at a large multi-coloured target, resembling the Imperial German Eagle, which was composed of several separate parts. The target was raised on a mast and the crossbowmen, using special blunt-headed bolts, attempted to knock down the various sections, each of which had a different points-value.

The first specially made target crossbows seem to have been produced in the Low Countries in the later 16th century. Based upon the typical late medieval war bow they were of robust construction with a stout steel bow spanned by means of a windlass. The most distinctive feature of this

1. *Flemish target crossbow of the 17th century with its windlass attached. Note the typical down-curved hand-rest beneath the string; the raised portion of the tiller behind the string, notched for the thumb of the trigger hand; and the double set trigger mechanism protected by a trigger guard made in the form of the old lever trigger.*

2. *Swiss target crossbow of the mid-19th century. Similar bows are still in use. Note the ring attached to the fore-end for attachment of the fitted "pusher" bending lever; and the backsight, in this example equipped with a plumb for levelling.*

3. *Target crossbow of the type made in Brussels at the beginning of this century. Note the fore-sight adjustable laterally for windage; and the lugs on the side of the tiller.*

type is the downward swelling of the tiller just in front of the release-nut, which served as a left-hand grip to help steady the aim. This was often decorated with carved scroll work and sometimes, especially in the 17th century, with applied sheets of brass or steel pierced and engraved with armorial bearings. To increase accuracy and sureness of aim, these target bows were usually equipped with double-set trigger mechanisms and sometimes with adjustable sights. This form of crossbow retained its popularity in northwestern Europe until the 19th century, later bows being generally of plainer form.

2

3

1

Bows

The crossbow system could be adapted in various ways, and makers produced a number of weapons which owed something to the firearm.

1. Combined wheel-lock and crossbow, c. 1620.

2. Pistol crossbow, an ingenious idea but never a commercial proposition.

3. A barrel crossbow, which shoots a bullet from the slit barrel.

1

Unusual adaptations of the crossbow have, almost by definition, resulted in no improvement. The surviving examples have come down to us as curiosities. The first, and of course, the easiest, form of adaptation for the crossbow was to combine it with another weapon. The bow persisted for some time in use alongside the gun, and the combination of the wheel-lock with the crossbow was produced in the same period as the combinations of the wheel-lock and the matchlock long gun with secondary weapons. Another unusual adaptation, but a natural progression from the above, was to produce a pistol bow. This allowed the user to shoot single-handed from horseback, although to span a bow in the saddle cannot always have been easy. The pistol bow, probably introduced c. 1800 in Austria, was made only in very small quantities; a few English examples are known. They were probably chiefly used for target shooting.

Crossbows were also combined with staff weapons, but it was with guns that the majority were "married".

Mention has been made in the section on stone-bows of the late "invention" of the catapult gun in the early 1900s with the use of elastic rubber in place of the bow. This theme had been pursued by a number of earlier inventors, notably Richard Hodges in England during the 1850s, but the power obtained from rubber could never match the effect of a true bow.

Bows

Like the longbow, the crossbow has enjoyed a revival in the last few years, although its popularity never completely disappeared amongst devotees.

Like the modern longbow, the crossbow is hardly recognisable in the material used in its construction, although the shape of course is still very much the same. The use of plastics, plastic laminates, fibreglass and other man-made materials has allowed a more powerful and accurate weapon to be manufactured. To these advances made possible by modern technology have been added superior design of the stock and the fitting of sophisticated sights. The advantages have been lightness, combined with a high degree of accuracy.

Such has been the impression made by the modern crossbow that its use for military purposes has been mooted in various circles and experiments have taken place with a view to its serious adoption in a limited military role. The advantages of the modern crossbow are immediately obvious: its silence is paramount, but of course its accuracy is also an attraction. As a launcher it also has possibilities, indeed during World War I a number of crossbows were used as grenade-launchers as well as serving as conventional bows.

Below. *A modern crossbow, showing developments in butt shape and sights. The application of new technology has produced bows more powerful than were ever conceived before. German, 1981.*

FIREARMS

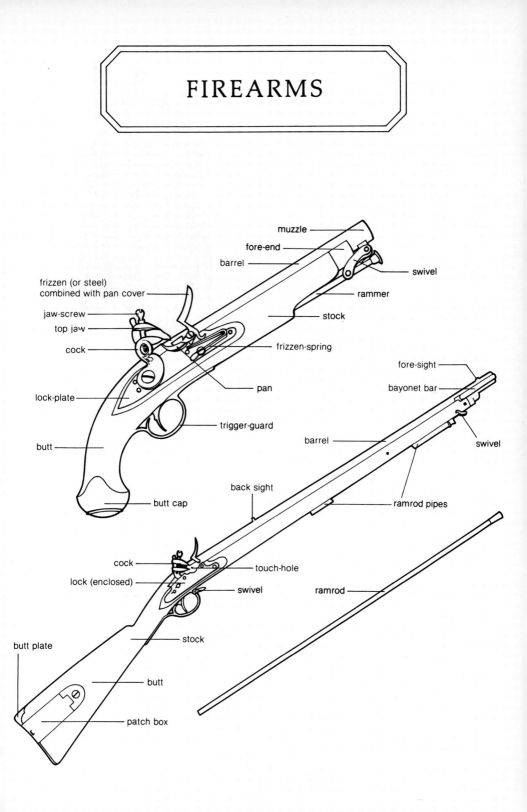

muzzle

fore-end

barrel

swivel

frizzen (or steel)
combined with pan cover

rammer

jaw-screw

top jaw

cock

frizzen-spring

stock

lock-plate

pan

butt

trigger-guard

butt cap

fore-sight

bayonet bar

barrel

swivel

back sight

ramrod pipes

cock

touch-hole

lock (enclosed)

swivel

ramrod

stock

butt plate

butt

patch box

Firearms

The origin of gunpowder is so obscured in a wealth of fact and fiction that it seems certain details of the actual discovery will never be known. Both the Chinese and the Arabs have been credited with the invention and it is probable that knowledge of gunpowder came to Europe via Arab traders. The actual inventor of the application of gunpowder as a propellant is impossible to identify but it is thought that it was Roger Bacon who in the 13th century made the properties of gunpowder and its force public in the book ascribed to him *Epistolae de Secretis Operibus Artis et Naturae et Nullitate Magiae*, but the crucial portion of text which completed the formula was jumbled in the anagram *lura nope cum ubre*. Once transposed these letters become carbonum pulvere, charcoal, the ingredient which when added to saltpetre and sulphur gives gunpowder.

The first reference we have to a machine firing a projectile is in a decree of the city of Florence which instructed two men to make *canones de metallo* in the year 1326. The first pictorial evidence dates from the same year and is to be found in *De Nobilitatibus, Sapientiis, et Prudentiis Regum* a manuscript presented to Edward III of England. This shows a knight in mail armour lighting a fuse in a large vase-shaped barrel loaded with an arrow. An actual vase-shaped barrel has been found (Loshult, Sweden) but the later hand cannons with stocks had barrels of what was to become the conventional shape. At first the smaller guns were strapped to planks and laid along the ground to be fired, but they soon acquired stocks or tillers, and there is a reference in 1373 to fitting tillers to eight guns "in the style of pikes". Among examples of this type of hand cannon that have been excavated perhaps the earliest is the Tannenberg gun (before 1399) now in a Nuremburg museum, which is constructed so that the pike or shaft fitted into a socket at the breech; the "Vedelspang" gun found in the ruins of a castle destroyed in 1426 has an iron shaft forged into the barrel but it also has a hook under the barrel which when rested on a castle wall acted o check the recoil. (The German term for this type of "hook gun", *Hackenbusch* – hackbut or hagbut in England – is the origin of the French *harquebus* or *arquebus*; the latter term covers both the heavy early matchlocks used with a barrel-rest and 16th- to 17th-century wheel-lock carbines for use in the saddle.) In later 15th-century handguns the barrel (or barrels – there were experiments with multiple-fire even then) was held to the wooden tiller or stock with iron bands, thus tentatively heading towards a more modern arrangement of barrel and shaped stock.

1. *"Vase gun" of the same type as that illustrated in the 1326 de Milernete manuscript. Cast bronze, found at Loshult, Sweden; early 14th century.*

2. *"Hook gun", an advance on (1) – the hook could be used to steady the gun, which probably originally had a wooden stock or tiller – a true handgun, unlike (1). Mid- to late-14th-century, found in the sea near Mörkö, Sweden.*

3. *Rare horseman's gun, with loop on tiller or stock (gun is all iron) to prevent dropping it. North European, 14th century. (Bend is later damage.)*

4. *Bronze "hook gun" (hackbut). An advance on (3), this would have had a wooden stock, and the priming pan is now at the side, where it is more convenient, and looks forward to the introduction of the matchlock. North European, early 15th century.*

5. *Soldiers with early guns, from an early 15th-century manuscript.*

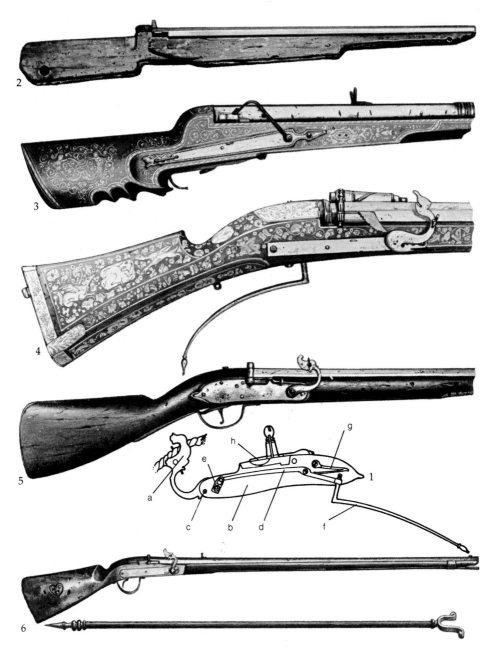

The Matchlock

*The matchlock was the first
ignition system that employed a
trigger mechanism and a
lock-plate rather than the
plunging of a hot igniter into the
touch-hole on the barrel.*
1. *The parts of the sear matchlock
(see text): a) match-holder; b)
lock-plate; c) screw; d) sear lever;
e) tumbler; f) trigger; g) spring; h)
pan and cover.*
2. *Early 16th-century matchlock
of primitive design. The lock is
missing. German.*
3. *Later matchlock with cast
barrel, and inlaid full stock with
finger grips. German, early 17th
century.*
4. *Inlaid Dutch matchlock with
long trigger-arm and rectangular
lock-plate.*
5. *English matchlock musket of
the type issued to musketeers in
the second half of the 17th century.
Note the simplicity and sturdiness
of construction and the use of a
trigger-guard.*
6. *17th-century matchlock musket
with rest, an essential part of the
equipment in all armies for a
steady aim with this hefty
weapon.*

The earliest ignition system other than the direct touch-hole was the matchlock. While basically doing mechanically the same job with a match that had been done by hand, it did allow the hands of the user to take a proper grip on his weapon and thus more freedom to aim, and also facilitated the design of a more manageable firearm.

The earliest form of matchlock was a jaw at the end of an S-shaped metal arm that was fitted with a central hole and through this screwed to the stock. Into the jaw was fitted slowmatch, which burned at the rate of perhaps a foot every three hours. The gunner then pulled on the lower part of the S-shaped piece of metal and pivoted the smouldering match onto the touch hole, so igniting the charge. This simple pivot "serpentine", so called because of its shape, seems to have first appeared around 1410.

The true matchlock, a lock with spring enclosed and let into the stock, appeared in 1475, according to contemporary German documents. The new improved matchlock took two forms, the snap, or the safer sear, lock. The latter used the top part of the old S-shaped piece, which was cut off at the central curve and fitted to a plate with a screw. The inside of the lock consisted of four parts: a lever inside was linked via the screw to the outside jaws; a second long lever, fitted to the end of the first, was activated by the right hand near the butt of the stock; a return spring, against which the lever was pushed to fire, raised the jaw back up from the pan on release of pressure on the trigger lever.

With this new system, handguns or muskets became streamlined in form, stocks were shaped better for firing from the shoulder, with a recess cut into the butt to give a better grip for the right hand; a ramrod or scouring rod was fitted in a channel beneath the stock; and above all the lock mechanism was protected from breakage by being let into the woodwork. The matchlock, efficient and cheap, enabled armies to modernize their equipment and tactics.

With the use of the musket through Europe came other innovations, the main one being the cartridge. This was a rolled piece of paper with enough powder for a single charge, and usually contained the bullet also. The cartridge end was bitten off, the charge poured down the barrel, and the paper screwed up and rammed home to act as a wad. The ball, which in battle might be taken from the mouth where a number of loose balls had been placed, was rammed down. This procedure meant that no loose powder was about and no accidents could occur from the ever-burning slow match.

Firearms

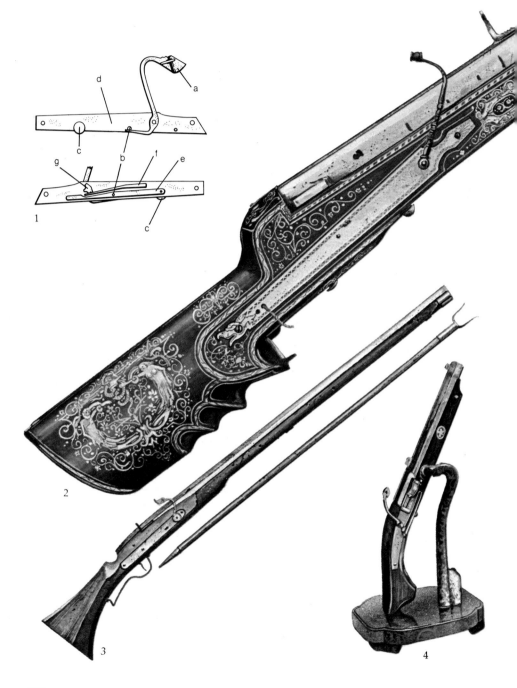

1

2

3

4

The Matchlock

As with all technical innovations in weaponry, the makers of matchlocks employed variations both in the mechanism and in the degree of decoration to cater for the rich with the use of carving and inlay work. The snap matchlock, a variation of the basic theme, involved the reversing of the internal mainspring, so that the serpentine holding the smouldering match could be cocked and kept in the ready-to-fire position. To fire, a button on the side of the plate was pressed and the serpent with match was released and thrust by the power of the spring into the pan of priming powder. While this gave a steadier aim because of the shorter time between pressing the trigger and ignition, it was also more dangerous – not only was the match often extinguished on its speedy downward journey but the priming powder could be struck with such force that it showered all over the place. (This mechanism is sometimes referred to as the button lock.)

For the hunter armed with a matchlock, sitting or still game were the only possible target, and speed of ignition was essential so as not to risk scaring away the prey. There are a great number of contemporary sporting prints with matchlocks drawn by Johan Stradanus in the latter part of the 16th century. These show heavy-barrelled, thick-stocked weapons with abruptly curving butts, and a long trigger without guard. The butts of these weapons are very reminiscent of hockey-sticks. While many were plain, a large number were highly decorated, with ivory, bone or staghorn inlay on the stock; yet the metalwork was remarkably plain.

Because of their use as hunting weapons for sitting prey, sights were introduced, usually consisting of a rudimentary "bead" at the muzzle-end and a peep-sight at the breech. The peep sight was usually a small tube which the firer looked through, lining up the "bead" with the target. Up until this period the sporting weapons had been swords or spears, and bows and arrows, but the improvement of the matchlock over the hand cannon now made it an effective hunting weapon. Although short-lived with richer sportsmen as a serious hunting weapon, because of the introduction of the more sophisticated and advanced wheel-lock, the matchlock continued in limited use as a target weapon and remained common amongst the poorer peasants in rural areas until at least the middle of the 18th century.

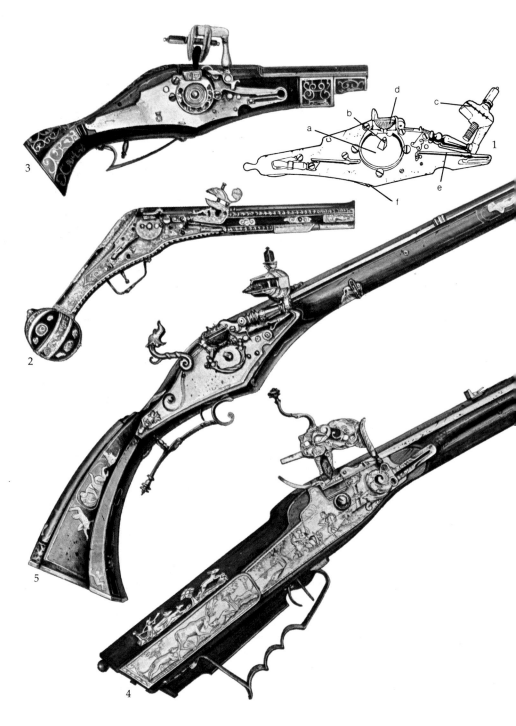

The wheel-lock, unlike the matchlock that preceded and the flintlock which superseded it, was never general issue to troops because of the expense of the intricate mechanism and its unreliability when neglected.

One of the earliest drawings we have of what appears to be a wheel-lock is that by Leonardo da Vinci in the *Codex Atlanticus,* done between 1500 and his death in 1509. It is not certain whether the drawing is his invention or taken from a mechanism already in existence. We do know that by 1517 Maximilian I of Germany had issued an order forbidding the manufacture and use of the wheel-lock system, in order to stop the carrying of a weapon which could be concealed, rapidly drawn and fired. While the matchlock was practical and cheap as a long gun, it was highly impractical and dangerous as a pistol.

The wheel-lock worked in a similar fashion to a modern cigarette-lighter; a serrated steel wheel acted on a piece of pyrites or flint to produce a spark. To fire a loaded wheel-lock, the owner pulled the "dog" holding the stone down onto the pan cover. This was, so to speak, the full-cock. When the trigger was pulled, it opened the pan containing the priming powder and allowed the stone to rest on the serrated wheel, which started to turn rapidly, having previously, like a clock, been wound with a key or spanner. This action showered sparks into the priming powder which in turn fired the main charge.

Early forms of this type of lock were fitted with a safety device which was in fact a matchlock mechanism built into the same lock-plate. This enabled the user who had lost the all-important spanner or key still to use the firearm. The main drawback to the wheel-lock was that the mechanism was delicate and could fail in the springs on the inside or in the external winding mechanism, so besides the use of an auxiliary matchlock system, some makers made their locks with two jaws holding the pyrites, in case one should shatter. Wheel-locks were also fitted to maces, halberds and other weapons to give a back-up defence should the weapon misfire at the crucial moment. Again, the new lock design enabled the gunmaker to improve the firearm as a weapon, and made the provision of a pistol for the horseman feasible.

Wheel-lock long guns in their early and most basic form naturally have a stock similar to that of the matchlock. In the plain musket style this is apparent, but in the sporting styles different patterns of stock and barrel abounded. The highly decorative stocks which came into fashion with the

The wheel-lock was a great advance on the matchlock. It allowed loaded weapons to be carried without the hazards of accidental discharge because of the smouldering match, but more important it allowed the introduction of the pistol into man's armoury.

1. *The wheel-lock: a) serrated wheel; b) squared end of spindle to take key; c) jaws of "dog" to hold iron pyrites or flint; d) pan and spring-loaded pan-cover; e) spring to hold cock against pan-cover; f) mainspring behind lock-plate.*

2. *German, 1530. Wheel-lock pistol by Stopler of Nuremburg with large lock-plate and inlaid stock with ball butt.*

3. *Italian, c. 1610–20. The stock is in walnut with simple inlay work and incorporates a trigger-guard.*

4. *German, c. 1620, wheel-lock rifle with trigger-guard with finger grips, typical short stock with inlay and patchbox, and leaf rear-sights.*

5. *Italian, c. 1620, combined wheel-lock and matchlock gun with single trigger. The pressing of the trigger activated both mechanisms simultaneously. The wheel-lock is activated by the internal mainspring while the match-holder works against an external coiled spring.*

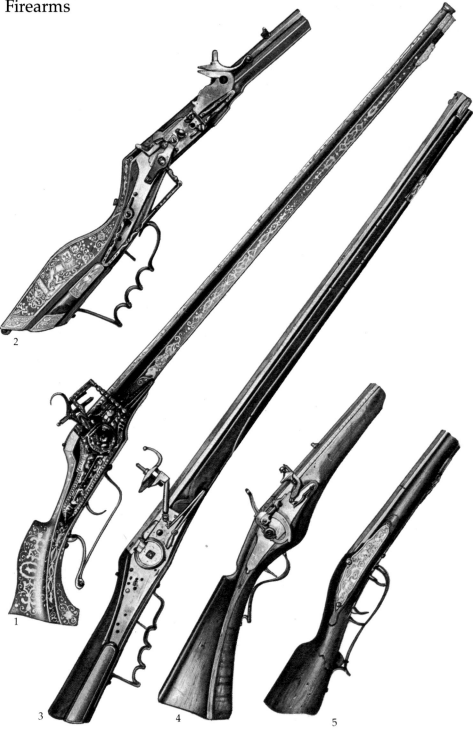

2

1

3

4

5

The wheel-lock system allowed firearms to develop further and it also produced styles of stock suited to different types of gun. Hunting and target rifles and guns soon became popular, and the design reflects the sport for which the weapon was used.

1. *German wheel-lock, c. 1600, with inlaid stock and chiselled barrel. This is typical of the style of hunting gun and the shape of the stock shows clearly how the weapon was held.*

2. *Tschinke. With the shape of its stock, inlaid as is common in wheel-locks, this weapon is a noted variation of the wheel-lock.*

3. *Wheel-lock with straight short stock and trigger-guard with finger grips. Typical of many of this popular style.*

4. *Butt and lock of an Italian segment lock wheel-lock rifle with fore-sight and rudimentary rear-sight. The stock is unusually plain but the style of butt is slowly altering with the change in shooting habits.*

5. *German enclosed wheel-lock, c. 1725.*

matchlock and the crossbow, the carved woods and the inlay, continued in the wheel-lock long gun.

One most important "invention" which dates from the beginning of the 16th century was rifling, the grooving of the internal bore of the barrel to impart spin to a bullet, thus increasing its accuracy, range and velocity. Although the principle had in part been known earlier – as shown by crossbow bolts with the flights set at an angle – it is not known who applied this thought to the gun. One of the earliest rifles was made about 1500 for the Holy Roman Emperor Maximilian I, and was originally a matchlock. The rifle became popular for hunting in the second half of the 16th century and many were produced in the great arsenal of Europe, Germany. These have distinctive stocks with heavy, usually octagonal, barrels, and awkwardly shaped butts with a ball finial for resting on the ground when loading, to protect the decorative butt plates. The shape of the butt did not, however, hinder the user at all, as the left side of the butt had a shaped cheek-piece. The firing position was adopted by holding the fore-end of the stock in the left hand, and gripping the usually indented trigger-guard in the right with the fore-finger on the trigger; the butt was not pulled back into the shoulder but held so that the cheek rested firmly on the cheek-piece. Because these rifled weapons required a tightly fitting ball, they also required lubrication before being loaded. This task was carried out with the use of heavily oiled patches, and as a convenient place for housing those a trap was cut into the wood of the butt – opposite the cheek-piece – which usually had a decorated bone sliding lid. Another innovation, brought about possibly because of the weight of the gun and the position in which it was held, was the double trigger incorporating set and hair triggers. The first trigger set the firing mechanism and the slightest pressure on the hair trigger fired the gun.

Target shooting was another popular pastime. Special rifles with sights were made for use on ranges usually of 500 feet with targets formed by a 16-foot high wall. It was a very popular sport in Germany, Austria and other countries in middle Europe.

These heavy wheel-lock hunting and target rifles continued in manufacture well into the 18th century and examples are known made in the 1730s. In these later guns all parts of the mechanism are usually housed in the body of the stock, behind the plate. However, the last known wheel-locks, also with concealed locks, were a pair of pistols made by Le Page of Paris in 1829.

Firearms

While the wheel-lock revolutionised the use of firearms on foot, a more far-reaching consequence was the shortening of the barrel and the shaping of the stock so that the weapon could be used single-handed by a man on horseback. The mechanism was "safe" in that it did not require a burning match clamped in the jaws of the cock before it could be used, and so it could be carried ready for use in a holster or belt.

The earlier wheel-lock pistols were decorated in similar style to the long guns. They had heavy barrels and more or less plain locks. The butt style was again similar to the end of a hockey-stick but usually terminated in a ball. This gave a surer grip to the butt and made it easier to draw from the holster. With the wheel-lock system a pistol could not only be safely kept ready for immediate use but could also be concealed about the person. A number of monarchs forbade the carrying of pistols on these grounds.

The shapes of the stocks started to change after 1550. The bulbous butt gave way to a more slender grip and finally, towards the end of the century, a stock with a gentle curving butt, more akin to the later flintlock style of pistol and swelling out to a flattened butt cap.

The wheel-lock used by the mounted man had more than the advantages already mentioned. Surprise attacks from a concealed position were now possible. The tactics used by cavalry lucky enough to have an issue, or to have purchased their own (wheel-lock pistols were never general issue), was to charge the enemy, turn about at the vital in-range distance, then fire first one and then the other pistol before retreating in the direction from which they had come, reloading as they did so. Given the difficulties of reloading on horseback, and the limited numbers available of cavalry armed with pistols, it seems likely that this style of fighting was used as shock tactics.

The origin of the word pistol is hard to define, but it is generally accepted that the term derived from the Italian city of Pistoia, although other sources have been suggested such as the term *pistala* (pipe), used in the 15th century to describe a short Bohemian firearm.

During the early part of the 17th century many of the wheel-lock pistols produced were plainer and less decorative, of a more functional military type. While this lack of inlay and decoration obviously lowered the price, the wheel-lock pistol was never sufficiently cheap to be available to all cavalry during the English Civil War in the 1640s, by which time the flintlock which had developed from the snaphance was already well established.

1. *Early wheel-lock with external bridle for wheel spindle. The straight stock was not conducive to good aiming. This pistol was made in 1534 for Charles V, Holy Roman Emperor.*

2. *The developed form of German ball butt wheel-lock holster pistol, with large ball pommel for ease of drawing from the saddle-holster. These sometimes highly decorated weapons influenced design in other countries (see no. 6). Mid-16th century.*

3. *A century later perhaps than (2), this 17th-century French weapon shows the final form of the wheel-lock holster pistol, particularly as made in France and the Low Countries (and probably England). The slender form requires a projection for the wheel, but is similar to early flintlock stock forms.*

4. *This masterpiece of mechanical ingenuity is essentially a conventional German pistol, but with two barrels and two complicated locks to accommodate. Note the single trigger, only introduced to double-barrel shotguns from the late 19th century.*

5. *The fashion for very straight stocks never entirely died out. This is a German example of 1608.*

6. *English wheel-locks are extremely rare. When made they show, as in this c. 1590 example, German influence, but with English decorative detail.*

7. *A small early 17th-century German pistol. One answer to the weakening of the stock entailed in removing the woodwork in small weapons was to use metal for the stock for greater strength, as here.*

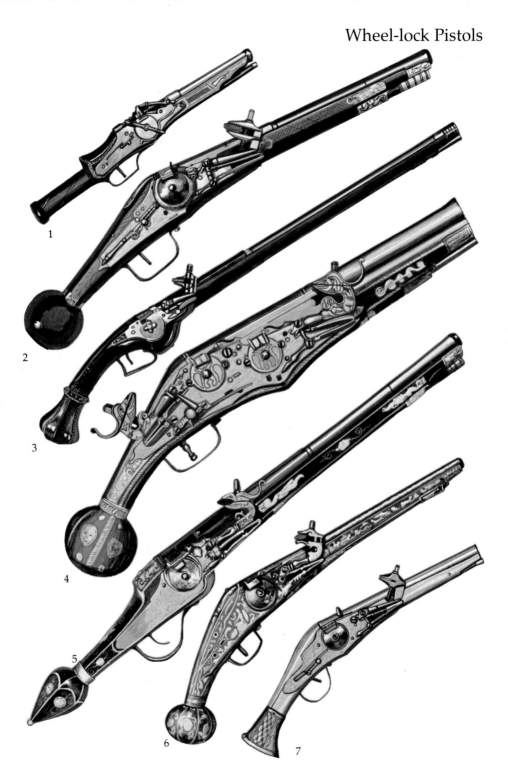

1

2

3

4

5

6

7

Firearms

The snaphance lock originated, probably in the Low Countries, about the middle of the 16th century and, like the wheel-lock, functioned with flint and steel. In the snaphance the action was similar to the snapping match-lock; the pan was primed and the cover shut over it, the cock holding the flint was pulled back and a steel on an arm shut over the covered pan and held there by a spring. To fire, the pan cover was opened by hand, and the trigger pulled, the flint striking the steel and showering sparks onto the priming powder.

Not only did this system further the development of firearms, leading eventually to the flintlock system, but it was cheaper and easier to make than the wheel-lock, less prone to breakages and required no winding key that could be lost. The snaphance was soon adopted and continued in use alongside the wheel-lock and the matchlock. Because, in this evolution of firearms, the snaphance was prominent only for a relatively short period, it never ousted the wheel-lock or matchlock. The Dutch spread its use via their trading fleets to the Mediterranean and North Africa, where the snaphance system was readily adopted either in the exported form of either complete firearms or just the locks. In North Africa the snaphance survived well into the 19th century.

The Dutch influence was not confined to North Africa. It was deeply felt in England and Scotland, where there was a history of importing arms from Holland. By the end of the 16th century, however, the Scottish arms industry was manufacturing its own snaphance weapons, producing pistols and long arms in a distinctive style. While the stocks of Scottish long arms of the period have a vaguely Moorish look, their provenance is shown by Celtic carving and flutes or channels carved in the butt. These weapons had long barrels and usually no trigger-guard. Very few survive to this day and many were probably destroyed following the Acts of Parliament aimed at disarming the Jacobites after the rebellions in the first half of the 18th century. The pistols, too, were distinctive. At first they had wooden stocks but soon all-metal stocks, the trademark of the Scottish pistol, were adopted.

The developed snaphance was improved by fitting a mechanism which did away with having to open the pan by hand. When the trigger was pulled, the pan cover was opened as the cock fell.

The next step in the evolution to the true flintlock was the Spanish Miquelet lock. In this system the pan cover and steel were combined in a reversed "L" shape.

1. *The parts of a snaphance lock: a) mainspring acts on b) tumbler connected to c) cock; cock falls when d) horizontal sear is retracted through e) hole in lock-plate, thus releasing the heel of the cock. The pan-cover (f) opens as the cock falls; the flint hits the frizzen or steel (g) and sparks fall into the pan (h) igniting the priming powder.*
2. *English snaphance, c. 1600, reflecting the styles of the Low Countries, where the mechanism was probably invented.*
3. *This 1572 weapon, like some other early snaphances, is supplied also with a matchlock in case the snaphance failed to fire.*
4. *Scottish, 1614, with Celtic motifs but reflecting English and Dutch styles.*
5. *This splendid gun was made c. 1610–15 by the Frenchman Marin le Bourgeoys, who is credited with the first "true flintlock": the pan-cover and steel are in one piece making an L-shape, and the sear acts vertically directly on the tumbler.*

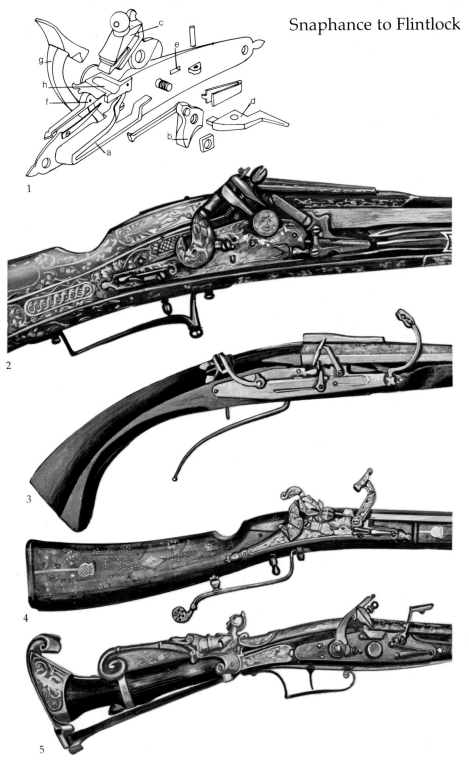

1

2

3

4

5

Firearms

As the snaphance system was transformed into the flintlock with steel and pan cover combined in one piece, regional variations of the flint-and-steel idea were developed. Distinctive features of the Miquelet included combined mainspring and frizzen spring set externally on the lock-plate, the upright striking surface of the frizzen heavily grooved and the cock, similar to those employed on the earlier wheel-locks. The grooved striking surface of the frizzen enabled the user to pick up and use any suitably shaped flint; the cock was fitted with a screw and ring to tighten the jaws together. This form of lock was also in use in the Caucasus but the style of stock differed from the Spanish version and pistols from southern Russia usually had an ivory ball butt and numerous barrel bands, all engraved and blued.

The Italian snaphance pistols were far more ornate and slender, and were made long after the introduction of the flintlock elsewhere. The true artistic skill of the gunmaker was lavished on these weapons. The cock is more conventional and the jaw screw without the ring at the top. The mainspring was fitted inside the lock-plate and the only spring on the outside was that which acted on the steel. As in the Spanish lock, a horizontal sear acted through the lock plate on the cock, holding it in place until the weapon was fired.

The Baltic lock is another variation on the same theme. The cock on these weapons is distinctive, being long and slender and having a steel which could be angled, so that no accidental discharge was possible. This form of lock also found favour in Russia.

In England the regional form was termed the "dog lock". While this is in fact a flintlock with combined steel and pan cover, it was a variation on the French true flintlock system invented in the 17th century in Normandy by the famous gunmaker Marin le Bourgeoys. In this type of lock the internal mainspring did not act on the cock directly but indirectly via a tumbler. The tumbler was fitted to the cock and shaped so that when it was rotated as the piece was cocked, the sear pushed against it until it engaged in a slot at either half-cock or full-cock. In this French system there was no longer any need for the sear to act through the lock-plate. In England the system was adopted, but the tumbler arrangement obviously gave cause for doubt and English locks were fitted with a pivoted hook behind the cock, and the cock itself had a notch cut in the back to engage the hook at half-cock, an early and simple form of the safety catch.

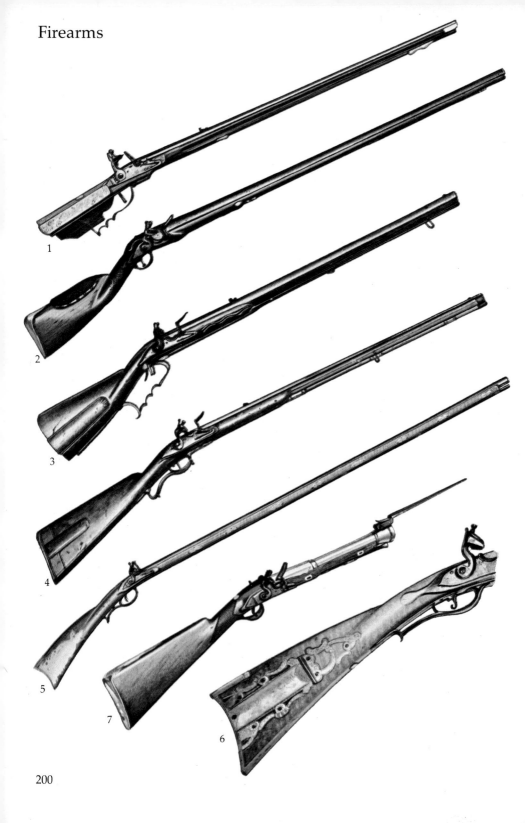

1

2

3

4

5

7

6

Once the flintlock had become the universal ignition system, numerous types of long gun were made to suit different civilian needs, for hunting, target shooting, self-protection and wildfowling.
1. *German-style flintlock rifle, with stock reminiscent of the wheel-lock period.*
2. *English fowling piece with "banana-shaped" lock-plate and padded stock, c. 1690.*
3. *German target rifle with patchbox, and a pronounced trigger-guard again reminiscent of the wheel-lock.*
4. *German hunting rifle with set trigger and patchbox, c. 1770.*
5. *American "Kentucky" rifle, c. 1800 and* **(6)** *detail showing the crude style of lock compared with English guns but the fine inlay to the stock.*
7. *Brass-barrelled blunderbuss with "flick" bayonet, by Henry Nock, London, c. 1795.*

Early flintlock long guns were long-barrelled and fully stocked; sporting guns very rarely had two side-by-side barrels. Other forms of flintlock long guns were the short blunderbuss and, slightly shorter than long gun, the carbine for the mounted man.

The sporting guns, smooth-bored and long-barrelled, were favoured by the gentry. Unlike earlier systems with which the prey could only be shot when it was still, the speed of the flintlock and the design of the stock made it possible in particular to shoot birds on the wing.

The blunderbuss had a wide variety of uses, military and naval, in home protection and stage-coach protection. Early examples have a cumbersome stock and a heavy bell-shaped barrel in steel. The idea of widening of the barrel was to spread the shot, but in fact it had very little effect in this direction, so perhaps ease of loading was a more important consideration, as well as the quantity of shot that could be fired from the large bore. Later blunderbusses had brass cast barrels turned like the outer contours of artillery cannons, and the locks and stocks conformed more to the styles in vogue, being more slender and more manageable. Many of the later ones were fitted with spring bayonets.

With the new flintlock system, the idea of rifling, already well known as we have seen, caught on for the sportsman shooting deer etc. A variety of forms of the flintlock rifle are known including the well-known German *Jaeger* rifle, sturdy, full-stocked, with an octagonal barrel and deep rifling, and its offspring the so-called "Kentucky" long rifle made in the Americas long before the American War of Independence, which had a long slender barrel, a slender down-curving butt decorated with inlay and had an inset patch box, and perhaps a set trigger and trigger-guard with an extra finger bar for better grip. Even in the percussion era, the style of this weapon did not change. Most were made in America using imported locks from Birmingham.

Towards the end of the 18th century and at the beginning of the 19th, the slender styles were all apparent in shotguns and in rifles for both target and game shooting.

Naturally different countries developed their own styles not only of their particular weapons but in their manufacturing processes. This is most striking in the making of barrels. In Britain twist barrels were considered the best, whereas in Germany and France barrels never had the twist exposed by delicate browning, these two nations leaving them plain or blued. Noticeable national characteristics are the design of the stock and the lock, as will be apparent from the accompanying illustrations.

Firearms

The comparative simplicity of the flintlock mechanism made possible something approaching mass production in the large arms centres of Birmingham, London and Liège. As the fashion declined for wearing a sword (first the rapier, then the small sword) protection could be obtained by carrying a pocket pistol or two. At first, in the early and middle 18th century, these were scaled-down pistols with conventional side locks, but soon the so-called "box lock" appeared. This had no external spring for the frizzen, and no side hammer or frizzen and pan to snag on the pocket when the weapon was needed in an emergency. The box lock which soon dominated all styles of pocket pistol had a centre-mounted cock and frizzen. There was no ramrod but a turn-off barrel, which for loading was unscrewed, the powder put in to fill the chamber and the ball placed on the recessed hemispherical portion of the breech. The barrel was then screwed back on and after priming the pistol was ready to fire. Variations on this theme include double barrels, with or without a tap (hence tap action) to fire one and then another, duck's-foot pistols with a spread of barrels, and three- and four-barrelled tap-action pistols. Other popular pistols were the horseman's or holster pistol and the travelling pistol, usually cased in pairs.

The most elegant was the duelling pistol, an essential part of any gentleman's wardrobe, to judge by the numbers of surviving examples. These were hand made by leading gunmakers with great care and attention to detail. The stocks were designed to ensure that the weapon came "on target" with minimum conscious effort, the barrels well bored and polished, and browned or blued to cut out distracting glare, and the locks made and fitted with the utmost care. The trigger was of the set type which could be adjusted by a screw to the owner's finger pressure so that on the word "Fire" only the slightest pressure was needed. Various styles of stocks were used, all carefully chequered to give a better grip; some, called saw-handle butts were popular, with projections over the top of the hand, as the name suggests.

The all-metal pistol abounded in Scotland, with steel replacing the usual brass stock, from the mid-17th century. The metal was often engraved with Celtic, thistle and other motifs. The stock bore a belt-hook opposite the lock, and the always unguarded trigger was, from the 1650s, of spherical form. All-metal pistols for military use lasted into the last decades of the 18th century. As levée wear for the military and court wear for civilians, percussion versions lasted into the 1870s.

The flintlock was the first firearm to be owned by large numbers of people. Various nationalities evolved their own form of lock and stock, and styles were made to suit military and duelling requirements, and those for self-protection when on foot or in a coach.

1. An elegant French pistol, the butt cap with ears and fine work on the fore-end. By Mazelier, Paris, 1708.

2. One of a pair of Dutch ivory-stocked pistols with ornate butt and work on the stock; 1720.

3. A typical English concealed-trigger box lock pocket pistol with rounded butt and frizzen spring, together with a top lock safety catch, c. 1810.

4. English "Queen Anne" style turn-off barrel pistol with silver mounts, c. 1730.

5. German pistol, by Johann Jacob Kuchenreuter, c. 1760, one of a pair with superb gilt mounts.

6. Scottish flintlock pistol, one of a pair by Thomas Murdoch of Edinburgh, c. 1775.

7. English cased pair of duelling pistols by John Manton, using a pair of barrels by Johann And. Kuchenreuter. This is a typical cased pair of pistols for the duel or target use, with all needed items; c. 1790.

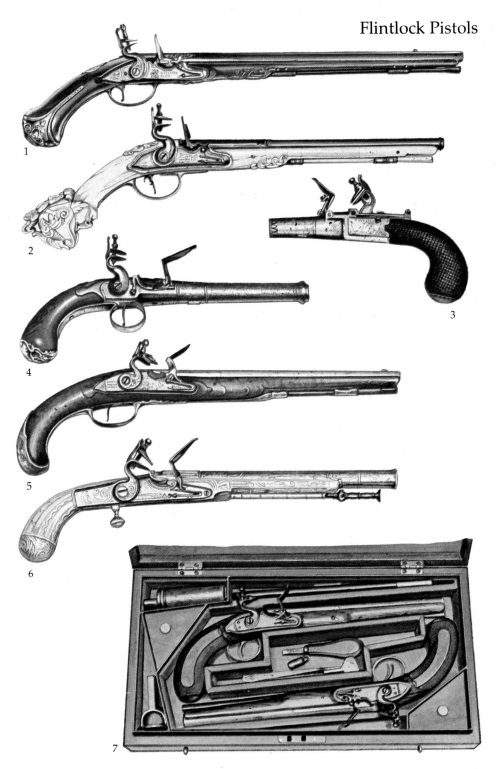

1

2

3

4

5

Flintlock Military Long Guns

The flintlock system provided cheap firearms to the world's armies.

1. *British Sea Service musket. Made from Land pattern parts with no provision for a bayonet, this was the poor relation of the military weapons. The Navy until the 1850s took the surplus of land weapons, often in made up or cut down form.*

2. *Prussian model 1782. Replacing the model 1720, this was more modern in design and more like the British pattern musket, having no barrel bands but the barrel fixed by pins.*

3. *French 1785 musketoon for cavalry, designed for light cavalry but still too long in the barrel to be really useful for the mounted soldier. Britain and Prussia had adopted the carbine, a lighter and shorter weapon.*

4. *British New Land pattern musket. Adopted in 1803, this was the more streamlined version of the "Brown Bess", but the war with France made its introduction a slow one and the "India pattern" musket was more widely used.*

5. *The Austrian Jaeger rifle, the style typical of rifles adopted by a number of countries, most of which were designed on this or hunting rifle lines.*

The flintlock system changed the tactics of the world's armies. With the flintlock everywhere replacing matchlock and pike by the end of the 18th century, surprise attacks became possible, as there were no glowing matches to give away the attackers' intentions, especially at night, and ambushes and skirmishing by infantry were now possible. While the weapons issued to infantry were fairly basic and smooth-bored, they did allow a more rapid rate of fire. From soldiers grouped in either line, square or column, the effect of volley fire was often devastating on attacking cavalry or opposing infantry.

The basic soldier's musket had to be simple and cheap. Simplicity was of paramount importance because of the lack of education and training and the background of the average recruit to the increasingly large armies. The military muskets had a simple yet solid stock, the butt ending in a metal plate to protect it when grounded, the ramrod fitted beneath the barrel in a tube, the barrel of large bore (often about 12 bore), browned on the outside to prevent glare and rusting, and of course a lock of solid construction, with the minimum of parts to go wrong and no refinements. The brass furniture, such as trigger-guard, side plates and barrel bands, was cast.

At the beginning of the 18th century, when the dog lock was superseded by the flintlock, the musket still resembled the cumbersome matchlock, there having been very little change in the design and shape of the stock. But during the middle and later years of the century, the stock became more streamlined, following trends in civilian design. While a new shape was assumed for ease of use, strength was never neglected. All muskets for foot soldiers were full stocked, the wood extending almost to the end of the barrel, allowing a short protrusion for the fixing of the bayonet. In most countries the barrel was held to the stock by a screw through the tang which connected with a thread in the trigger guard, and, in nearly all cases, barrel bands, often three in number with a fore-end cap as one of them. These bands also acted as pipes or holders for the rammer. In Britain and a minority of other countries the barrel was held by a screw through the tang and pins passing through the stock and through lugs brazed to the barrel.

Towards the end of the 18th century flintlock muskets were nearing the peak of their development. During the first three decades of the 19th century refinements such as reinforced hammers and better-made lock interiors brought this rugged military arm to the height of its excellence.

Firearms

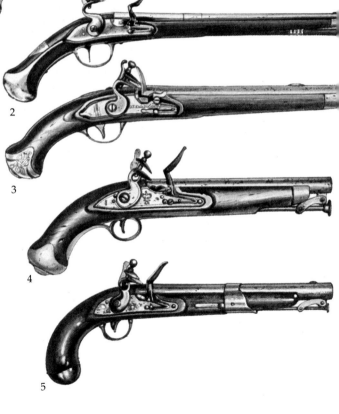

The flintlock cavalry pistol was a most effective and widely used arm, produced for light and heavy cavalry in every major army. Some cavalry regiments were provided with carbines, which had a longer range.
1. French cavalry pistol, model 1777.
2. Swedish cavalry pistol, model 1699.
3. Prussian cavalry pistol, 1787.
4. British New Land pattern cavalry pistol, c. 1800.
5. American cavalry pistol, model 1819.
6. Austrian carbine, model 1807.
7. British cavalry carbine, 1806.

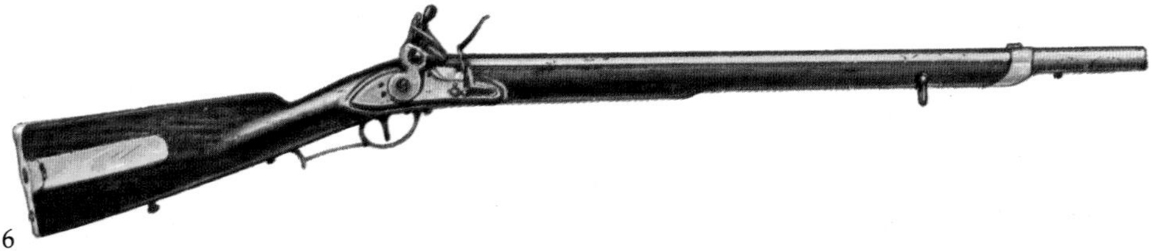

6

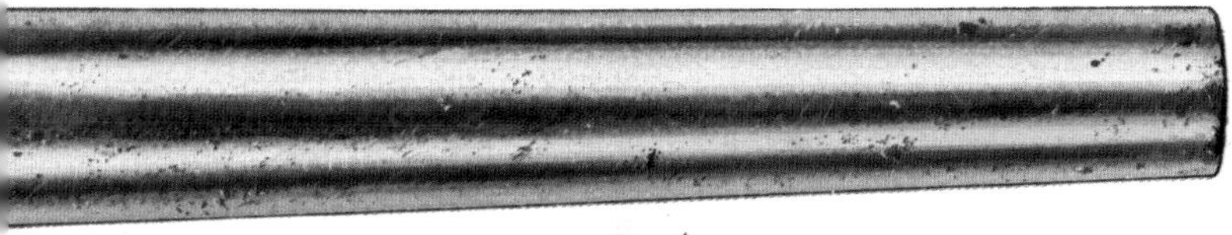

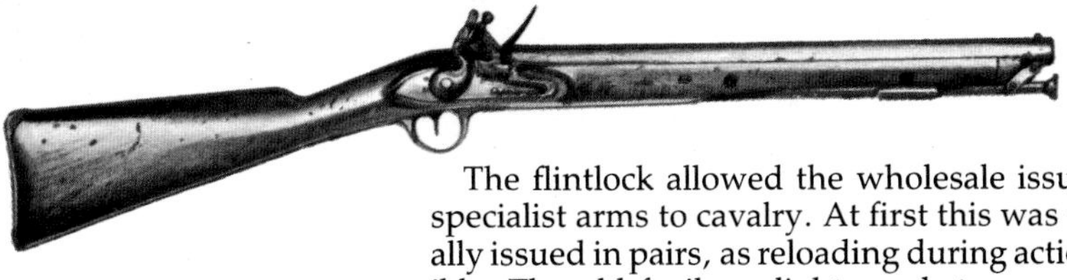

7

The flintlock allowed the wholesale issue of short and specialist arms to cavalry. At first this was the pistol, usually issued in pairs, as reloading during action was impossible. The old fusils or light muskets were not altogether withdrawn from use, but slowly a shorter arm was called for. In some countries, shoulder stocks were supplied to clip to the butts of pistols. Other armies, while retaining the pistol, supplied a shorter long arm – the carbine. Early carbines were sometimes fitted with swivels which attached to hooks on the carbine ammunition pouch belt to avoid loss, or with a long "staple" opposite the lock along which ran the ring of a sling. One vital part of the pistol or carbine was the rammer; without it the weapon could not be loaded. In early forms of pistol the rammer did not lie in a groove beneath the barrel but was carried by the man either in the holster or in the belt. Later versions of both carbines and pistols avoided this fault by having the rammers fitted to the weapons by a swivel link at the front.

A noticeable mark of all cavalry pistols was the large heavy butt for ease of drawing, usually with a large metal butt cap. The carbine, which was used with two hands, provided the mounted soldier with additional firepower both when he was on the move and when he dismounted.

During the mid-19th century, there were many experiments with breech-loading carbines. There were fewer such trials with pistols, as these were rarely intended to be reloaded while on the move, and the carbine continued even alongside the revolver as the general cavalry firearm. The carbine continued in many armies as the cavalry arm and it was only when in some countries the infantry rifle was shortened and made a general issue weapon, and when the horse gave way to armoured vehicles, that the carbine slowly faded away. It was, however, later revived for specialist troops and is much in evidence today in the new form of the sub-machine gun.

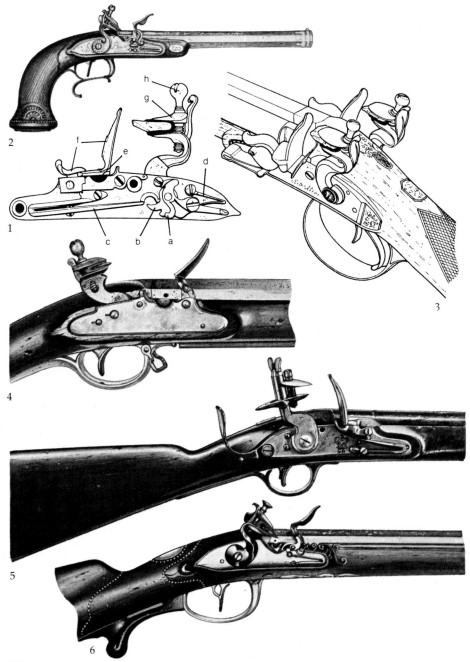

The Later Flintlock

By the end of the 18th century many gunmakers were experimenting with often ingenious ways of improving the efficiency of the flintlock system by not only devising means of smoother working of the lock parts, but also improving the pan, cock and also the actual construction of the lock itself.

1. *An 18th-century military flint lock: a) tumbler; b) vertical sear; c) mainspring; d) return spring; e) pan; f) pan-cover and frizzen; g) cock; h) jaw screw.*

2. *French duelling pistol of 1792, showing certain refinements to the lock and the French style of stock and barrel.*

3. *A superb example of the workmanship of locks in the last years of the flintlock system. A double fowling piece by Manton, 1810.*

4. *Henry Nock's screwless lock (1796), undoubtedly one of the finest contributions to the late flintlock era. Destined for military arms, it was, however, never taken up on a large scale.*

5. *British musket (1806) with reversible jaws to the cock, to enable the soldier to keep firing without the need to change the flint. The idea was never taken seriously.*

6. *A German flintlock, c. 1820, showing lock refinements such as raised pan and roller on the frizzen spring. The stock, along military lines, is however inlaid and studded.*

The beginning of the 19th century was the heyday of the flintlock. It had been in service for nearly two centuries, and gunmakers and inventors were eager to refine and make it more efficient. This desire was noticeable in the manufacture chiefly of duelling pistols and fine presentation pieces, sporting guns and target rifles, particularly in the many and varied inventions put forward to improve the flint lock itself. The most far-reaching was the waterproof pan which protected the priming powder from damp.

Other innovations included gravitating stops, rollers to the frizzen and spring, and double-jawed locks in which, in the event of the flint ceasing to spark or of a part breaking, the second cock could be swung into action.

Besides refining the workings of the lock and adding safety catches, there was it seems little that could be done until the London gunmaker Henry Nock introduced his screwless lock. Enclosed within plates, the lock had no external mechanism that could be damaged. It required few tools to dismantle it, and for the first time parts could be easily changed. Nock's enclosed lock relied on a single internal spring (the trigger return spring excepted) which activated both cock and frizzen, and the number of components was thus lessened. On the outer plate Nock added a guard on the side of the pan.

The refinements made to the internal working parts of the lock were carried out at this period in fine weapons particularly, but also in some military arms. The attention to the finish of the lock components is perhaps the most noticeable improvement, with highly polished parts, each one mirror-polished and exact in every dimension.

Other parts of the lock also came in for attention, such as the pan – of which there were numerous waterproof types available, and the hammer shape. Another breakthrough was the introduction in 1787 by Henry Nock of his patent breeching. Rather than the usual method of having the simple touch-hole or vent connect with the barrel direct, Nock produced a breech with a chamber just inside the vent before the main breech area. This allowed the sparked priming powder to ignite the charge more rapidly.

Soon many other gunmakers introduced similar breeches which not only speeded up the ignition time but, because of the hotter flame produced, burned the main charge faster and thus produced more range and a flatter trajectory for the ball. So efficient was this system that as late as the 1820s Nock's son-in-law James Wilkinson was still offering to fit it to barrels of the ordinary type.

At the turn of the 19th century, the Scotsman Alexander John Forsyth tried substituting fulminate for priming powder in a flintlock, but it was a failure. Remembering that it detonated when struck with a blow, he thought of ways to contain enough fulminate to ignite the main charge. He built a small receptacle, in the shape of a pivoted "scent bottle" from which a small amount of fulminate was deposited over the touch-hole. The "scent bottle" was then pivoted, to bring its other end containing a spring-loaded striker over the powder, the flat-topped hammer was then released, the fulminate ignited, and the flash sent to fire the main charge. Forsyth in 1806 persuaded the Master General of the Ordnance to allow him to work at the Tower of London. But his lock of 1807 failed to impress, and with a change of Master General, Forsyth was asked to remove his "rubbish" from the Tower. Setting up on his own and

3. *The pellet lock, patented in 1816, relied on a small pellet of fulminate being placed in the recessed nose of the hammer, to detonate upon striking the hollowed nipple. English.*
4. *The Forsyth "scent bottle" lock. showing the swivelling magazine containing the fulminate.*
5. *American Maynard patent tape primer lock, 1855, one of many attempts to avoid the risk of losing the small percussion cap, and to speed up firing.*

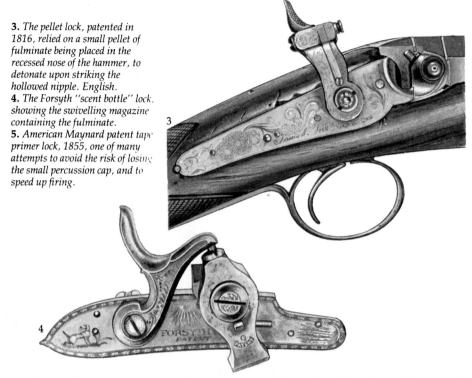

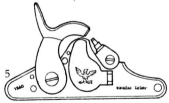

taking out a patent, he produced pistols and long arms for the civilian market. In 1821, with Forsyth's patent expired, other makers produced various percussion systems, including Webster's improved magazine and the Westley Richards improved magazine. Prior to these were developed the tube lock, with the fulminate contained in a rolled tube, and the pill lock, with the fulminate in pills. Some sandwiched the fulminate between pieces of paper – in one form this resembled the roll of "caps" for a child's gun. But eventually they all gave way to the copper percussion cap, although the "tape-primer" was adopted for a while by the U.S. forces. The title of inventor of the cap has many claimants, including Joshua Shaw, an Englishman living in America, and Purdey and Egg, two famous London gunmakers. The first patent for percussion caps was filed by the Frenchman Prélat in 1820, but only reflects common knowledge of the time, at least in England. The copper cap was detonated by the hollowed head of the hammer over a drilled steel nipple connected to the main charge chamber by a narrow hole.

1

2

3

4

5

6

Percussion Long Guns

Percussion long guns were similar to their flint counterparts when the new system came into popularity and many were in fact converted. During the century these new guns developed new types and styles.

The most popular of sporting weapons was the smooth-bored double shotgun, more practical as a percussion than as a flintlock weapon, with its elegant stock and perfectly aligned barrels, which had emerged in flintlock days and has indeed retained its overall lines to these days. It was made in a variety of bores, many more than today, and great use was made of patent breeching and of wadding of various types, and much attention was given to shot sizes and powder charges. The greatest change in the percussion era was the manufacture of large-bore game rifles. These monsters of ten bore had thick, heavy rifled barrels, double percussion locks and pistol grips to the stocks, as well as an innovation for civilian long guns – swivels or loops for slings.

Another innovation was that of more sophisticated sights for target shooting, an increasingly popular sport during the middle and later years of the 19th century, as a result of the general introduction of the rifle. The military, and the nationalist spirit in many European countries from the 1840s, fostered the mastering of firearms.

Yet another form of double gun, well favoured in southern Africa, was the Cape rifle, a percussion muzzle loader with double 40 or 52 bore. Made by a variety of makers in varying calibres, they are normally plain, almost military-style weapons, devoid of the engraving and finish expected on the best London sporting guns. Later in South Africa a double-bore gun with one smooth and one rifled barrel was popular. French sporting weapons in the percussion era carried on the flintlock tradition of highly decorative work, notably inlay, chiselling, blue and gilt and the carving of the stock, especially behind the trigger-guard. French barrels tended to be blued and inlaid with gilt, rather than browned as in the British styles; they also took a certain characteristic appearance with octagonal breeches. Germany also continued with its own forms, the *Jaeger* rifle surviving well into the percussion era. This heavy, well-balanced weapon, still appears clumsy alongside a slender London-made gun.

Among the many advantages enjoyed by the user of guns in the percussion era over his counterpart of the flintlock period was the range of innovation, including under-hammer systems, concealed lock systems, centre-fire percussion shotguns, and superb target and match rifles.

Although the percussion lock did not drastically alter the shape of firearms at the beginning, within a few years weapons had become more streamlined and better designed. The various types of the flintlock era continued, especially in the field of long guns. New butt designs and complex sights were soon common.

1. *American underhammer target rifle with typical style of stock and sights, c. 1850.*

2. *Detail of an elaborate sporting gun with carved and studded stock and chased lock detail, European, c. 1860.*

3. *English Vivian double-barrelled carbine for constabulary use, 1836.*

4. *German target rifle with elaborate hand-guard and heavy barrel, c. 1850.*

5. *English 46-bore target rifle by John Rigby with micro-adjustable rear and fore-sight. This style was popular in the 1860s.*

6. *English percussion walking-stick gun, a type of weapon that became feasible with the percussion system.*

Firearms

The chief forms of percussion pistol at the time of change from the flintlock in the 1820s and 1830s were very much the same as those evolved during the flintlock era – pocket, travelling, holster, duelling, blunderbuss pistols etc. While the percussion system itself did not generally change the design of pistols, they became as a result of its adoption easier to carry and to draw from a holster, and there was no longer any necessity to change the flint after a number of shots.

The new system did however bring new forms of pistols, one such weapon being the "bootleg" pistol reputedly so called because it was carried in the boot. This was possible because the maker had made the weapon an under-hammer. In this system the hammer is housed centrally beneath the barrel and in front of the trigger. The percussion cap nipple is screwed straight into the underside of the barrel and positioned in a protected recess in the woodwork or stock. With the curve of the butt protecting the hammer instead of a hammer at the side or top to snag, this was a popular weapon.

Along with percussion came the French and Belgian saloon pistols in small calibres, designed for indoor shooting. These became very popular and the style continued long after the percussion system had given way to the cartridge, remaining in manufacture in France, Belgium and Britain up to the early part of the 20th century.

Flintlock weapons were converted to the new system by the removal of pan and frizzen, replacing the cock with a hammer, drilling out a vent and fitting a block or drum with a percussion nipple that connected with the chamber.

By the 1840s, however, certain changes in style were apparent, mainly in duelling pistols. No longer were they full-stocked as they had been. In the half-stocked percussion duelling pistols some of the elegance of the flint duellers had disappeared, to be replaced by a more functional design. Most pocket pistols were changed little in appearance, and many sported folding bayonets, and a new form of pocket pistol emerged in the United States. While it was only a small wood-stocked side-lock percussion pistol, Deringer's pistol was to achieve immortal fame not only as the weapon used to shoot President Lincoln but as one of the most popular small pistols in the United States. So popular was the Deringer that it was copied by a host of gunmakers, the word "derringer" becoming a generic term. The 1860s saw the beginning of the decline of the percussion pistol, especially in civilian styles, as the revolver had arrived.

1. *English box lock pistol of c. 1840. Note the flat-sided "slab" grip very popular in the 19th century and the spring bayonet beneath the barrel, patented by John Waters in 1781.*
2. *Belgian-made turn-off pocket pistol, c. 1845. Similar in design to the English pocket pistols, but with the following typically Belgian features: black ebonised grip, symmetrical engraving on the frame, and decorative etching of the twisted structure of the barrel. On the left of the frame is the proofmark of Liège, which appears on most Belgian-made guns.*
3. *American pocket pistol made by H. Deringer, c. 1850. Note the typical "derringer" features of a full stock and beaked pistol grip.*
4. *English pistol of c. 1840, a typical box lock pocket pistol with barrel and frame in one.*
5. *A Dublin-made "over and under" pistol of c. 1835. Note the curved nipple-guard attached to the lower part of the frame to prevent accidental firing of the lower barrel.*

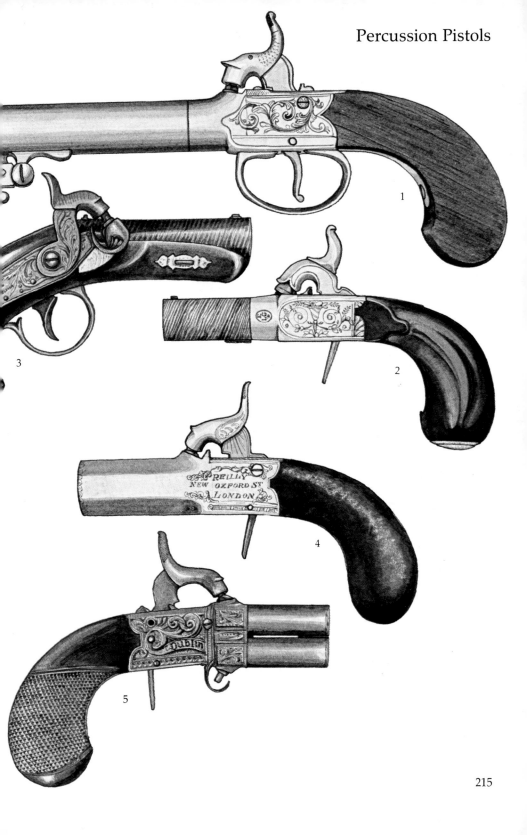

1

3

2

REILLY
NEW OXFORD ST
LONDON

4

Dublin

5

1 2 3 4 5

The percussion system, despite all its advantages, was not at first adopted by the armies of Europe and America in the way sportsmen took to it. When it was adopted, the percussion system was found to be not only easier to make but also less prone to breakages and misfires. It was during this period that the general adoption of the rifle came about.
1. *French rifled sharpshooter's carbine* à la Pontcharra *model 1837.*
2. *Prussian musket, model 1839.*
3. *Austrian Jaeger rifle, model 1842.*
4. *British Brunswick rifle, pattern 1836.*
5. *British Enfield rifle, pattern 1853, the first general-issue rifle of the British army.*

Military authorities of all countries were usually slow to adapt to technical changes and new inventions, and so it was with the percussion system. The flintlock had served for many years and given little trouble, and many asked why they should change to this new system which perhaps was no better. Nevertheless, the change had to come, and it did in the 1830s, in various countries. But as there were large stocks of flint firearms, the authorities sought an easy and cheap method of converting these to percussion. The first issued percussion arms were such conversions, although in some countries the earliest percussion issue was made up from converted flint parts.

Once in the hands of the troops, the percussion system was found to be easier to handle than flint, less prone to damage and misfires, and with fewer external parts to snare on foliage etc. or to tear clothing. The advances made in gunmaking, the adoption of the percussion system, and the slowly changing attitudes to war heralded in the general introduction of the rifle. In most countries, the rifle, even if percussion, remained for some years the arm of the specialist rifle or *Jaeger* troops, who still performed the same role as they had done with the flintlock rifle. By the early 1850s, the general introduction of the rifled long arm had been made in most armies. The British introduced their 1853 pattern Enfield for general issue in that year, while the French, the Danes and the Swedes and the Americans had introduced general-issue rifles by the 1850s. It was only the Prussians who had short-circuited the percussion system era. Percussion arms served little time in their army, because in 1841 the Prussians introduced the bolt-action breech-loading needle rifle. (See pp. 226–7).

The old complaint about the rifle barrel becoming fouled after a number of shots, needing extra force on the rammer to drive the ball home, was overcome in the 1840s. There were many types of bullet made to answer this problem, the most important being that produced by Minié in 1849 and its derivatives. In this type, the base was hollowed and an iron cup placed in it. The bullet was smaller than the bore so that, in spite of any fouling, it could be easily loaded; on firing, the plug expanded the bullet and made it bite the grooves of the rifling, so imparting the required spin. Later Minié bullets simply had a carefully designed cavity without the iron cup.

Naturally this new accuracy of fire and the increased range, together with a fire-rate equal to that of smooth-bore guns, made some impact on military thinking.

Firearms

By the beginning of the percussion era, the cavalry pistol had for a variety of reasons been withdrawn from some units in favour of the carbine but those troops, usually lancers, who were not equipped with carbines were still issued with pistols. In the French army pistols were still essential issue for heavy cavalry and some light cavalry, and this was true also in Scandinavia and Austria. On the whole, Prussian cavalry preferred the carbine. In the United States, pistols were issued on a limited scale, but once the percussion revolver had become popular this was issued with sword and carbine. Percussion pistols were also issued to other bodies such as police, the *Gendarmerie* in France, customs officers and coastguard officials. These usually followed the military pattern, although most were specially made for the service requiring them rather than cast-off military issues.

Some countries preferred to try to combine pistol with carbine, as had been done on occasion in the days of the flintlock. The weapons were essentially fairly long-barrelled but not too long to use single-handed; they had a slot for the attachment of a butt to make the weapon into a carbine. A notable example of this style was the American Springfield rifled pistol with stock, while as a pure carbine the British Victoria carbine could be used single-handed.

Tradition mostly dictated that cavalry should be armed with a percussion pistol, although its range was poor compared with that of the carbine. Despite this, authorities still issued muzzle-loading smooth-bore pistols to some cavalry units well into the 1860s. These issues were mainly to the native cavalry of colonial powers, one such example being those made in Birmingham in the late 1860s and early 1870s and issued to native cavalry of the Indian Army.

The carbine, however, because of its popularity, received much attention from gunmakers with a view to its improvement. Most strove hard to find a suitable breech-loading system, as did Westley-Richards with his so-called "Monkey Tail" breech (also produced as a cavalry pistol) and Sharps and others in America, and the American Civil War proved the heyday for the capping breech-loader. In France, Scandinavia, Austria and Italy similar experiments were conducted to perfect the cavalry carbine.

Most of the breech-loaders or capping breech-loaders only reached the experimental stage, some even being experimentally issued. Some survived, like the American Sharps, which went on to take a centre-fire cartridge. Even with the advent of the revolver, the carbine still remained the cavalry firearm well into the 20th century.

Although the pistol had dropped in popularity as a cavalry weapon, it was still widely issued. The carbine remained a popular and standard issue and efforts were made to combine pistol and carbine in a number of armies.
1. United States Springfield rifled pistol carbine, model 1856.
2. British Victoria pattern carbine, 1844.
3. French musketoon model 1822.
4. French navy pistol, 1840.
5. British coast guard pistol pattern 1842.
6. Prussian cavalry pistol model 1850.

One method of increasing firepower was to speed up the loading procedure, and so the breech-loader was born. It has persisted through early hand-fired guns, through matchlock, wheel-lock, flint and percussion and remains today the most effective method of loading a firearm.

1. *English 16th-century, Henry VIII's breech-loader with hinged breech mechanism. The lock is now thought to have been a wheel-lock although in this renovation a matchlock has been fitted.*

2. *Egg's breech-loading system modelled on that invented by Giuseppe Crespi of Milan in the 1770s. British.*

3. *The Ferguson screw-breech system. This method did away with ramming and was extremely effective but never widely used. It was copied with slight differences by other makers.*

4. *Breech-loading flintlock with separate chamber incorporating frizzen and frizzen spring. This system was never popular for obvious reasons.*

5. *Sharp's breech-loading carbine, patented in 1848, had the breech-block activated by the trigger-guard. So popular was this capping breech-loader that it survived the arrival of the self-contained cartridge and was adapted to fire it.*

6. *Westley-Richards "monkey-tail" system for military and civilian arms, one of the few systems adopted by the military for limited use. British, 1858.*

The only way rapid fire could be obtained was to increase the rate of loading the piece. From the 16th century onwards gunmakers attempted to accomplish this by adopting various breech-loading systems. The main problem encountered was how to produce an effective breech seal and, considering the ignition systems in use at the time, many made a creditable effort to overcome the problem.

Some types of breech-loaders utilised separate chambers which were preloaded, one such example being that made for Henry VIII, dated 1537. In most early forms of this system, the hinged block was moved over and a loaded steel chamber similar in shape to a modern cartridge inserted in the breech. From the mid-17th century the reusable chamber was inserted in the rear end of a drop-down barrel.

Another type was the pivot breech – the most famous being that invented by Giuseppe Crespi of Milan in 1770. In this system the separate breech-block was hinged to allow loading, but the seal was poor. Crespi's idea was however copied and adapted by many makers such as Durs Egg in London and the Americans Hall and Thornton. The Hall rifle was adopted by the U.S. army in 1817 as a flintlock, and despite its drawbacks was later made in percussion form. One system of this type which perhaps could have answered the problem was patented the same year by Urbanus Sartoris of Paris. In this the hinged breech was linked to the barrel by an interrupted screw thread.

Another, better-known, type of early breech-loader used a movable breech-plug, one of the earliest known examples dating from 1593 and made by Freiherr von Sprinzenstein of Munich. The system involved having a hole in the top, bottom or side of the breech-end of the barrel. The barrel was loaded through this hole, depending on its position, in the usual way or in reverse order, the ball being inserted before the powder. The hole was then blocked by the breech-plug, which had a screw thread. The best-known weapons on this system are those of Isaac de la Chaumette (invented c. 1704) and later the improved version of Captain Patrick Ferguson (1776). In both systems a hole was bored from top to bottom right through the breech of the barrel and stopped with a plug which was threaded and attached to the front of the trigger-guard, which acted as the turning lever. In the Ferguson, unlike the de la Chaumette, one turn of the guard was sufficient to unscrew the plug, which also had a stop at the bottom preventing its entire removal.

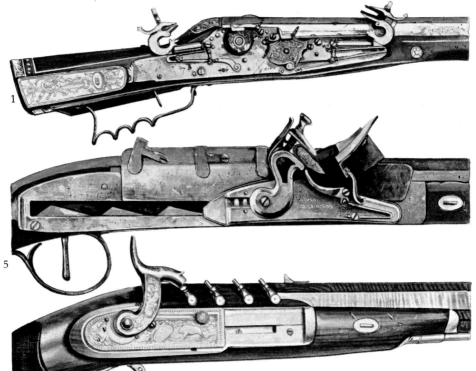

1

5

6

Another method of increasing firepower, more popular until the advent of the cartridge and the revolver, was the use of multiple fire, either by many barrels firing at once, as in the case of volley guns, or by firing a series of charges in one barrel or a number of separate chambers.
1. *Wheel-lock with two superimposed charges in the barrel, one in front of another, both fired by different pans and pyrities in the jaws; c. 1650.*
2. *Four-barrelled flintlock gun, all barrels designed to fire at once; c. 1650.*
3. *Henry Nock's seven-barrelled volley gun for the British Navy, c. 1780.*

Some saw the breech-loader as the answer to rapid fire, but the early makers saw an increase in the number of barrels as the answer. Some early 15th-century handguns had four barrels, each with a touch-hole. Others of this multi-barrel style unleashed the contents of all the barrels in one roar at the unsuspecting enemy or game. A notable example of this type of weapon, made originally for naval use but also found in civilian sporting versions, was the seven-barrelled volley-gun. Attributed to Henry Nock, the gunmaker who supplied all 600-odd military versions, it was in fact the brainchild of one James Wilson. This lethal weapon discharged seven musket balls at the pull of a trigger. Another weapon of this type was the so-called "Duck's-foot" pistol. A box-lock pocket pistol in style, the gun was equipped with four or five barrels, all firing at once, and spread fan-like.

In pocket pistols, the tap-action was favoured by those who required anything up to four barrels to be fired one after the other, but for larger pistols and long guns, some makers preferred the use of a superimposed load. In this system, the barrel is loaded with anything up to, say, four rounds, one on top of the other. On the outside, at the right points at the breech-end of the barrel, there would be the corresponding number of touch-holes. In one type of weapon, the lock was made to slide so that each time it was

4. *Lorenzoni system repeating flintlock with magazines holding both powder and bullet charges, c. 1680–85.*

5. *A four-shot superimposed charge flintlock gun with a single lock sliding from touch-hole to touch-hole, c. 1810–15.*

6. *Four-shot superimposed percussion rifle with sliding lock, c. 1825.*

7. *Superimposed charge system with fixed lock and bar firing first charge and keeping hammer off second, c. 1850.*

positioned, cocked and fired, the topmost of the charges was ignited. In another version there were four separate locks, one for each touch-hole.

Yet another form of multiple fire was the use of a magazine inside the gun to store powder and bullet. Perhaps the most famous early system using this principle was that often attributed to Michele Lorenzoni, a Florentine gunmaker, but made also by others.

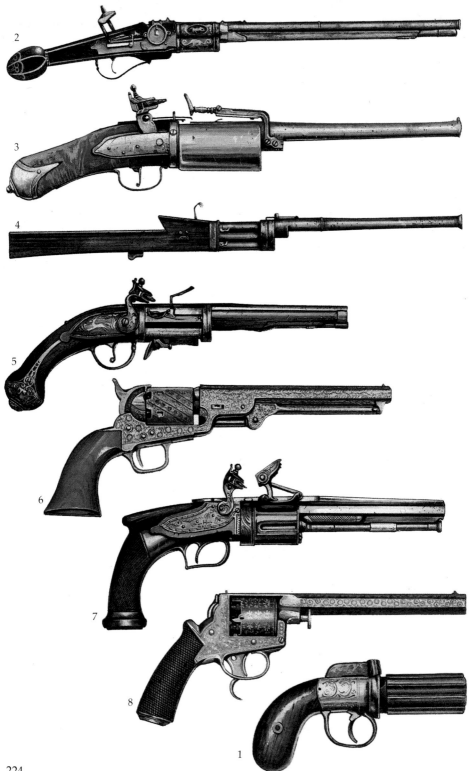

On the earliest wheel-lock pistols and carbines with revolving cylinders, the cylinders had to be revolved by hand, and between each shot the lock had to be re-wound and the hammer cocked. Although a longish performance, it still speeded up the rate of fire.

An important precursor of the true revolver was the pistol with revolving cylinder made in England, probably by John Dafte, in the second half of the 17th century and now in the Tower of London. This was a snaphance mechanism, in which the cock when fired activated a link which opened the pan cover to allow the flint as it struck the steel to ignite the priming powder. The one great advantage of this early revolver was that the act of cocking turned the cylinder from the empty chamber just fired to the next loaded one. During the next century a number of weapons were devised using the cylinder system, some with each chamber having its own pan already primed and a steel, but it was not until 1818 that a real advance was made, in the system patented by the American Elisha Collier. In this system, the cylinder originally revolved automatically to bring up the new charged chamber when the hammer was cocked.

The earliest widely popular revolver was the so-called pepperbox. In this arm there was no separate cylinder, in fact the whole set of barrels was the cylinder. In earlier flintlock versions the barrels were hand-rotated, but by 1837 the American Ethan Allan had patented a system for a double-action trigger that cocked and fired with one pull and was coupled to a pawl and ratchet to rotate the cylinder. The main drawback of the pepperbox was the bulk of the barrels.

It was Colt and his later rivals in America and Britain who brought the revolver as we know it into prominence. Colt patented his first revolver in 1835, and after an initial failure with manufacture in 1841 resumed production in 1848. From then he went from strength to strength with various models from the Paterson to the Navy, the Army, one with external hammer, the Rootes, and later the centre-fire Peacemaker. In Britain Colt's rivals, such as Adams, Tranter, Deane, Webley, Bentley, etc., were all hard at work. Some said that because the majority of the British revolvers were closed frame (Colt had an open frame) they were sturdier; certainly British makers did introduce larger calibres and, unlike Colt, produced revolvers with a double-action trigger that cocked the hammer, revolved the cylinder and set the hammer falling on the percussion cap.

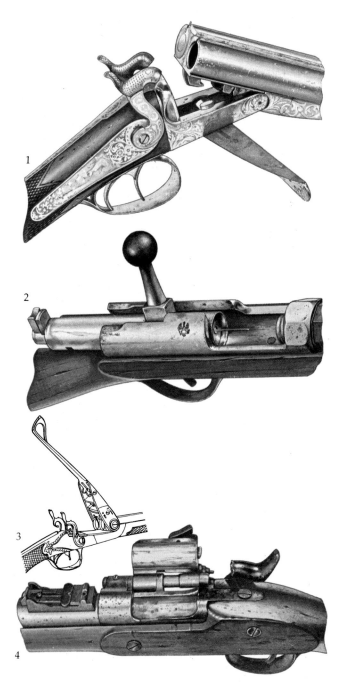

Rapid fire was attempted by many methods, but it was only with the coming of the self-contained cartridge and a safe gas-tight breech that the way was opened for further development.
1. *Typical pin-fire shotgun of the 19th century. This shows the breech open with cartridge in one barrel and the "pin" protruding.*
2. *Prussian Dreyse needle gun, the first breech-loader issued by the military.*
3. *Breech-loading shotgun designed by Pauly, patented in 1816. Years ahead of its time, it was never taken seriously.*
4. *The first issued British army breech-loader, the Snider-Enfield of 1865, using an existing muzzle-loading Enfield with a breech designed by Jacob Snider.*

Achievement of Rapid Fire

From the beginning of the 19th century inventors were attempting to produce a weapon that did away with the external mechanism of the flintlock by combining the igniting charge with the propellant and projectile in one. The Swiss Samuel John Pauly invented such a self-contained cartridge and a breech-loading arm to fire it, and patented this in France in 1812. Leaving France in 1814, he came to Britain, where he took out a patent in 1816. The system was very advanced for its time and was inevitably too radical for it to gain ready acceptance; it was also very expensive to make. The pity was that what Pauly had designed and patented was almost identical in principle to the modern cartridge we know today. The weapon he invented opened with a trap at the breech which exposed the breech-end of the barrel; here was inserted a paper cartridge with a reusable brass base containing priming agent, in this case a small pellet of fulminate (percussion) powder; the rest of the cartridge held the powder charge and bullet or shot.

Pauly made little or no money from his invention, but one of his Paris employees was to change the nature of firearms with a similar idea, Johann N. von Dreyse. In his "needle gun", adopted in the Prussian service in 1840, Dreyse employed a bolt action and a self-contained cartridge with priming agent in the base of the bullet itself. Far ahead of its time, the invention was instrumental in the Prussian defeat of Denmark in 1864 and Austria in 1866 and was the forerunner of bolt-action military rifles.

Early variations of cartridge breech-loading design included the "capping breech-loading" combustible cartridge with standard percussion nipple and cap; Pottet's "centre-fire" with percussion cap in the cartridge base, similar to modern practice; the "rim-fire" of Robert and Houiller; and "pin-fire", patented by Houiller (see also pp. 250–51). Casimir Lefaucheux's drop-down barrel system with under-lever locking (1832) set a pattern for shotguns which, with improvements, remains the basic form for modern side-by-side double-barrelled shotguns.

It was also necessary to convert the existing arsenals of thousands of percussion muzzle loaders to a single-shot breech-loading system. In America, the thousands of Springfield muskets were converted with the E.S. Allin system with trapdoor breech, while in Britain a side-opening breech, invented by the American J. Snider, was adopted. France soon went for an entire new system, the 1866 Chassepot bolt-action rifle similar to the Prussian needle gun but with the detonating cap in the base of the cartridge.

1. *Hammeli .22 target rifle with refined style of butt and stock hold now demanded on the target competitions.*
2. *Winchester 1866 carbine, the forerunner of the famed 1873 and others of the underlever type.*
3. *10-bore lever shotgun by Winchester, 1887, one of a variety of weapons that emerged from the underlever action.*

Once a breech-loaded centre-fire cartridge and effective breech sealing had become a practical reality, the hunt was on for the perfect breech-loading system. Some favoured the bolt action, used as early as 1835 by Dreyse, others the swing-out breech, the falling breech-block, the raised breech-block, the drop-down barrel. All manner of systems were tried, favoured by some, rejected by others. Three that have stood the test of time are the bolt action, drop-down barrel action, and the falling-block action. The muzzle-loading weapon was obsolete by the 1870s except with diehards, although the military had converted quantities of muzzle-loaders as a stop-gap. Breech-loaders were adopted earlier for sporting use.

There was a large variety of both bolt-action and dropping breech-block action rifles such as the Carter and Edwards nearly adopted by the British army, an excellent rifle which would have easily converted to magazine use, the Money Walker, an awkward falling-block rifle, the Henry

4. *A hammer shotgun with bar action by Wilkinson. The hammer did not strike the pin but was linked to a bar with a pin on the end which struck the cap on the cartridge.*

5. *A "London made" hammerless sidelock ejector gun showing the best of the London gun trade skills, c. 1920.*

6. *The famous .461 Metford-Farquharson breech-loading sporting gun.*

7. *Bolt-action Mannlicher big game rifle, c. 1910.*

with its falling block and external hammer, the American Remington, and many more, some famous and others whose names have disappeared. Other famous rifles included Lebel, Schmidt-Rubin with its pull-push bolt, Ross, Lee, Mauser, and Mannlicher, and in America a host of breech-loaders included the famous Winchester, the Sharps, and the Savage, amongst others.

In the search for efficient breech-loading there were two schools of thought. The first was to have a single-shot cartridge breech-loader, as the use of black powder with its inherent disadvantages of fouling mechanisms and clouds of smoke made a reliable magazine or repeating rifle difficult to make. The second school of thought persevered with the magazine or repeating rifle, such as the Winchester. In 1886 the French introduced smokeless powder. This quickly changed the whole thinking behind magazine or repeating rifles, especially for military use.

The single-shot rifles, however, such as the Gibbs-Metford-Farquharson, were still in constant demand for target and match shooting until the turn of the century, when sporting riflemen started to adopt versions of various military magazine rifles such as the Lee-Enfield, the Mauser, and the Mannlicher.

Firearms

With the coming of the self-contained metallic cartridge, a host of revolvers and pistols appeared in the arms markets of the world. Smith and Wesson were quick to see the potential of cartridge revolvers and they were followed by established makers such as Colt, Remington, Francotte, and Webley. The Belgian trade produced vast numbers of pin-fire revolvers. Some of the earlier percussion revolver makers, notably Adams and Tranter in Britain, although producing the new breech-loading revolvers, dropped out in the 1880s, and many other smaller firms in America, France, Spain, Germany and Britain lasted only a few years.

Alongside the revolver, the pocket pistol for self-defence still found a place in the guise of the cheaper derringer. The word, the trade name of one maker and subsequently of the general type of pistol, was applied to many small weapons, such as the Remington .41 over-and-under pis-

During the late 19th century a large variety of pistols and revolvers was produced, the revolver eventually ousting the pistol as a more convenient form of handgun. By the beginning of the 20th century, the revolver and automatic were the two types left.
1. English .577 double "howdah" pistol. A popular weapon for officers in India, this one presented by the Prince of Wales in India in 1875.
2. American Smith and Wesson revolver.
3. American Remington derringer .41 two-shot pistol.

230

4. *American Remington, model 1875.*
5. *American Colt New Service revolver, model 1917.*
6. *English Wilkinson-Webley, model 1911.*

tol still made today. Target pistols, usually single-shot, were also produced, as were .22 saloon pistols for indoor target shooting. Target shooting with pistols or revolvers was a growing market in the 1890s, and many manufacturers such as Colt, Smith and Wesson, and Webley produced target revolvers, with longer barrels and more attention to finish and sights.

While the revolver was much favoured by the military and civilians there were obvious limitations to the size of bullet it could fire if it was to be manageable and to have enough shots. The idea of more than five or six shots was developed in Belgium by the firm of Henrion, Dassy and Heuschen who produced a massive 20-shot double-barrelled revolver. It was never a success as the automatic pistol could do better and was lighter.

The supreme example of large-calibre pistol must be the .577 howdah pistol. Massive, short-barrelled, with a shotgun-type breech-loading action, external hammers and shotgun fore-end, it was a popular pistol of the 1870s and 1880s in India for big game hunters and others. Carried either by the hunter in the howdah on the back of the elephant, or more often in a holster on the belt or saddle, the pistol was intended for self-defence rather than offence. Against a charging wounded tiger it was ideal, and the military ammunition was readily available, being that of the regulation British Snider-Enfield rifle.

Firearms

While there were breech-loading military guns in some armies before the introduction of the modern cartridge, most had been issued on a limited or experimental scale. All were flintlock or percussion weapons with the breech taking a preformed powder-and-ball charge without built-in means of ignition.

Until the 1870s many military breech-loaders were conversions from percussion with breech-blocks such as the Snider and Allin systems referred to previously. As we have also seen the first purpose-built breech-loader was the Prussian Dreyse needle gun.

All converted weapons, the Snider-Enfields, the Springfields and many others, served as stop-gaps while the war departments adjusted to the new system and searched for a gun, or a gun combining the best from a number of makers, to suit their armies for a good number of years. The new weapons had a drastic effect on warfare. The flatter trajectory of the bullet improved its velocity, range and accuracy.

In Britain, 1871 saw the introduction of the Martini-Henry rifle in .45 calibre with a chamber of .577, while 1874 was the year the French abandoned the Chassepot for the Gras system with ejectable case. The armies of the world followed suit, adopting systems such as the German Mauser, the Remington (used in various countries as well as the U.S.A.), the Italian Vetterli, the Austrian Werndl, the Portuguese Guedes and the Russian Berdan, these being a few of the new breed of single-shot breech-loaders.

Soon, however, the search was again on for rapid fire and various countries including Britain tried to convert their single-shot weapons to multiple fire with clip-on magazines. Most, if not all, failed to meet the needs of the military. In America the tubular magazine had gained much popularity in the Spencer carbines, which had a tube containing a number of rounds loaded through the butt. This weapon had a somewhat antique look, with its external hammer. Perhaps the most famous of all magazine weapons of the time was the Winchester, also with tubular magazine, taking up to 20 rounds.

Other countries, ever-mindful of ammunition expenditure and of course the prevailing tactics and strategy, opted for a magazine that held fewer rounds but affected the balance of the rifle less during shooting, the box magazine being beneath the bolt. This system was adopted in various arms such as the Mauser, the Lee-Metfords and Lee-Enfields and the French Lebels as well as the American Krag and later Springfield rifles.

The introduction of the self-contained cartridge for breech-loading systems brought about a rapid change in the arms of the soldier as well as the methods of warfare. The new systems, adopted by all countries, allowed a more rapid rate of fire with the single shot systems and heralded the arrival of the magazine military rifle whose increased rate of fire was to prove decisive on many occasions.

1. *British Martini-Henry rifle, pattern 1871.*
2. *American Spencer rifle, patented in 1860, model 1863.*
3. *French Chassepot carbine, model 1866.*
4. *Italian Vetterli rifle, model 1868.*
5. *German GEW 98 with enlarged magazine, model 1898.*
6. *Galland and Somerville revolver, model 1868.*
7. *French model 1892 revolver.*

1

2

3

4

5

6

7

The various powers entered World War I with the magazine rifle. The Lee-Enfield and the Mauser came through with flying colours. Undoubtedly for speed the Lee-Enfield had the edge on the probably more accurate Mauser. In the hands of trained men it was a formidable weapon, surviving in the British and other armies until recent times.

Firearms

The ultimate in multiple fire, and the dream of many an inventor and gunmaker, was the automatic weapon which would fire for as long as the trigger was pulled and the ammunition was there. With the self-contained cartridge the dream became a possibility but it took many experiments to perfect the idea. Most early automatic weapons harnessed the recoil engendered when the bullet is fired to produce the ejection of the spent case, the reloading of a new round and the cocking of the piece ready for the next shot. Fully automatic weapons provide continuous fire, while in semi-automatic weapons, it is necessary to press the trigger again after the reloading.

The first automatic pistol was produced in Spain by Orbea in 1863. It worked from gas pressure rather than recoil and was a revolver-styled weapon. The first practical true automatic pistol was invented by an Austrian, Anton Schonberg, who produced a clip-loading 8mm-calibre weapon which worked on neither the gas nor the recoil system, instead using movement engendered by the primer to activate the mechanism. It was perhaps the 1893 product of the German-born Paul Borchardt, a naturalised American who could find no backing in his new homeland, that put the automatic system on the map. Produced by Lowe in Berlin, the new automatic pistols, although of unusual and awkward appearance, had some commercial success. The box magazine it used was revolutionary and the ammunition was rimless. Bergmann, one of the giants of automatic weapons manufacture, ranking with Mauser and Browning, was quick off the mark with his product, as was also the firm of Mannlicher with a weapon taking a

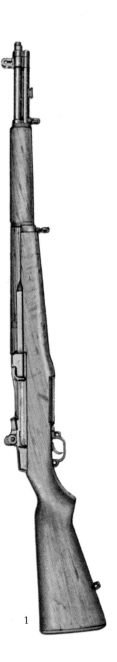

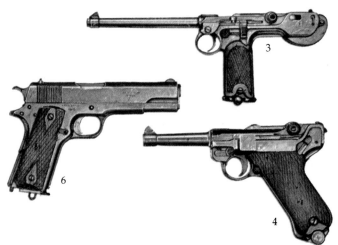

Automatic Guns

The development of the cartridge breech-loader and the machine gun allowed inventors to combine the two to produce automatic weapons of all types, pistol, carbine and rifle. Today in the military field, the bolt-action magazine rifle has bowed to the semi- and fully automatic rifle, while the machine carbine or sub-machine gun and the automatic pistol have replaced the carbine and revolver.

1. *American Garand rifle, model 1936.*

2. *Browning 9mm pistol. Current issue with the British army, this model 1935 is termed the model 1946 for military use.*

3. *German Borchardt pistol, model 1893.*

4. *German Luger, model 1908.*

5. *American Thompson sub-machine gun, model 1928*

6. *American Colt pistol, model 1911.*

7. *Spanish Astra pistol, 1921.*

rimmed round. In the United States, where the revolver was the supreme hand-gun, there was little interest initially in automatic pistols, but by 1900 Colt had decided to investigate the question of automatic hand-guns. After producing weapons in, among other years, 1900 (experimental) and 1902, Colt finally produced in 1911 one of the most enduring automatic pistols, designed by John Browning. The Model 1911 is still in use over 70 years after its introduction. Among many other names famous for their automatic pistols are Beretta, Astra, Mas, Luger (whose Parabellum was adopted in 1908 by the German army), Mauser, and Steyr.

The automatic principle was also applied to carbines and long arms. During World War I the German army issued the Bergmann "Musquete" automatic carbine and this was followed by the Italians' Beretta 1918. The Thompson sub-machine gun or "tommy-gun" entered production in 1921 and was used in World War II by both the U.S.A. and Britain. The first sub-machine guns (two-handed relatively short-barrelled automatics firing pistol ammunition) were produced by Italy in 1915, and by Germany in 1918 with the MP 18 (*Maschinen-pistole*). Developments in the interwar period resulted in the American Garand, the first self-loading rifle to be adopted as standard issue (in 1936 in the U.S.A.), and early World War II sub-machine guns included the German MP 40, the British Sten, and the Austen (Australian Sten) and the Owen in Australia.

Firearms

Since the end of World War II, advances in weapon design have been chiefly in the field of military and law-enforcement weapons. For the target shooter and sportsman, the rifles and shotguns they use remain virtually unchanged. The favourite rifles such as the Lee-Enfield Mark IV, the Mauser and the Mannlicher, and shotguns such as the side-by-side hammerless ejector, as well as the more modern over-and-under (with two barrels one above the other), the pump-action and automatic shotguns, are still in use world-wide.

The main trend in individual military arms has of course been away from bolt-action magazine rifles to semi- or fully automatic rifles, and a great upsurge in the development of the sub-machine gun, the machine pistol and the automatic pistol. The revolver, however, because of its sturdy construction and simplicity of mechanism, has often cast doubts on the suitability of the automatic pistol with its jamming problems.

In long guns, mainly the military arms, the trend has been towards smaller calibres, such as the 7.62mm NATO round and especially the American 5.56mm calibre, which

1. *Russian Tokarev TT 1930, incorporating the basic Browning swing-link locked breech.*
2. *German Walther PPK, successor to the Walther PP, introduced in 1931 as the PPK (Polizei Pistole Kriminal) in 7.65mm calibre but extended to .22 LR, 6.35mm and 9mm short calibres. Copies widely available today.*
3. *United States Colt Python model 1955. This leading Colt weapon was the first of its type to differ from the conventional revolver in its shrouded barrel housing, integral ejector rod and adjustable rear sight. Chambered only for the powerful .357 magnum round, it has a flat hammer face and an internal firing pin in the frame.*

4. *United States Smith and Wesson model 16. This target revolver with 6-inch barrel was in .32 calibre, finished in blue, with adjustable sights.*

5. *Schmiesser sub-machine gun, the MP 38, one of the outstanding automatic weapons produced by the German weapon manufacturers before and during World War II.*
6. *British Lee-Enfield Mark V (Jungle Carbine), a shortened version of the Mark IV without the supporting woodwork to the fore-end. First of the Mark IV types to be fitted with a knife bayonet.*
7. *British L1A1, the SLR or self-loading rifle, today the infantry weapon of the British army. The weapon depicted has special sniper's sights.*

nevertheless with very high velocities still have greater hitting-power than the previous larger .303 and .30 (of an inch) calibres. There has also been a tendency towards the design and production of semi- and fully automatic rifles which take box magazines and which include the use of stampings rather than castings to assist mass production.

The other great advance has been made with military sub-machine guns. The British Sterling and the Israeli UZI are among various well-known designs of sub-machine gun developed in the U.S.A., France, Italy and Germany which are the tools that modern forces use. Usually using 9mm parabellum ammunition, these weapons have a high rate of fire, are easy to handle and, using modern methods of manufacture, are made in quantity.

Firearms

Leonardo da Vinci knew all about the use of air as an alternative driving-force for firearms, but his surviving description of how to make such a weapon deals only with the construction of the barrel. The vital detail of how the air was to propel the projectile is unfortunately not recorded.

By the early 17th century the air-gun was being taken quite seriously. It is known that one such weapon was purchased in the Low Countries for an assassination attempt on Oliver Cromwell, and from the middle of the century air-guns were made in quantity.

There were two chief ways, both in use at this time, of creating the compression of air required to propel the projectile. The first was the simple method (less common in early air-guns but used in most modern air rifles) of using a crank to compress a spiral spring attached to a piston; on pulling the trigger the piston shot down a cylinder, compressing the air within it to propel the projectile. The other principal method stored compressed air in a metal reservoir either in the butt of the weapon or in a sealed outer barrel around the barrel proper. The reservoir was filled by a hand pump and depending on size had enough air for so many shots, the last ones of course being weaker than the first. After its heyday in the first part of the 17th century the barrel reservoir gave way to the butt reservoir and its Austrian equivalent, the ball reservoir situated under the stock forward of the trigger-guard. A third type of air-gun in the 18th century used a bellows-and-spring mechanism. When the trigger was pulled the spring immediately compressed the bellows, sending a short burst of air into the barrel to expel the projectile. In all these systems, particularly the last, because of the small amount of pressure it was possible to build up, the calibre had to be small and the range was relatively short.

By the 18th century the butt and the ball reservoirs were extensively used in air-guns, the ball version being mounted not always under the stock but sometimes on top of the barrel. Many of the 18th-century air-guns were fitted with lock-plates and "hammers", or even complete flintlocks.

The simplicity of the mechanism allowed some makers to experiment with multiple-fire air-guns and rifled barrels. A repeating magazine air rifle invented by the Italian maker Girandoni was adopted by the Austrians to arm a regiment of *Jaeger* sharpshooters in 1780. It had a butt reservoir capable of powering 40 good shots. By all accounts it performed well, but the weapon's delicate nature caused it to be withdrawn in 1815. Sporting versions were made by some of the best Viennese gunmakers.

From the 16th century, gunmakers were experimenting with the use of air as a propellant to replace gunpowder. Some advantages, such as lack of smoke, silence, and a plentiful supply of raw propellant, are obvious, but the disadvantages were the lack of penetrating power and the mechanism.

1. *German bar-lock air rifle by Johann and Valentin Zigling of Frankfurt, 1753, with reservoir and hand pump.*
2. *English 64-bore air rifle with skeleton stock and dummy flintlock mechanism, again with ball reservoir and pump-up action.*
3. *Bohemian crank-up air pistol, c. 1850.*
4. *Austrian military magazine air-gun with the reservoir fitted in the butt, c. 1780.*

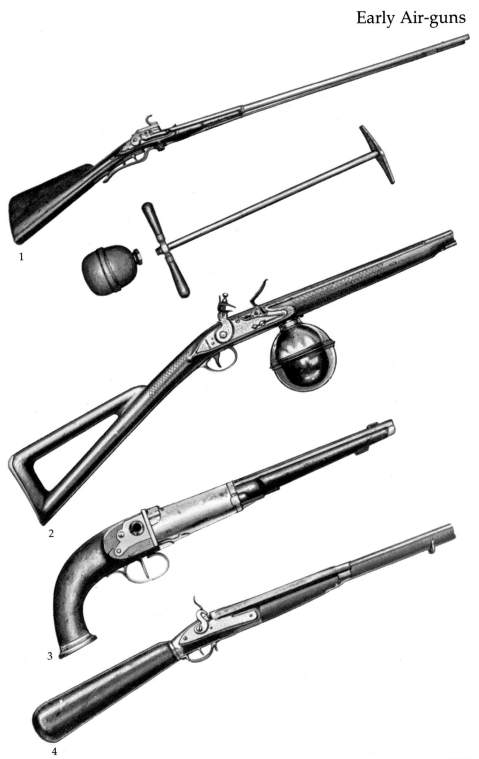

1

2

3

4

1

2

3

Improvements in design and an increase in power and range during the latter years of the 19th century established the air-gun amongst those not able to afford a firearm and amongst the young. The various types of gun and pistol that emerged at the end of the century all employed air compressed by a piston and spring. The compressed air was stored at the rear of the barrel with access to the bore by means of a valve controlled by the trigger. There were two main ways of creating this compressed air. In the first there was a loading trap in the breech end of the barrel reminiscent of the tap on a tap-action pocket pistol. In the open position this received the pellet and when turned through 90° it presented the pellet to the bore. The air was compressed by a lever which cocked the gun and compressed the air. The other method was to combine loading and cocking in one movement. This was the split-barrel system where the barrel was "broken" as one would open a shotgun, the barrel taken to 90° from the horizontal to cock the trigger and compress the air, by the action of a

Air-guns have in the past enjoyed success and even been adopted by the military. The coming of the .22 rim-fire partially eclipsed the air-gun, but with firearm legislation, the air-gun again came into its own. Today weapons are a far cry from those offered even 20 years ago.
1. *Simple target pistol with forestock designed for two-handed shooting.*
2. *American air rifle designed to look like the American .30 carbine.*
3. *American air rifle with break barrel action.*
4. *BSA .22 air rifle.*
5. *Sophisticated target air pistol with sights.*

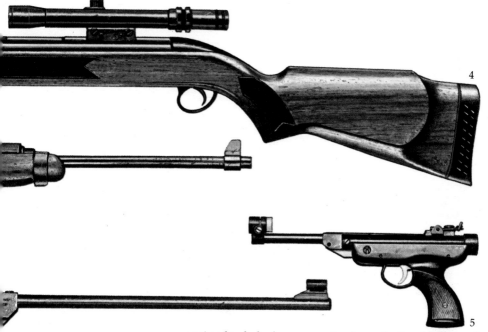

4

5

spring-loaded plunger, and returned after inserting the pellet, to mate with the breech.

While these basic methods were used by most air-gun manufacturers, there was still room for the inventive pioneer. One such was the American Quackenbush who produced an air rifle that could not only fire pellets by compressed air but with a simple conversion could also fire .22 short rim-fire cartridges. The conversion consisted of introducing a striker in the place of the leather washer seal; on firing the piston moved forward, pushed the striker home and fired the cartridge. When required as an air-gun, the striker was removed and the leather washer replaced. Of course Quackenbush's rifle was in .22 calibre, now one of the most popular for air-guns, although the older .177 and the BB (.175) have their devotees.

Another innovation first popularised, in France, by Paul Giffard about 100 years ago was the use of cartridges of CO_2 gas, such as those used in refillable soda syphons. Housed in the butt of pistols, these provide the propellant to fire the pellet. While effective, they are more expensive and, although they may provide more shots than the earlier reservoir systems, like them they have a finite life. Unlike other types of firearms, including some air-guns, old methods seem to be the best, and the spring-and-piston system is not only simple but effective. Air-guns today are popular for indoor target shooting, training in handling weapons, for control of small pests, and they also serve specialist functions such as the firing of tranquilising darts.

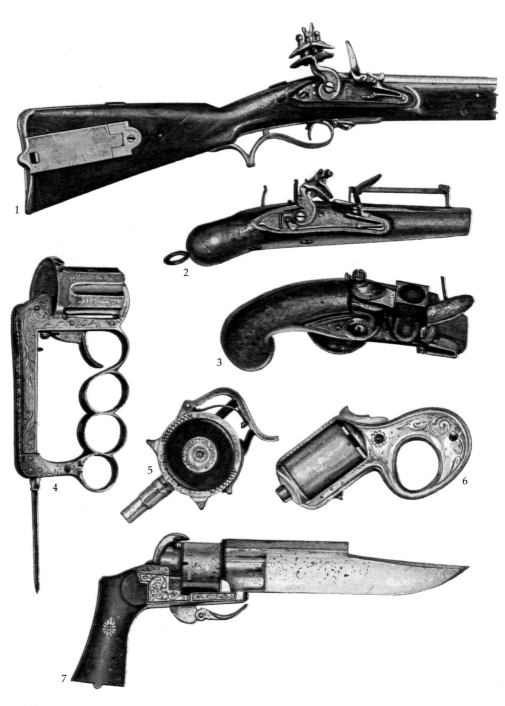

Unusual Guns

1. British Baker rifle with double
jaw to cock. Never adopted.
2. Early English alarm gun,
meant to be set with trip wire etc.
to announce the presence of
poachers.
3. Signal pistol. Designed on the
lines of a tinder pistol, this one
was meant to fire coloured smoke
from the deep brass chamber.
From the austere appearance it
could perhaps have been used by
coastguards.
4. United States combination
pepperbox revolver, knuckle
duster and dagger, a handy
close-combat weapon. It was not
as popular as the derringer but it
had its followers.
5. United States squeeze palm
pistol, c. 1885. Not as popular as
the derringer but with the
advantage of concealment, it was a
favourite of the Mississippi
gamblers.
6. A small-calibre pistol, designed
to be easily concealed. With the
solid metal frame and large
trigger-hole it was suitable as a
knuckle-protector. United States.
7. A pin-fire revolver with blade
beneath the barrel, one of many
such arms manufactured in
Belgium using the pin-fire
system.

While some of the many "unusual" weapons made since the early days of firearms were the brainchild of inventors and gunmakers, some were designed for a specific need. With the advent of the flintlock system, "unusual" weapons proliferated, such as the cannon igniter, a pistol butt and lock attached to a long tube for placing in the vent of the cannon to fire it; the grenade launcher, comprising a cup fitted to a musket which fired a blank charge to propel the grenade; the combination of rifled and smooth-bored barrels in one weapon; or the more common knife pistols, etc.

The percussion system enabled more specialised weapons to be made, and, with the coming of the cartridge, this variety was expanded. The opening up of empires and the thirst for big game hunting led the gun-maker to develop new weapons to "bag" the kills. Undoubtedly the percussion elephant gun with its massive bore and weight was a triumph of the gunmaker's art, usually in 10 bore, the thick barrel made to withstand the extraordinary charge and deeply rifled. Popular in India and Africa these weapons lost much of their weight when technology came to cartridge design.

In response to the increased need for whale oil and blubber, harpoon guns with percussion systems were perfected. These sturdy weapons, manufactured in Belgium and in Birmingham (by, for example, the great W.W. Greener, son of the inventor in 1836 of a rifle bullet which anticipated Minié's), were mounted on a crutch or rowlock-type holder on a pillar and used a large charge to throw the harpoon a considerable way. Even when on land the self-contained cartridge had overtaken the percussion system, these large harpoon guns continued to be manufactured until the 20th century.

Other unusual weapons included the American Chicago squeeze palm pistol dating from the 1880s which worked, as the name suggests, by squeezing the bar trigger in the palm of the hand; key-pistols with matchlock, flintlock or percussion mechanisms fitted for them to act as both jailers' keys and self-protection; and a great variety of combinations of pistols and other weapons, especially blades (see pp. 138–9), but also staff weapons (pp. 100–101) and crossbows (pp. 180–81). Of the firearm and blade type perhaps the Unwin and Rogers pocket knife with .22 calibre barrel was the most famous, although in the U.S.A. the Elgin cutlass pistol of .54 calibre, with an 11¼-inch "butcher" style blade fitted under the barrel, achieved some prominence.

1

2

3

Ever since men had a gun at their disposal, they had to have a means of carrying the essential gunpowder and projectile. After the clumsy bags, the first containers made were of cows' horns, which had the advantage of being a convenient shape that was simple to use and in abundant supply. The large end of the horn was blocked with wood, the tip of the horn removed and a small wood bung made. For the more expensive decorated guns powder horns were engraved, carved and inlaid to complement the gun decoration. These horns had their heyday in the era of the wheel-lock in the 16th and early 17th centuries, and in North America for a further 100 years.

In the late 18th century, there was a swing to the work of copper- and tinsmiths, who produced embossed or plain flasks. Like their often richly decorated predecessors made of a variety of materials, these were more practical than the simple horns (from which many sportsmen measured powder with the discarded bowl of a clay pipe),

4

5

as they incorporated a nozzle with an exact measuring device. The nozzle was notched so that it could slide up and down, the notch engaged over the fixed head of a screw. The various notches varied the powder charge that the nozzle would hold when filled. To load, a finger was placed over the open end of the nozzle, which had been set to the charge required, the thumb pressed the spring lever on the cut-out that kept the powder in the body of the flask and the flask was inverted. The lever was then released, the flask placed over the muzzle and the finger removed to allow the charge in the nozzle to fall into the barrel. In the 19th century a number of companies specialised in nothing but powder flasks, including in England firms such as Dixon, Sykes and Hawksley.

This type of flask with a cut-off also had other applications, the most obvious being for the wildfowler and his shot. Again the nozzle was notched and marked to correspond with the amount of shot required for a particular load. These flasks for shot came in a variety of forms, the most common of which was similar in shape to the powder flask but made of leather. Others with the same form of nozzle were made like a long leather tube, for wearing across the shoulder and round the body. Another popular

The powder container was one of the most important pieces of equipment for the firearm, and many designs were made.
1. *The cartouche, much favoured in the Middle East to carry powder and shot.*
2. *The bandolier, the ideal way in the 17th century for the military to carry a number of pre-measured charges. The containers were usually of wood.*
3. *Italian powder flask in embossed leather with steel fittings. This incorporates a spring mechanism at the neck.*
4. *Bohemian staghorn powder flask with engraved and raised hunting scene. The neck is stopped with a staghorn cap on a chain.*
5. *Carved ivory powder flask of a typical form with steel fittings and neck stopper.*

Firearms

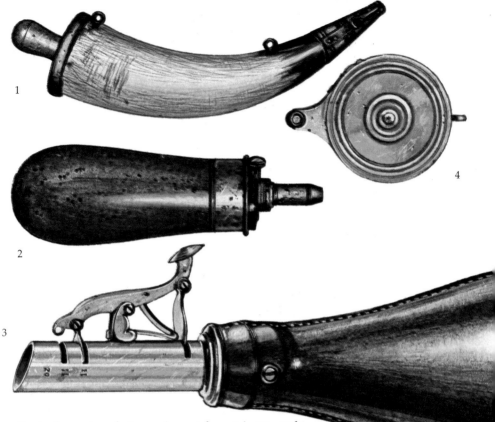

method of carrying shot was in metal containers, each made up with the shot charge.

With the arrival of the percussion cap, the shooter was provided with yet another contraption, the cap dispenser. Rather than keep the caps loose in a pocket or pouch, the dispenser was filled with caps and when the leading cap was placed on the nipple a spring automatically pushed the next one to the "loading" position. These, like flasks, came in many shapes – often a flat circular, or teardrop or more elongated form, of brass, copper, or tin alloy – most shapes having a ring to attach to the chain, perhaps of a watch.

The military had less use for flasks. With loading-rate vital, the early musketeer wore a bandolier to which were attached a number of small containers, usually of wood or metal with a screw top, carrying pre-measured charges, a shot pouch and a small priming flask or touch box. Later the military used a sturdy leather pouch with a wood block inside drilled out to take the paper-wrapped charges and the combined projectile and powder cartridges. With the coming of the cartridge in the world's armies, all these extras disappeared.

For the sportsman or soldier, the tools and other extras were as essential as the flint, powder or percussion cap, to keep the weapon in good order, to effect repairs, and cast bullets.
1. *18th-century powder horn, the brass dispenser with spring-loaded catch.*
2. *19th-century flask, typical of the hundreds of thousands supplied with cased gun sets. The neck is graduated in drams for powder measuring.*
3. *19th-century leather-covered shot flask, with the neck graduated in ounces for shot charges, the dispenser activated by a spring lever operated by the thumb.*

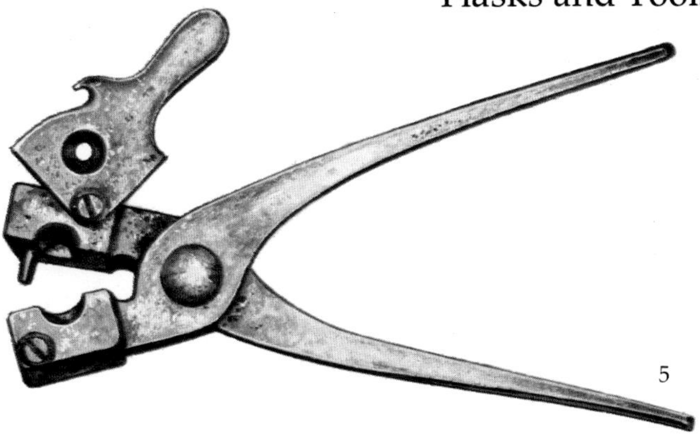

5

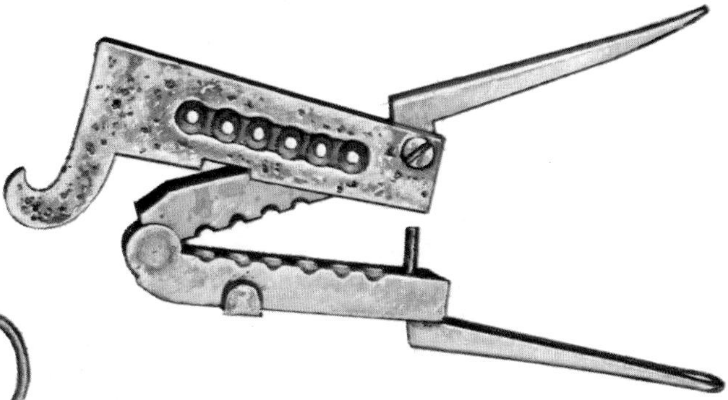

6

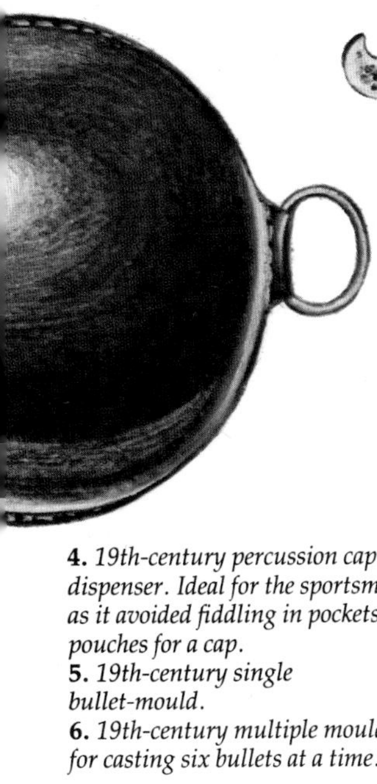

4. *19th-century percussion cap dispenser. Ideal for the sportsman, as it avoided fiddling in pockets or pouches for a cap.*
5. *19th-century single bullet-mould.*
6. *19th-century multiple mould for casting six bullets at a time.*

No firearm could function with rapidity and ease unless, like a car, it was serviced. To this end gunmakers in the past provided tools which were either enclosed with cased sets or available separately. These were fundamental tools to enable the owner to service his gun without recourse to the gunmaker. Locks had to be cleaned and oiled, barrels cleaned and bullets and patches made. The variety of tools would bewilder the modern sportsman with his double-twelve and his cartridges made up ready for use.

Of prime importance was the turnscrew or screwdriver. In most cases these were made in hardened steel from broken main springs, and excellent they are. The bullet-mould, which varied calibres had made necessary since the 16th century, was supplied to enable the shooter to make his own ammunition. A set of tools would also include cleaning or scouring rods with numerous jags, for the barrel, a corkscrew-like "worm" for extracting an unfired charge, a pricker to clear the vent, brushes to dust out the pan, and, later, nipple-keys to unscrew the percussion nipple for cleaning the nipple and chamber. Many also had mainspring clamps, and military armourers were provided with "combination" tools incorporating mainspring clamps, nipple-keys, jags, even spikes for clearing nipples.

247

Firearms

Many tools found today come from cased sets, sold complete with all accessories for loading, cleaning, stripping down or effecting minor repairs.

1. *Combination tool (see text).*

2. *Mainspring clamp to depress the mainspring for its removal from the inside of the lock-plate.*

3. *Nipple key with, concealed in the cross-piece, a pricker for clearing the nipple and, in the screw-on ends of the cross-piece, spare nipples.*

4. *Powder measure from cased gun with the holder graduated in drams.*

248

8

There were other tools for the care of the gun, such as the brushes for the barrel, and yet further tools which were important when shooting. These included the moulds mentioned above, but also the wad-cutter. This was in the form of a punch designed to be struck by a mallet on a piece of cloth, to make the wrapping on the ball for a rifled arm, or on a thick composition of card, to make the wad for a shotgun. Many weapons at this time had "traps" or patch-boxes in the butt for wadding and cleaning patches so that they were ready to hand. Among other tools which graced each cased weapon along with the flasks, mould, and spare springs, hammers, caps, etc., were the oil bottles, usually in zinc.

For sporting long guns, the accessories were for home maintenance because the cases were not carried about; in the field perhaps the most useful tool was again the turn-screw.

Finally, from the earliest days the essential loading stick was stored under the barrel, initially in a hole in the full stock, then in metal tubes or "pipes", and often from c. 1800, secured by a swivel device at the fore-end. From the late 18th century in military weapons steel ramrods replaced the metal-tipped wooden rods which had been so prone to breakage.

5. *Zinc oil bottle.*
6. *Wad punch and wads, which were made to be wrapped around the bullet.*
7. *Military combination tool for Enfield rifle with turnscrew, jag for extracting bullet and charge, and nipple key.*
8. *Eprouvette or powder-tester with graduated dial to record the explosive strength of the powder under test.*

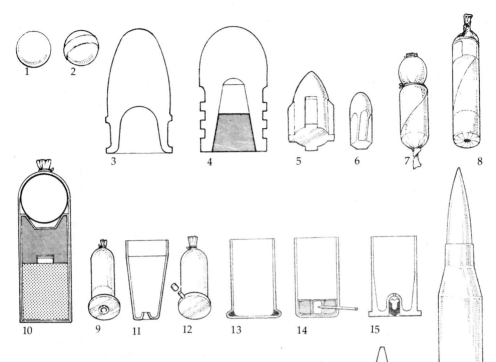

Ammunition, now thought of as a self-contained cartridge, was originally simply loose powder and ball. The combined bullet and powder charge wrapped in paper to form a simple cartridge was a late entry in the history of the gun and then mainly only used by the military. Early forms of pre-measured powder charge – carried in bandoliers – had been used with the matchlock, and pre-measured powder charges wrapped in paper were introduced by Gustavus Adolphus, king of Sweden 1611–32. The next development was to enclose the bullet with the charge. In this way ammunition could be made up in large quantities for various calibres with an accurate charge. The propellant was wrapped in cartridge paper (hence the name) which was sealed at one end, and the ball tied into the other. Loading was carried out by biting or tearing off the end containing the ball, which was removed, putting some of the powder in the pan and pouring the rest down the barrel. The paper was crumpled up, the paper acting as a wad, and rammed home, with the ball last.

The earliest self-contained cartridge that loaded complete into the barrel was that patented by the Frenchman Pauly in 1812. It had a base made from brass with a paper

Ammunition

body forming the front portion in which the propellant and ball were loaded. In a recess in the base there was a pellet of detonating powder. In the pistol cartridge, the entire affair was made of brass. The combustible cartridge of the capping breech-loader (see pp. 226–7), a successor to Pauly's, enjoyed some popularity, for example in the Civil War in the U.S.A.

Another breakthrough came with the Dreyse needle gun (see p. 226) and its cartridge which had powder and projectile wrapped together in paper; placed at the base of the bullet was the fulminate primer which, when struck by the needle, fired the charge. An extension of this principle was the pin-fire cartridge patented in 1847 by a French gunmaker, B. Houiller. In this a metal cartridge containing powder and ball had a small pin protruding from the base which passed through a small hole in the top of the breech. When struck by the hammer, the pin was thrust against a fulminate cap which fired the charge. The case itself was of thin metal which expanded on being fired and acted as a seal for the chamber. Houiller also showed in his patent a rim-fire cartridge (popularised by another French gunmaker in 1851) in which the rim was filled with fulminate which also acted, when struck through a slit by the hammer, as the propellant. The American company of Smith and Wesson elongated the case and added a powder charge in 1854.

The centre-fire cartridge, the most common in use today, was a combination of ideas by various inventors in both America and Europe. It was in 1865 that Colonel Boxer obtained a patent for the centre-fire .577 military cartridge he developed at Woolwich. The body was made of sheet brass over which a layer of white paper was fitted. The base was formed and placed within this. In the following year this base was improved upon with a solid brass disc and later in the following year an iron disc was substituted. In the 1870s, coiled brass cases, some bottle-necked, were developed, but the modern cartridge owes its design to the engineers who perfected the drawing of brass. All modern cartridges from the 1880s onwards have the basic elements in the same places, i.e. projectile, case, propellant and, in the base of the case, the cap on which the whole depends.

Bibliography

Alm, J., "Europeiska armborst. En översikt",
  Vaabenhistoriske Aabøger, no. Vb, Copenhagen, 1947.
Ascham, R., *Toxophilus*, London, 1545.
Blair, C., *European Armour c. 1066 to c. 1700*, 1958,
  reprinted London 1970.
Clark, J. G. D., "Neolithic Bows from Somerset,
  England, and the Prehistory of Archery in North-West
  Europe", *Proceedings of the Prehistoric Society*, XXIX,
  London, 1963.
Ffoulkes, C. J., *The Armourer and his Craft from the 11th to
  the 15th Century*, London, 1912.
Gay, V., *Glossaire archéologique du Moyen Age et de la
  Renaissance*, 2 vols., Paris, 1887, 1928.
Grose, F., *A Treatise on Ancient Armour and Weapons*,
  London, 1786.
Hewitt, J., *Ancient Armour and Weapons*, London, 1956.
Hogg, I. V. and Weeks, J., *Military Small Arms of the
  Twentieth Century*, London, 1973.
Laking, G. F., *A Record of European Armour and Arms
  through Seven Centuries*, 5 vols., London, 1920–22.
Meyrick, S. R., *A Critical Inquiry into Antient Armour*, 3
  vols., London, 1824, 1842.
Payne-Gallwey, R., *The Crossbow, Mediaeval and Modern*,
  reprinted London, 1958.
Peterson, H. L., *The American Sword, 1775–1945*, revised
  edition, London, 1968.
Peterson, H. L. ed., *Encyclopedia of Firearms*, London, 1965.
Rausing, G., "The Bow", *Acta Archaeologia Ludensia*, 6,
  Lund, 1967.
Reitzenstein, A. von, *Der Waffenschmied*, Munich, 1964.
Roads, C. H., *The British Soldier's Firearm, 1850–1864*,
  London, 1964.
Robinson, H. R., *The Armour of Imperial Rome*, London,
  1975.
Robson, B., *Swords of the British Army: The Regulation
  Patterns, 1788–1914*, London, 1975.
Stone, G. C., *A Glossary of the Construction, Decoration and
  Use of Arms and Armor in all Countries and in all Times*,
  Portland, Mne, 1934.
Taylerson, A. W. F., *The Revolver, 1865–1888*, London,
  1966.
Taylerson, A. W. F., *The Revolver, 1889–1914*, London,
  1970.
Taylerson, A. W. F., *Revolving Arms*, London, 1967.

Principal Collections

The following list includes some of the most important
collections containing examples of the weapons and
armour discussed in this book. Many local and
regimental museums also contain interesting pieces.

Austria Graz: Steiermarkisches Landeszeughaus. Vienna:
Heeresgeschichtliches Museum, Kunsthistorisches Museum.
Belgium Brussels: Musée de la Porte de Hals, Musée
Royal de l'Armée et d'Histoire Militaire. Liège: Musée
d'Armes.

Canada Toronto: Royal Ordnance Museum.
Denmark Copenhagen: Tøjhusmuseet.
France Paris: Musée de l'Armée.
Germany Berlin: Zeughaus. Dresden: Historisches
Museum. Solingen: Deutsches Klingenmuseum.
Hungary Budapest: Nationalmuseum.
Italy Florence: Museo Nationale, Museo Stibbert. Turin:
Armeria Reale.
Netherlands Leiden: Nederlands Leger-en
Wapenmuseum.
Norway Oslo: Haermuseet.
Poland Cracow: Museum Nardowekràkowice, Warsaw:
Polish Army Museum.
Spain Madrid: Armería Real, Museo del Ejército, Museo
Naval.
Sweden Stockholm: Kungl Livrustkammaren, Kungl
Armenmuseum.
Switzerland Berne: Historisches Museum. Chur:
Rüstkammer. Geneva: Musée d'Art et d'Histoire.
Lucerne: Musée Historique. Solothurn: Zeughaus.
Zurich: Schweizerisches Landesmuseum.
United Kingdom Birmingham: City Museum and Art
Gallery. Canterbury: West Gate. Edinburgh: Royal
Scottish Museum, Scottish United Services Museum.
Enfield: Pattern Room, Royal Small Arms Factory.
Glasgow: Kelvingrove Art Gallery and Museum.
London: National Army Museum, National Maritime
Museum, Rotunda (Woolwich), Tower of London,
Victoria and Albert Museum, Wallace Collection.
United States Boston, Mass.: First Corps Cadets Armory.
Chicago: George F. Harding Museum. Cleveland, Ohio:
Museum of Art. Fort Oglethorpe, Ga.: National Military
Park. Newhaven, Conn.: Winchester Museum.
Springfield, Mass.: Armory Museum. Washington:
Smithsonian Institution. West Point, N.Y.: U.S. Military
Academy. Williamsburg, Va.: The Powder Magazine.
Worcester, Mass.: John Woodman Higgins Armory.
U.S.S.R. Leningrad: State Hermitage. Moscow: State
Historical Museum, Kremlin Armoury.

Acknowledgements

Photographs were supplied by the Bodleian Library,
Oxford p. 38; British Museum, London p. 12; Cooper
Bridgeman Library, London pp. 14–15 (British Library);
Department of the Environment pp. 16–17, Crown
Copyright Reserved; Ekdotike Athenon S.A., Athens
p. 8; Michael Holford, Loughton pp. 7, 9, 10, 11t, 11b,
13, (all British Museum); National Gallery, London p. 2
(frontispiece).
    All armour artwork by Malcolm McGregor, all others
by Peter Sarson and Tony Bryan except as follows:
Sarson and Bryan 56–7; 78–9; 86–7; John Ronayne
pp. 72, 90, 179, 215; Tony Hadler pp. 76–7, 185, 195, 197.
    Line drawings for pp. 19, 89, 103, 163, 183 by John
Brennan.

253

INDEX

*The principal entries (**armour** etc.) are preceded by a line space, and subentries within these entries are not indented. Numerals in italic indicate illustrations.*